Summit Fever

Summit Fever

*The Story of an Armchair Climber on the
1984 Mustagh Tower Expedition*

Andrew Greig

Hutchinson

London Melbourne Sydney Auckland Johannesburg

Hutchinson & Co. (Publishers) Ltd

An imprint of the Hutchinson Publishing Group

17–21 Conway Street, London W1P 6JD

Hutchinson Publishing Group (Australia) Pty Ltd
PO Box 496, Hawthorn, Melbourne, Victoria 3122

Hutchinson Group (NZ) Ltd
PO Box 40–086, Glenfield 10, Auckland

Hutchinson Group (SA) Pty Ltd
PO Box 337, Bergvlei, 2012 South Africa

First published 1985
© Andrew Greig 1985

Set in Sabon by Wyvern Typesetting Limited, Bristol

Printed and bound in Great Britain by
Anchor Brendon Ltd, Tiptree, Essex

ISBN 0 09 162060 0

For my father, Donald Stewart Greig, 1899–1984, and Mr Rocky Moss of Los Angeles, without whom, no Expedition.

With warmest thanks to Malcolm, Sandy, Tony, Adrian, Kathleen, Alex, and Jon, without whom no climbing, no fun and no shuffling doss.

The author gratefully acknowledges the support of the Scottish Arts Council during the writing of this book.

Contents

List of Illustrations

List of Maps

Foreword

The characters who appear in this book may bear only a passing resemblance to any actual persons living or dead. On a long mountaineering expedition each member becomes a myth to the others, grotesquely enlarged like a Brocken Spectre projected on the mist. Each member has their own expedition. This is an account of mine.

Until the November evening when Mal Duff banged on my window, I was purely an armchair climber, happy to enjoy mountaineering from a comfortable distance. (After that, common sense deserted me.) But I'd found that most climbing books left me vaguely dissatisfied in the same way as the freeze-dried meals we were to eat on the Mustagh Tower – something was always left out.

Climbing books are written by dedicated climbers, people for whom mountaineering has become second nature and habitual. The result is there is much they have ceased to consciously notice, and an equal amount that they notice but don't think to mention. They also have to observe the general ethos of mountaineers, and so adopt a certain style towards danger, fear, loneliness, endurance, ambition, exultation – usually jokey exaggeration or complete suppression in favour of purely factual accounts.

The upshot is that, as with those cursed freeze-drieds, the contents are there but the whole juice and inner substance of the experience is missing. So I have tried to write about this adventure freshly, as it all happened to me for the first time. Having nothing to prove as a climber, I can afford to be honest about how it felt.

There is a very narrow ridge to walk between honesty and tact. My companions on this adventure have allowed me generous access to their diaries, time and inner lives. I have tried not to abuse their trust, but without glossing over (as many books naturally do) the emotions, irritations and incidents contained there. Himalayan climbing is an intense experience, and the mountains intensify rather than dissipate emotions. A small group of people are living and striving together in isolation for a long period under a great variety of stresses. Little generosities, selfishnesses and tensions become magnified. One gets it in proportion later, but an honest account of the experience necessitates recording how it felt at the time.

All climbing, and Himalyan mountaineering in particular, is not just about the final summit push. The preparations, the walk in, the mountain villages, vacant slog, arguments, the porters singing and the stars at night, food, fantasies, memories, personal relations, summit fever, the walk out – all are part of it. It is the totality of the experience that I have tried to pack between the covers of this book.

Andrew Greig
South Queensferry February 1985

Principal characters

Malcolm Duff	*A Leader of Men*
Sandy Allan	*Alpine Bin-Men*
Jon Tinker	
Tony Brindle	*Mr Keen*
Andrew Greig	*An Author*
Adrian Clifford	*A Doctor*
Kathleen Jamie	*A Bright Young Thing*
Alex Reid	*An American Slave*
Captain Shokat	*A Liaison Officer*
Mohammed Ali Changezi	*A Guiding Star*
Burt Greenspan	*Mr Phone*
Donna	*A Climber*
Sybil	*A Trekker*
Jhaved asnd Abdul	*Cooks*
Haji Mahdi	*Headman of Askole*
The Man from Lahore	*The Man from Lahore*

I

It's There If You Want It

In which a near-stranger makes an outrageous offer
17–23 November 1983

Climbing was something other people did.

I was quite content that it should stay that way, until one wet November evening Mr Malcolm Duff walked in and turned my life upside down.

An evening at home in South Queensferry, idly watching television. Kathleen was reading, the wood stove hissed, the cats twitched in their dreams. Life was domestic, cosy and safe – and just a little boring. But what else could one expect? Then a sharp bang on the window made us start. Enter Malcolm: alert, weathered, impelled by restless energy. We'd met briefly twice and he'd reminded me of an army officer who was contemplating becoming an anarchist. He seemed, as always, to be in a hurry; a brief Hi and he went straight to the point.

'It's there if you want it, Andy.'

I looked at him blankly. 'What's there?'

'The Karakoram trip. The Expedition will buy any gear you need, pay your flight out and any expenses. What you do is climb on the Mustagh Tower with us and write a book about the trip. Rocky's really keen on the idea.' He prowled restlessly round our kitchen. 'Well, what do you think?'

I couldn't think. I was running hot and cold together inside, like a mixer tap. Turning away, registering what had been offered yet unable to take it in, I went through the motions of making coffee, asked if he took sugar. That was how little we knew each other. I remembered now a drunken evening over my home-brew, how he'd said he'd liked my book of narrative climbing poems, *Men On Ice*, that he was going on an expedition to Pakistan. And I'd made some non-sober, non-serious remark about how it would be interesting to go on a mountaineering trip and write about it. And he'd said he would phone a man called Rocky Moss who was financing the climb . . .

'Er, Malcolm . . . you do realize my book was purely metaphorical? I can't climb.'

For a moment he looked taken aback. 'I'll teach you. No problem.'

'And I'm scared of heights. They make me feel ill.'

'You'll get used to it.'

'To heights, or feeling ill?'

'Both.' The sardonic – satanic – grin was to become all too familiar.

'It's just . . .' Just what? Wonderful? Outrageous. Exciting? Stunning. I played for time and said I'd need to think about it.

'Sure,' he replied. We leaned against the fridge and chatted for a few minutes. I wasn't taking in much. He drained his coffee, stubbed his cigarette and made for the door. 'Let me know inside a week.' Then he paused, grinned. 'Go for it, youth,' he said, and was gone.

Leaving me sweating, staring through the steam of my mug at a mountain I'd never seen or even heard of – the Somethingorother Tower – waiting for me on the other side of the world. A week to decide.

What does an armchair climber feel when offered the chance to turn daydream into reality? Incredulity. Euphoria. Panic. Suddenly the routines of ordinary life seem deeply reassuring and desirable. Why leave them? Familiar actions and satisfactions may at times seem bland, but they are sustaining. Armchair daydreams are the salt that gives them savour, nothing more.

And yet . . .

I talked it round and round that evening with Kathleen. She was torn between envy and worry. She didn't want me to go. She wanted to go herself. I didn't know what I wanted. If I stayed to finish a radio play – about two climbers, as irony would have it – we could afford to go somewhere interesting, hot and safe.

As we talked it out, I wondered how often this scene had been enacted. It's the one the adventure books always omit. Conflicting desires and loyalties, leaving someone behind. Any adventurer who is not a complete hermit must go through that scene. It makes some apparently callous and ruthlessly clear about where their priorities lie.

I had none of that certainty. Yet how could one turn down an offer like this?

'Try saying No,' Kathleen suggested.

I phoned Malcolm the next evening to say I hadn't made up my mind but maybe it would be a good idea for me to find out more about the Expedition. Such as what, where and who. At the end of five minutes my head was spinning and my notepad was crosshatched with names, dates and places, and some alarming vertical doodles.

The mountain was called the Mustagh Tower. It had been climbed only twice, and that twenty-eight years ago; we were going for the Joe Brown–Tom Patey route. I tried to make knowledgeable, approving noises. It was just under 24,000 feet high, in the Karakoram which were apparently part of the Himalayas, 'third turning on the left before K2'. At least I'd heard of that.

We'd be leaving in June, for two or three months. Our second objective was called Gasherbrum 2, some 26,000 feet high. I was pleased to hear I wasn't expected to do anything on it. That 'gash' bit sounded vicious, and the 'brum' was resonant with avalanche. At the moment there were four British lead climbers, a doctor and myself, four Nepalese Sherpas and three Americans whose experience was limited largely to being guided. One of them was the intriguing Rocky Moss who was paying for the trip. I wondered what he had against writers. The plan was to fix ropes on the steep section up to a col at 21,000 feet – that would be my summit – then the lead climbers would try to finish the route, establishing one or two more camps on the way, and the Sherpas would give the less experienced climbers a chance of the top. No oxygen, except two cylinders at Base Camp for emergency medical use. An American Slave, to serve us at Base Camp.

Even from my limited reading of mountaineering books, it sounded a very strange expedition, more like a circus. I'd never heard of anyone being guided up a demanding Himalayan peak.

I sat by the fire, frowning at the notepad and trying to

memorize the jumble of figures, names and places. They all sounded vague, unlikely, entirely fanciful. Yet these names could acquire faces, the places could be all around me, and they could all become part of the most powerful experience of my life. The rap on the window, the surfeit of home-brew, my book of metaphorical climbers, could propel me into the one great adventure we all daydream about.

Or into fiasco, failure, or worse.

A week to decide. The world outside me went on, but neglected as a flickering TV during a barroom brawl. I went through the motions of living and working, blind to everything but my inner debate. A couple of climbing acquaintances eagerly filled me in on the quite astonishing variety of ways of croaking in the Himalayas. Falling off the mountain seemed the least of my worries. Strokes, heart attacks, pulmonary oedema, cerebral oedema, frostbite, exposure, pneumonia, stone fall, avalanche, crevasse, mountain torrents and runaway yaks – each with a name and an instance of someone who had been killed that way. Climbers seemed to love good death-and-destruction stories, and at first their humour appears callous and ghoulish.

I could picture them all, every one. My fingers turned black from frostbite while clenching a fork, ropes parted as I pegged out the washing. I stood on the col bringing in the milk, then was bundled into oblivion by avalanche as I let in the cat. I chided myself for being melodramatic; the truth was I had no idea what I was up against. All I knew was that many people had died in many ways in the Himalayas – how prepared I was to take a chance on it? Life was too pleasant and interesting to lose, yet to turn down an experience like this . . .

My enthusiasm diminished noticeably by nightfall. By the time I lay in bed, exhausted by visions of blizzards, bottomless crevasses, collapsing cornices, avalanche, it was clear I wouldn't go. The only realistic decision. I was not a climber, nor meant to be.

In the morning, contemplating another quiet day at the type-writer set against the adventure of a lifetime in the great mountains of the world, it was obvious: go, you fool. Enough shifting words around a ghostly inner theatre. I'd always hungered after one big adventure. Then I'd come home, hang up my ice axe and put my boots in the loft. There was some risk, but that was the condition of adventure. It seemed inevitable that I'd end up going.

On the evening of 20 November, Kathleen threw an I Ching hexagram.

'This is uncanny. Want to see?'

I looked at the reading:

Hexagram 62. Hsiao Kuo: Preponderance of the small.
Success. Perseverance furthers.
Small things may be done; great things should not be done.
It is not well to strive upward,
it is well to remain below.

My eye skipped on.

. . . Thunder on the mountain. Thunder in the mountains
sounds much nearer.

I put down the book, thought about it. 'Were you asking about yourself or me?'

'Both of us.'

'Doesn't pull any punches, does it?'

Silence from Kathleen. Then, quietly, 'Please don't go.'

I visited a climbing acquaintance to sound out his opinion. My wellbeing and safety rested largely on Mal Duff's judgement and abilities. I scarcely knew him as a person, and not at all as a climber. What was his reputation in the climbing world?

'Mal Duff? Can't say I know him that well. A lot of people

would put a question mark beside his name, but I don't know why. Envy, maybe – he's one of the very few who almost make a living from climbing. There was some kind of financial screw-up . . . No one's ever suggested he can't climb.'

I accepted a whisky and let him talk on. The climbing world appeared very intense, gossipy yet reticent, full of allegiances and rivalries. I was just beginning to learn to read the coded messages, and to try to sort out a sound assessment from bias.

'He's done a lot in Scotland in winter, some in the Alps. I think he was out on Nuptse twice, so he's had some Himalayan experience. He's possibly not as good as he thinks he is – but nor am I! I've heard of this other chap, Sandy Allan, but the rest of the Brit climbers mean nothing to me. The Mustagh Tower is a classic – did you know it was once called "the unclimbable mountain" and "the Himalayan Matterhorn"? – but it sounds a very odd expedition with these semi-climbers along. I'd be very surprised if anyone gets to the top.'

I nodded, looked into the bottom of my glass. How much of what I was hearing was envy? How much was climbing bullshit and how much accurate assessment? We talked a while longer about Malcolm and the trip – in that warm, Edinburgh flat it all seemed extremely hypothetical – till I asked the obvious question: is it possible for someone with as yet no mountaineering experience at all to go to 21,000 feet on a Himalayan peak?

'Yes, it's possible. Whether it's desirable . . .' He laughed, seemed to find the whole project amusing. But then he'd found being shipwrecked off Patagonia amusing. He'd obviously lost a few brain cells along the way. 'Yes, if you're very fit, can take the altitude, have considerable determination and are lucky – '

'That doesn't sound like me at all,' I interrupted him.

' – there's no reason why not. It may blow your mind a bit, but you'll be safer than you think. Mind you, the Himalayas make the Alps look like a kiddies' playground – but you've never seen the Alps, have you? And of course,' he continued, smiling, 'if something doesn't go according to plan – and that's bound to happen – you could be in real trouble. You've maybe one chance in twenty of snuffing it.'

We had another whisky and I looked over the photos on his wall. Douglas crawling beneath stomach-turning overhangs, Douglas on Patagonian mountains, Douglas and friends steering a 12-foot inflatable through a Greenland ice pack. A lump of quartz from a Patagonian first ascent. Mementoes of another world. Nice to have some souvenirs like that . . .

It's the little vanities that get us going.

'The trip's a freebie,' Douglas said. 'Take it.'

After five days of indecision – or rather, of constantly changing decisions – I went home to Anstruther to talk it over with my parents. I wanted to hear their opinion; perhaps that would clarify my thoughts.

So, should I go?

Dad paused so long I thought he hadn't heard me properly. A long, awkward silence, my mother at the other end of the table, waiting for his response. Then he said very slowly, 'I'm too old to be asked a question like that.' He looked at me, his eyes pale blue and slightly fogged over, set deep among the ridges, wrinkles, creases and weathering of eighty-four years. 'You see,' he said simply, 'I can no longer see any appeal in experience for its own sake.'

How had I failed to see how old, how very, very tired he'd become in the last year? The hand that held the glass of wine had shrunk to skin and bone. He took a sip, grimaced. 'I've even lost the taste for this. But in your position, at your age . . . Yes, you should go.'

Then he began to pull out from the vast, shadowy storehouse of his memory bales of stories of scrambling in the Cairngorms as a medical student in the 1920s, seeing the colossal Grey Man of Ben MacDui, the early days of the Scottish Youth Hostel movement, escapades in Ardnamurchan, taking the first motorcar over the old drove road to Applecross, hurrying five miles across a snow-bound moor in the dead of winter to deliver a baby in an Angus bothy . . .

And vitality came back to him like a fitful companion as he talked, and I sensed it was all happening again for him, behind the eyes of this most unsentimental of men. It had been these tales, together with his recollections of dawns in Sumatra and hurricanes in the China Seas, that had first made me long for my own adventures, for those experiences of youth that nothing, not even extreme old age, can take away from you as long as you breathe.

Listening to him confirmed in me what I'd always known. When it came down to it, I'd take the chance.

'Are you thinking what I'm thinking, Kath?'

'Yes.'

Pause. Me leaning on the door frame, her grinning on the settee.

'We're going then?'

'Yes.'

And that was the decision made, in an instant, on an impulse. The impulse of life that says, 'Why not?'

Mal had just gone out the door, and taken most of my reservations with him. He'd filled us in on more details, and they were largely reassuring. He'd promised my Glencoe initiation would not be terminal. I was very aware that my life would depend largely on his priorities and his judgement; in the end, on his character. I'd been watching and listening to him closely. I'd liked him from the start for his great enthusiasm for life. He was interested in practically everything, not just climbing. Now I sensed behind the casualness considerable determination. Behind the romantic was a hard-nosed realist. Behind the restless energy that kept his fingers tap-tapping a cigarette and his right knee jumping as he sat, there was a sense of self-possession. These were not nervous mannerisms, but those of someone who revved his way through life. The sardonic grin, the offhand climber's humour, the thoughtful frown into the mug of coffee – they all seemed in balance with each other.

He struck me as the kind of person who might get you into scrapes but would probably get you out of them again. (And how prophetic that turned out to be!)

I'd trust him.

A deciding factor was Kathleen's inclusion. She asked if she could come along with the trekking group who were to accompany us on the walk-in to Mustagh, and cover her costs through writing articles about her trip. Just flying a kite . . . Mal took it quite seriously and said he saw no reason why not, subject to Rocky's agreement.

We hadn't actually said Yes to him but, grinning wildly at each other, we knew we'd decided.

The world was transformed. Being alive felt dramatized and vivid, vibrant with challenge. We couldn't sit still. Adrenalin propelled us outdoors into a mild November night. We walked fast and aimlessly past moonlit stubble fields, dark cottages, a hunched country church. An owl glided between us and the moon. An omen? The night felt huge and elating as we talked, half giggling, spilling out plans, images, anticipations and fears.

It was like being a teenager again. The same pumped-up energy, the fancies and fantasies swirling through the body, the sense of the world being wide open and there to be explored. The ordinary things around us seemed vivid and precious, shining as the map Kathleen drew with a finger dipped in beer on a polished table in the Hawes Inn that night. 'Here is Pakistan,' she said, 'and here's Islamabad where we fly to.' She wetted her finger again and drew a squiggly line. 'And *here*, I think, are the Karakoram.'

We sat and stared at the table, silent for a minute as the crude map of our future shone then faded.

2

A Glencoe Massacre

In which a novice is initiated
20–26 January 1984

As we head north on icy roads in mid-January, Mal enthuses about the conditions. A substantial fall of snow, a slight thaw, now freezing hard. 'Glencoe will be crawling with climbers this weekend.' I'm less enthusiastic; if anyone will be crawling this weekend, it'll be me. The van heater is broken so I huddle deep in my split-new climbing gear, watching our headlights skew out across deepening snow. We don't speak much, each absorbed in our own thoughts.

I'm keyed up, anxious yet oddly elated. To shut out the cold I mentally run through everything Mal had shown me about the basic mechanics of snow and ice climbing, in the warmth of his flat a day before. It had been quite bewildering – the knots, the principles of belaying, the extraordinary array of ironmongery, the pegs, pins, channels, screws, plates, nuts, crabs, slings . . . An evocative litany but especially confusing when everything seemed to have several alternative names. This was starting truly from scratch.

I try to review it all logically. First, the harness. I smile to myself in the dark. With our harnesses belted on and the full armoury of the modern climber dangling from them, we'd looked like a cross between gladiators and bondage freaks. Then the rope; I tried to picture again the basic figure-of-eight knot used for securing the rope through the harness loops.

Then the basic sequence of events for climbing. The leader climbs up, more or less protected by his second, who's on a hopefully secure stance at the other end of the rope. When the leader reaches a secure position somewhere near the rope's full extent, he in turn protects the second who climbs up after him. Simple and reasonably safe. At least, I hoped so.

We'd rehearsed it on the passage stairs. We stood roped together at the bottom of the stairs. Mal tied a 'sling' – a loop of incredibly strong tape – through the bannister and clipped it to my harness with an oval metal snaplink, the karabiner or 'krab'. This secured my belay stance. Then he took the rope near where it came from his harness, threaded it through a friction device, a descendeur, and clipped that to my harness. Then with a 'see you at the top, youth' he solemnly walked up the stairs while I paid out the rope through the descendeur. About 20 feet up he stopped and pointed out that if he fell now, he'd fall 40 feet in total before the line between us came tight. 'So I put in a "runner".' He looped another sling round a bannister rail, then clipped a krab to it, with the rope running freely through the krab. If he fell now, he'd only go down twice the distance he was above the runner till he was brought up short by the tight rope between us being looped through the karabiner.

I thought about it a couple of times till the logic of it sank in. Yes, it made sense. The runner was there to limit the extent of the leader's fall.

It was at this point a woman came bustling up the stairs and gave us a very strange look.

With the merest blush, Mal continued on up, putting in a couple more runners till he got to the top. There he tied himself securely to the rail. 'On belay!' The cry floated down the spiral staircase. I unclipped the descendeur, tried to remember the appropriate call. 'Take in slack!' I shouted. He took in the rope till it came tight between us. I waited as he put his descendeur onto the rope. 'Climb when you're ready!' With some difficulty I unclipped myself from my belay stance, shouted 'Climbing!' and set off up after him.

Some 20 feet up I was going great guns, then was suddenly brought up short with a jerk. I couldn't go any further. 'Try taking out my runner,' Mal called down. Of course, the first runner was preventing me from continuing above it. I unclipped the krab, untied the sling and continued.

At the top, we shook hands most movingly.

And that seemed to be the basic principle and practice of belay climbing. I hoped I'd remembered the calls correctly. I mumbled them over a few times in the freezing van. The rest of the gear – the pitons in various shapes and guises, the screws and nuts –

were for use when there was nothing convenient to loop a sling over to set up a belay stance or a runner. We'd gone around wedging them into cracks in Mal's fireplace. It had all been wonderfully ludicrous, but next time it'll be for real. How did I get into this?

After Callander the glimmering countryside grows wilder and more desolate. Long slopes suddenly swoop upwards, the snow deepens as we skirt the wilderness of Rannoch Moor and wind down towards Glencoe. As we near the infamous Clachaig Inn I think back on the last time I was here, sixteen years ago. High on adrenalin, youth and Pale Ale at 2s. 3d. a pint, I'd stood in a corner in full hippie regalia – the gold cloak, quilted tea cosy for a hat, peacock feathers, the strawberry tunic, oh my God – and thrashed out Incredible String Band songs into a small bar dense with steam, smoke and climbers so large and hairy it was hard to tell where beards ended and sweaters began. Climbers must be exceptionally tolerant, and such was the confidence of youth and the mood of the times that I got off with it, even had a few drinks bought me. Then at closing time walked out with a nurse from Glasgow into the black night to try yet again to lose my virginity, mind intoxicated with Pale Ale, adventure and the great sensed bulk of the mountains . . .

Now I can't even recognize the interior. The clientele are much the same, only now they look younger and smaller. A motley crew: straggly hair, gaiters, training shoes, bare feet, old jeans, blue fibre-pile salopettes, bright red Gore-Tex jackets, moving from table to table talking gossip or snow conditions, arm wrestling, playing pool. A number of girls too, some looking decorative and bored, others decidedly capable.

Mal's clearly well known and respected here. A constant stream of people come up to our table. Climbers' talk. 'Tower Ridge . . . still seconding all the time . . . solid for its grade . . . knew he was going to lob, so . . . Whitesnake . . . the crux after the chockstone . . . wiped out in Peru . . .' It's all new to me, exotic and bewildering, but I sense some interesting interactions behind these casual exchanges. Allegiances and rivalries, the seeking and withholding of information, put-downs and half-acknowledged challenges. How much a casual remark such as 'I thought it a soft touch at Grade 5' can imply! It suggests that for the speaker the climb was easy, that he is familiar with *real*

Grade 5s, it inquires after the listener's capability and casts aspersions on his friend who first climbed and rated the route. Just how good are you, anyway? 'I found it hard enough last time,' Mal might reply mildly. This counterstroke makes it clear that he has climbed it, and more than once, that he doesn't need to pretend a hard climb was easy to bolster his reputation . . .

In fact, it's just like the literary world. Competition and cooperation; jostling over places in an invisible league table; ideological, personal and geographical divisions. The Aberdeen crowd here to show the others what real climbing is, the hard men up from the North of England to make their point, the Central Scotland boys protecting their patch . . . Yes, very familiar.

'Who are you?' one youth asks me, uneasy he can't place Mal's new partner. 'I'm a guitar player.' Pause. 'What are you doing up here, then?' 'Learning a few new chords.' He looks baffled, scowls and retreats. Mal grins and agrees that though climbing itself may be a pure activity, there's nothing pure and disin-terested about the social side of it. Everyone seems extra-ordinarily vague about what they're going for tomorrow.

Tony Brindle and his climbing partner Terry Dailey walk in the door. Tony's one of the lead climbers for Mustagh, the only one I've met other than Malcolm. Handshakes all round, it's good to see a familiar face. I'd seen him last at Mal and Liz's wedding, carried off to do a Dashing White Sergeant by two tall girls and grinning wildly. Even sober as now, he's still bouncy and hyper-enthusiastic. As he chatters away about past and future routes it suddenly strikes me who he reminds me of: Davy Jones of the Monkees. Small, looks as if butter wouldn't melt, innocent brown eyes, hair in a neat fringe, something about Tony makes one want to pat him on the head. He's twenty-three and looks about fifteen. I think he both resents and plays up to it. It's hard to imagine that he's recognized by his peers as having quite excep-tional stamina and self-reliance. There must be steel somewhere behind that baby face. Who or what put it there?

'So where are you taking Mal tomorrow?' he asks me, for the benefit of Mal who's locked in conversation about this season's big challenges on 'the Ben', i.e. Ben Nevis.

'Oh, I don't know, we'll just poke around,' I reply in the prescribed vague manner. 'Maybe warm up with Smith's Gully and see what he's up to. Then we'll take a look at something more serious.' Now we have a few attentive ears at the next table. Mal twitches slightly but can't get out of his conversation.

Tony grins, replies in his Lancashire accent, 'Yeah, he's a bit lazy is Duff. The old fella's buggered. Still, he'll second anything you lead.'

'Thought I'd maybe give him a couple of leads if he's shaping up . . .'

Mal is saved from further roasting by the arrival of more friends I recognize from the wedding. A big boozy night that was; the climbers there all gravitated towards the corner of the room and spent the night talking about the only relevant subject at such occasions – climbing. They're obsessed, but it's an interesting obsession, for the first couple of hours at least.

And so that first night at the Clachaig rolls on. Red faces, swollen knuckles, diminishing pints, growing excitement and anticipation as hopes and plans build for tomorrow. At least they don't train on orange juice and early nights. Their regime seems to be one of alcohol, nicotine, late nights and systematic abuse, both verbal and bodily. Suits me.

I stand outside our chalet door for a few minutes before going to bed. The air is clear and cold, smelling unmistakably of snow. Clouds move across a three-quarter moon and sweep enormous shadows over the glimmering slopes across the glen. Passing voices ring hard in the frost. Orion is rising, the wind whispers over the snow, distant echoing water. I feel uplifted and self-forgetting before the irresistible forces of moon, shadow, mountains, snow. This alone was worth coming here for. I shake my head and go inside. See what tomorrow brings. Hope I'm up to it. I've been training two months for this.

The wind's gusting spindrift into our faces, but my new gear keeps me surprisingly warm as we plod up through soft, deep snow into Lost Valley. We go over ice-axe braking and the placing of 'deadmen', which are in effect snow anchors. Then the fun's over. Time to do some climbing.

My heart thuds wildly as we gear up, I have to force myself to breathe slowly and deep. Concentrate. I buckle on the harness, tie in the rope, get the knot right on the second attempt. Then strap the crampons onto my cumbersome rigid-soled double boots.

The cramps are like heavy-duty running spikes, with two addi-
tional fangs projecting out in front. Then I sort out my two ice
axes. Both have sharply inclined picks with teeth notched
towards the tip; the head of one ends with a hammer for knocking
in and removing pitons, while the head of the other ends in an
adze for cutting steps. Apparently this is largely redundant, as the
combination of front-pointed crampons and inclined picks make
step-cutting unnecessary in most situations.

I feel absurd and overburdened, like a deep-sea diver in a
paddling pool, as I follow Mal up the steepening slope. It's not
steep enough – he says – to merit belaying. I keep my gaze
determinedly at my feet. Slip, flurry, recover. Continue. Untangle
these stupid axes. Stop tripping over the crampons. Up and
across, don't like traverses, getting pretty high now. Don't look,
watch your feet, time for doing, not thinking. How clear the
sounds are: scrape of crampons on rock, scrunch of boots in
snow, jingling harness, echoing wind, a faint mewing cry . . .

We look up and spot a figure waving awkwardly further up
John Gray's Buttress. 'Looks like he's got gripped,' says Mal.
'Kick yourself a ledge and wait here.' I feel a moment's pleasant
superiority over the incompetent up ahead, then a surge of fellow
feeling. Mal tries to persuade him to climb down, but the shake of
the head is vehement even from here. I look down. Safe enough
really, but just the same . . . Mal climbs further up, secures a
belay. In crabbed, awkward movements the man picks his way
down. When he finally passes me, he's white-faced and embarrassed. 'Snow's tricky in patches,' he mutters apologetically. I
agree politely.

A shout from Mal. He's waving me up towards a ledge on the
left beside a steep drop into a narrow gully, then adds something I
can't catch. By the time I reach the ledge, he's disappeared. The
rope runs over the edge into the gully, then drops out of sight. I
wait. And wait. And wait.

Thirty minutes later there's still no sign of him and the view
downhill is beginning to impinge on me, nagging like a toothache.
I shout tentatively, feeling foolish. No answer. Adrenalin wears
off and muscles stiffen. Now what? Don't think. Wait. Odd
feeling alone up here . . .

He finally appears below me, plodding up the hill looking
puffed and not very pleased. 'Dropped my glove belaying that

wazzock, it slid right to the bottom of the gully.' I ask what had happened to the man he'd rescued. 'Gripped,' he says shortly and indicates our next line. A traverse right across a distinctly steep snow slope. He sets off. Looks like I'm not going to be belayed. I've had a lot of time to get nervous and don't like the look of it, but follow on gingerly, thinking about avalanche, about falling . . .

I reach his stance, a narrow ledge beside a boulder, panting hard. Nerves, mostly. 'Right, better clip in now, Andy.'

I put him on belay through the descendeur as we rehearsed on his stairway a lifetime ago. He checks my gear, goes over the call sequence and disappears round the corner. One day all of this will seem normal. I peer round to see where he's making for and find myself looking down the throat of an apparently sheer snow chute. I look away, feeling ill. How did we get so high? This fear is like seasickness, invading mind and body. Hands tighten, stomach lurches, legs feel weak, stare fixedly in front . . . 'Gripped' is the right word for it. One grips and is gripped by an enormous fist of fear. I can't do this. I'll have to cry off the Expedition. What a farce. Then angry at myself, at this instinctive fear and revulsion. A clinking sound drifts faintly back. He must be putting in a runner. Good man. Put in a dozen. Stare at the weave in my gloves, the powder snow caught in the cuff of the windsuit. All sharp and vivid, too clear. 'I'll put you in controlled freak-out situations,' Mal had said. 'You freak out and I'll control them.' He knows what he's doing. You trust him, don't you? Yes. So nothing to worry about, just don't make an ass of yourself . . .

The rope stops paying out. I start untangling myself, take off the descendeur and clip it to my harness. The slack's taken in, then tugs come down the line. If only we had to face just one moment of truth, not many. Here goes . . .

'Good enough, youth.'

I arrive at Mal's stance and subside, jittering with adrenalin. I've just learned that waiting is worst; climbing itself is too novel, too demanding and intense to leave much room for anxiety. Or for memory. Already the last twenty minutes are reduced to a floundering through whiteness, stinging knuckles caught between axe shaft and rock, a flurried impromptu tango when my crampons interlocked, a hurried pull-up, the surge of satisfaction when the pick thuds into frozen turf. All so clumsy and unfamiliar, but something in this lark, perfectly safe really . . .

Then I look down and that anxiety that is like drowning rushes up to my throat. We're poised out on the edge of space. Horrible. Unnatural. I shrink back into the slope. Mal points out matter-of-factly that the crampons can't grip properly this way. Clinging to the slope actually increases the likelihood of falling. I point out this may well be true and would make a sound Buddhist parable, but every instinct in my body shouts at me not to stand upright.

By now the weather's deteriorating fast; a greenish-grey sky and each gust fiercer than the last. And the pitch above us isn't filled in with snow and ice – Mal points it out, I shudder and try to sound regretful when he decides we've done enough for today. And oddly enough, I suddenly am. He belays my descent along a ridge and down the sheerest slope yet. Perhaps because down is the right direction, I enjoy it and even find the blinding spindrift exhilarating. Then turn outwards and step-plunge down, feeling positively elated. Great to be in the hills, feeling oneself so physically immediate, so simple . . . And there's something pleasing in the essence of winter climbing; a rope, axes, crampons, things to wedge in cracks, and with these one can go almost anywhere, in reasonable safety. Pointless maybe, but satisfying. And I like the way in which, quite unlike rock climbing, routes appear and disappear, may only exist for a few days every other year, are never the same twice.

In the valley we find an ice slab and mess around on that, reluctant to pack in for the day. Vertical and all of 12 feet high. My first fall of the day leaves me dangling helplessly from one axe wrist-loop, unable to go up or down, feet six inches off the ground, cursing a Duff helpless with laughter.

As we plod back, the wind redoubles. The combination of spindrift and fresh snow forms drifts in minutes. A couple of gusts simply knock us over. It's exhilarating. We do not know this is the beginning of the worst blizzard for years in the Highlands and that five climbers will be dead before it's through.

That evening in the Clachaig the sense of siege and drama mounted like the storm outside as one group after another staggered in, red-faced, dazed, plastered from head to foot, head torches making them look like negatives of miners. I floundered through chest-high drifts to our chalet, passed two tents reduced to mangled poles and shreds of material. And this on the sheltered floor of the valley. Rumours spread rapidly. All roads out blocked . . . sixteen head torches still on the hill . . . Mountain Rescue team on four calls at once . . . Hamish MacInnes stranded in his Land-Rover . . . someone's taken a fall, broken his collarbone . . . We drank on, increasingly aware of Tony and Terry's absence. They'd left at 5.00 a.m. to go to Ben Nevis. Mal was quite confident in them, but still kept glancing at his watch.

Finally, round 10.30, a small and a tall figure pushed wearily through the door. They looked as if they'd been tested in a wind tunnel, a mangle, a car wash, then hit repeatedly over the head for hours with a particularly substantial edition of *Being and Nothingness*. Which turned out to be pretty much the case as, drinks in hand, eyes still unfocused, they recounted their epic day. They'd succeeded in doing Vanishing Gully in appalling conditions ('Very vertical,' said Tony, eyes wide at the memory of it, '*very*'), abseiled off Tower Ridge where their lowered ropes flew straight up in the air like snakes charmed by the banshee howl of the wind, and made it to the CIC hut, mostly on hands and knees. There, unbelievably, they were refused shelter because they were not members of the Scottish Mountaineering Club, so they had to continue. From the hut to the road, normally an hour's walk, had taken them six and a half hours of tumbling, rolling, swimming, crawling, through a world gone berserk. 'I once took two and a half hours on that walk,' Mal said, 'and the conditions were desperate. For Tony to take six and a half hours . . .' He shook his head. Terry was slumped back, pale now, staring into his pint, completely drained. Tony was starting to recover, and entertained us with the absurdity of nearly being wiped out crossing the golf course ('Thought we might set a new record'), finally being slammed up against the fence ('I thought I was going to come out the other side as mince!'), getting to the car and realizing they'd have to dig it out. Then they'd driven through the blizzard, abandoned it on the road, and battered their way through to the Clachaig on foot.

A definite epic, a tale worth surviving for the telling of it. And sitting in that besieged inn in the wilderness, packed with dripping, excited, exhausted climbers, thinking back on the day and listening to the stories go round, I began to see something of what brings them there. Anxiety, adrenalin, physical endeavour, the surge of exultation; a day locked into the mountains, evening in the company of fellow nutters – after this, any other way of spending the weekend would be simply dull.

And one doesn't have to be a top-level climber to feel this. At any level the rewards and apprehensions are the same. This is what makes them risk life and limb, scrape, borrow, hitch, neglect work, lovers, family, the future. The moment you commit yourself to the next pitch all those ghostly chains of everyday worries fall away. Lightness in the midst of fear; all that exists is the next move, the mountain, and your thudding heart.

Come closing time we are invited into the Snug bar among the late drinkers. Something of a ceilidh starts; guitars come out and the songs go round. And looking round I suddenly see how this was the original bar I'd walked into sixteen years before. The door must have been here, the fireplace there. I see again the dartboard, the Pale Ale, my Glasgow nurse, myself singing out my teenage years into the hubbub of men. The place is recognizable though overlaid with changes. Me too. For a moment I long to go back, to have that night again, though I know I carry it inside me. Then one of the women's voices, trained and beautiful, lifts in a haunting Gaelic lament, and in the moment's silence at the end we are all briefly bound together by the silken, invisible rope of her song.

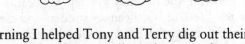

Next morning I helped Tony and Terry dig out their car. As we slithered towards Glencoe Village the car radio spoke of 2000 people trapped in Glenshee, marooned trains, three climbers found dead in the Cairngorms . . . Tony and Terry glance at each other, the slightest shake of the head. Nothing is said. It could have been them but it wasn't.

At the village I waved them goodbye and plodded to the monument to the Massacre of Glencoe. It's a simple pillar of stone on a hillock near the river. The inscription was unreadable, being plastered with spindrift. I thought of the sign in the Clachaig: NO HAWKERS NO CAMPBELLS. Life was precarious enough

in those days, no need for mountaineering. Climbing has some of
the adrenalin, the release, and the self-discovery of combat; the
difference is you're not being asked to kill anyone, and you take
no orders but your own. But war and climbing partake of the
same odd quirk in our nature – only when our survival is at risk
do we feel how precious it is to be alive. Tony and Terry's silence
came not from callousness but an acceptance of the risks
involved.

Mal spent most of the day in his sleeping bag, looking
haggard and listening to Frank Sinatra on his Walkman.
Apparently last night's session went on long and late. We ate and
slept, marking time. Climbers came, gossiped, picked up their
gear and left. Towards evening the snow came down again, thick
and swirling.

We went over to the pub for one beer, had several, and found
ourselves having a long and surprisingly personal talk about our
lives. Our paths have been so different, yet there are parallels. It's
hard to imagine now, but Mal worked in insurance in London for
five years. 'Then one day I looked around me, a long, slow look at
all the familiar faces reading the papers or looking out the
window, and I saw they were only existing, not living. And if I
carried on, I'd be like that in another five years. I thought, screw
that for a lark. I handed in my notice to quit that day.' He stared
down at his lager with his characteristic frown, part impatience,
part perplexity. 'That's why I could relate to you from the
beginning, because somewhere along the line you've chosen not
to live like most people.'

I nodded, knowing the unlikely kinship he meant. The turning point in my life had not been as sudden and clear as his.
My dissatisfaction with the life I was leading some years ago
grew slowly and unnoticed like an overhanging cornice until
finally I fell through. I kept on writing because there was nothing
else.

And the unhappiness we spread around us on the way makes it
all the more important that we do it well.

Climbing and writing seem poles apart, but we had both
rearranged our lives round a supremely satisfying central activity
that seems pointless to many – sometimes to ourselves. We were
both now doing what we wanted. That was our basis for mutual
respect.

That night he called out in his sleep, 'It's too late now.' And then, 'Better put some more runners in, Andy.'

Next morning loose snow still ruled out serious climbing. We spent it working on setting up runners and belay stances, and abseiling. There's something absolutely unnatural in walking backwards off a cliff. I found it also – when you're sure of the rope and the belay – surprisingly enjoyable. Just lean back and walk down, paying out rope through the descendeur. Pleasingly ingenious.

I spent some time on placing aids. Hammering pitons (blades, leapers, bongs, angles, channels, pegs, the wonderfully named RURPS – Realized Ultimate Reality Pitons) into cracks; wedging nuts (wedges, wires) into fissures. 'I lost a couple of friends here last year,' Mal remarked conversationally, fumbling with something on his harness. I didn't know what to say, made some sympathetic sound. 'They're worth nearly twenty quid now,' he continued. I stared at him. I know this is an age that sets a price on everything, but this is ridiculous. 'And even this one is a bit knackered,' he said, and held out a strange object to me with just the faintest hint of a grin.

It looked like a piece of particularly nasty dental equipment, like an adjustable wrench with its jaws turned inside out. They were spring-loaded so one could pull them back, shove them into a crack and then let them expand to grip the walls.

'It's called a "friend". Not totally reliable, but very useful at times.'

We went through the belaying sequence on the floor of a quarry. I was cumbersome and ponderous as I stumbled along pretending there was a 1000-foot drop on my right, placing runners along the rock on my left. When I shouted 'On belay!' my voice sounded absurd and lacking in conviction, like the first time you try to hail a taxi or call 'Waiter!'. Mal followed on round the corner, walking slowly, treating this charade with elaborate seriousness. He came to the first runner, removed the peg – then abruptly fell back. I instinctively pulled the rope back on the descendeur and he was held. He came on again, head down. When he arrived at my stance he looked up, shook his head. 'Whew, that was a bit thin, youth!' We laughed. It was a game.

The whole activity is an absurd and sometimes delightful game.

He led through and we did a couple of pitches on genuine slopes. It's clever and simple, this whole procedure, each climber alternately protecting the other. I was still getting tangled up and several times hit myself on the helmet with an ice axe, but it was beginning to feel more natural. Finding out what crampons can do, working out different moves, reading the slope ahead. The last pitch was a scramble; the snow deep and powdery, no purchase in it, then loose and shallow over rocks. Spindrift blowing up into my face, balaclava slipping over my eyes. The left axe pulled through and I was off balance, hacking away wildly for purchase, slipping ... An internal voice spoke very clearly, 'Slow down, look for it.' I spotted frozen turf, the inclined pick went in and held. Lovely. Pull up, across, come out on the top and find Mal sitting patient and immobile as a Buddha, wrapped in a cloak of spindrift.

We finished up by building a snowhouse. It was more of a beehive than a classic igloo, but the shelter it provided was impressive. Absolutely silent and windless inside. 'If those missing Army blokes have made one of these and stay in it, they'll be all right for days.'

Back in the gloaming, in high spirits, for tea and the latest disaster stories. A few casualties, but no fatalities in Glencoe. In the evening I borrowed a guitar and sang a few songs I'd written years before to go with my *Men on Ice*. Mal was very taken with them, insisted I put them on tape, and spent much of the rest of our time in Glencoe wandering about with the earphones on, bawling out the lyrics. When he was over in the pub I wrote some new verses to *Throw me down some more rope*, and a middle section. Mal was amazed on his return. 'How can you do that?' 'How can you solo Grade Five?' I replied. It was good to be reminded there were things I could do competently.

'We'll try a harder route tomorrow,' he said as I crawled into my bag. I lay thinking about that as he muttered over a new verse and the chorus, trying to memorize the words:

> *Halfway up 'Whitesnake' when the blizzard hits,*
> *Can't feel your nose or your toes, everything goes*
> *And nothing grips (except you);*
> *It's a funny desire, wanting to get higher,*
> *Sometimes you wish you'd stayed below,*

Sometimes you know that it's right,
Sometimes you know that it's wrong,
And sometimes you just Don't Know –
Throw me down some more rope (throw me down)
Throw me down some more rope (hey, youth!)
Throw me down some more rope 'cos I'm falling,
Yes I'm falling . . .

We set out in the half-light. No cloud, no wind, blue sky filtering through. The high ridges slowly become three-dimensional as we plod up the road in silence, our senses sharp and clear as the air. A flock of sheep freshly out of a snowdrift are encrusted with icicles; as they move, a delicate tinkling like wind chimes sounds across the valley. A buzzard circles into high sunlight, drifting on invisible currents. Three crows beside a frozen stream tear at a dead rabbit. Glencoe goes about its immemorial business.

It was a long day that, on the north face of Aonach Dubh, but only fragments of it remain lodged in the memory, like slivers of ice caught in a windsuit's creases. I was too caught up with what was happening to record, too present to stand back, too scared to take photographs.

The first pitch up a narrowing snow-choked gully made the first day's efforts seem child's play. Relief and exhilaration on arriving at Mal's stance, then half an hour clinging to a stunted rowan tree, fighting off paralysis and panic, hating it. Sitting still is the worst. Time to take in where you are, time to think, time to fear. I look down – too far, too steep, too empty. I glance up – too high, too steep, too endless. Contemplating going on this Expedition is absurd. My body hates this. Don't look, don't think. Keep the rope going. Where's Mal got to? If you think this is bad, imagine the sense of exposure on Mustagh . . . Extraordinary clarity of lichen on this branch, the precise angle of this fork . . .

It's a relief to be climbing again, traversing onto a buttress of steep rock, soft snow, patchy frozen turf. Gloves off, treating some of it as a rock climb, half-remembered techniques from childhood scrambling. Chunks of knuckle left on rocks, arms with all the resilience of blancmange. Concentrating hard, each movement dreamlike in its intensity. I call for tight rope and get it. Thanks, pal. Over a bulge, there he is . . .

Another anxious wait on belay, then another pitch. It's beginning to feel more natural. I cease tying myself up in Gordian knots of slings, rope, krabs and ice axe lines. Even relax enough to snatch a photo as Mal works his way up an angled cleft above me. After two hours fear starts to lose its urgency, and though I know this pitch is tricky by my standards I push up through soft snow, cross onto rock, find some lovely frozen turf and almost shout with satisfaction as the picks thud home. Hold an elephant, that would. Now pull up . . . Something in this lark, after all.

Until you pause and catch a glimpse of below.

An hour and two pitches later we come out on top of the ridge. I'm shattered, puffing like an old espresso machine, arm muscles like wet newspaper from working above my head all the time. In addition to the long approach plod, then the physical effort of climbing, I've put out enough nervous energy to light up Glencoe village for a year. But the weather's menacing and the light starting to go, so Mal hurries on and I plod after. We pause on the summit of Aonach Dubh – briefer than a kiss is this final pay-off, that's the joke of it.

Mal points down No. 2 Gully. 'Follow me as fast as you can – but concentrate.' I sense a certain urgency in his voice, and follow him down in the half-light. It seems steep, but I haven't the energy to care. Step, plunge, axe, step, plunge . . . It becomes endless, unreal, hypnotic. I begin to stumble, stuff snow in my mouth to stay awake. Somewhere along the line a crampon disappears. No time to look for it, carry on . . . I seem to have been doing this forever, stepping down through the gathering dark. In the distance Mal swings right and up onto a buttress. Eventually I join him. 'Well done,' he says briefly. Must have been harder than it looked. It's getting very dim now. We start feeling our way down over rock, scree and snow towards the yellow lights in the valley.

Finally his urgency relaxes, the rest is straightforward. We sit for five minutes on Dinnertime Buttress, munching biscuits and looking over at the glimmering slopes across the glen. We say nothing, but it is many months since I felt so at peace. 'What was that route called?' 'We can decide that in the pub,' he replies casually. Understanding comes slowly. 'You mean you . . . we . . .?' I splutter. He nods. 'I'd been saving that one up for a while.'

A new route for my first route. I'm outraged, flabbergasted, and not a little chuffed. Of course it wasn't hard – Grade 2 or 3 he reckons – and all I did was follow on, but the sense of delight and absurdity sustain me on the rest of the trudge back. 'Two Shakes' I say finally. 'Why?' 'Well, there was two tree belays on it, there's two parts to it – the gully and the buttress – and I'm lying about the amount of shaking I did!'

Finally, we push through the door of the Clachaig into a gust of warmth and light and laughter. Then the simple wonder of sitting down. We've been on the go for eleven hours. I slump back against the wall, totally blank.

'Tired, youth?' Mal asks.

I search for the right epithet.

'Massacred,' I say briefly, and with some effort raise the first pint of the night to my lips.

We left Glencoe two days later. I was relieved yet oddly regretful as the old blue van struggled out of the valley. Five days in this place had been a month of normal time. Grinding and slipping past abandoned cars, cottages up to their eyelids in snow, a snowblower moving across the wilderness of Rannoch Moor, followed by a tiny man in yellow oilskins . . .

We were silent as we worked our way south toward civilization and its dubious benefits. What had happened to me here, what had I learned? The extent of my fear, for one thing. It hadn't miraculously evaporated over the intervening years, like teenage acne. I felt weakened by that fear, yet strengthened for having coped with it. Perhaps one can never overcome fear completely – after all, it is often a sane and appropriate response – what counts is that it doesn't overcome you.

Being a novice climber is like having a weak head for alcohol: people may laugh at you, but you get high more easily. It didn't take much to get my heart thumping, whereas Mal has to push it a long way to get his kicks. Both novice and expert have the same experience, despite the huge gulf in their capabilities. Both know fear, exhilaration, satisfaction, relief. Both have to persist through discomfort and utter fatigue. Both have to recognize their limits, then push a little further. And both experience the great simplification of one's life that is the reward of all risk activities . . .

But I was thinking most of all about the two Army lads who were found dead today in the Cairngorms, and of the half-buried monument to the Massacre of Glencoe. Our 'massacre' by the elements is a self-imposed one, a piece of personal theatre. When it is over, all but a few get to their feet again and feel themselves, behind their fatigue, somehow stronger and more alive than before.

For those who do not rise again, there remains the unyielding pillar of stone, the inscription obliterated by drifting snow.

3

Sit-ups and Setbacks

In which we prepare to bottle up and go
November 1983–May 1984

I trained for our Expedition from late November till our departure in early June. I had not trained for anything in fifteen years. It was hard work. Sit-ups, pull-ups, press-ups, toe-ups, Bullworker, stiff hill walking with a weighted backpack. And, above all, running. Between three and eight miles, five days a week.

Picture one of those montage sequences used in films to indicate continued effort through time. At first we see an unfit, ungainly figure running through falling leaves, the last rags of autumn quivering in the trees. He emerges, panting and staggering, onto an open beach. Then the trees are bare, the light low and brief; it's a world drained of colour and sound; no birds sing, but the runner now seems to be moving more firmly and rejoices in the frozen sand as he turns for home in the half-light of 3.30. Then clots of snowdrops appear on the forest floor, then crocuses, birdsong, movements in the undergrowth. The runner has removed his gloves, then his sweater. He is moving faster and lighter than before, more upright. And suddenly the light is fresh and green, it is May, and as he turns for home at 8.00 on a sunlit evening – wearing only shorts and running shoes – he is running not towards his home and a cool shower but towards a tower of snow and rock some four and a half miles high, on the roof of the world.

I'd noticed the sudden proliferation of runners in the last few years. I could only shake my head and wonder at them. It all looked too mindless and too painful: an exercise in masochism. To my surprise it was not like that at all.

Not only did I stick to my schedule of running five days a week, but I found myself looking forward to it. After a couple of days off, I'd be edgy and irritable, obscurely dissatisfied. 'For God's sake, go for a run,' Kathleen would say, and her diagnosis was correct.

It was often uncomfortable, often painful, particularly for the first month, but other days were pure joy, a revelling in the sensation of movement, of strength and wellbeing. My regular headaches stopped. For the first time ever, I got through winter without even a cold. I felt incredibly well, began to walk and hold myself differently. When friends asked 'How are you?', instead of the normal Scottish 'Oh, not too bad,' I'd find myself saying 'Extremely well!'

How obnoxious.

On other days training was pure slog, the body protesting and the will feeble. The mind could see little point in getting up before breakfast to run on a cold, dark morning, and none at all in continuing when it began to hurt. Take a break, why not have a breather, why not turn for home now?

It is at times like that that the real work is done. It's easy to keep going when you feel strong and good. Anyone can do that. But at altitude it is going to feel horrible most of the time – and that's what you're really training for. So keep on running, through the pain and the reluctance. Do you really expect to get through this Expedition – this relationship, this book, this life, for that matter – without some of the old blood, sweat and tears? No chance. That's part of the point of it all. So keep on running . . .

The real purpose of training is not so much hardening the body as toughening the will. Enthusiasm may get you started, bodily strength may keep you going for a long time, but only the will makes you persist when those have faded. And stubborn pride. Pride and the will, with its overtones of fascism and suppression, have long been suspect qualities – the latter so much so that I'd doubted its existence. But it does exist, I could feel it gathering and bunching inside me as the months passed. There were times when it alone got me up and running, or kept me from whinging and retreating off a Scottish route. The will is the secret motor that keeps driving when the heart and the mind have had enough.

Mal would call it commitment. He'd said there was no point in going to a mountain with a 'let's see how it looks' attitude. One's commitment and self-belief had to be absolute. And yet that had to be balanced by clear, objective assessment of one's capacities and limitations. That balancing act is at the very heart of climbing. I noticed that most climbers didn't value bravado and boldness unless it was tempered by good judgement. One of the lads at Mal's wedding said, 'The hardest and bravest and probably the best mountaineering decision you can make is to say No.' I looked at Tony. The diminutive innocent nodded vigorously. 'That's right. Mountaineering isn't about getting to the top – it's about mountaineering.'

To call mountaineering a sport or a pastime is like calling monastic life a hobby. For those who become serious – though seldom solemn – about it, it is the core of their lives. Everything else is arranged around it. It affects their attitude to everything else. As time went by I gradually exchanged one obsession, writing, for another, climbing – though I denied and derided it to the last. I picked up the elements of Good Brit Style: not to be seen training, not to have gleaming new gear, to play down all but one's fears and fiascos. To drink too much too late, to get up reluctantly and late next morning, moaning and groaning, to arrive at the foot of the route with three hours' daylight left *and still climb it*: that was considered Good Style. I had little problem in acquiring that.

The substance was another matter. Due to poor weather I only had another four weekends' winter climbing in Glencoe. Yet the promise and threat of these changed my entire winter, made it something to be enjoyed rather than just suffered. Weekdays were a time for recovery and appreciation of home comforts, with the weekend to both dread and anticipate. My social life was suddenly full of climbers, climbing talk, climbing plans and reminiscences. Much laughter, drinking, abuse and friendship, shared experience. And gradually, the beginning of some composure.

It was, quite simply, very exciting. It dramatized my life.

By the end of the season, I'd done a grand total of six Scottish routes, none harder than Grade 3 or 4, and an amount of yomping about on the hills. It was an absurdly inadequate background for going to the Himalayas – the norm would be several Scottish winters, then a few seasons in the Alps doing the classics and adding some new routes, then one might consider Pakistan or Nepal.

My anxiety at exposure didn't disappear, but did diminish. I still disliked waiting on belay halfway up a route. And some days I had no appetite or nerve for it at all, when climbing was all slog and fear and trembling and wanting it to be over with, hating it. That too – and having to continue just the same – was valuable experience. But other days . . .

One day in particular remains with me, always will. A day when nervousness took the form of controlled energy, when I wanted to climb. When I had the appetite. A day of great intensity and joy. Then I rejoiced in the challenge of the crux of SC Gully; pulling up and over it and moving on, I was lifted up like a surfer on a great wave of adrenalin. The day was perfect: ice blue, ice cold, needle-bright. After two hours in the shadowed gully I finally pulled myself through the notch in the cornice overhanging the top, and in my eyes was a dazzling world of sunlight and gleaming ridges and all the summits of Glencoe clear across to Ben Nevis. Mal silhouetted against the sun, belaying me; a few climbers moving on the summit ridge; my panting exhilaration – in that moment I felt like a king, and what I saw in front of me was the earth as Paradise, blue, golden and white, dazzlingly pure.

The intensity we win through effort! In that pristine clarity of the air and the senses, the simplest experiences become almost mystical in their intensity. A cigarette smoked in the lee of a cairn, an orange segment squirting in the mouth and the smell of it filling the moment, making the world fruit, the patch of lichen inches from your face, the final pulling off of boots, at the end of the day – Glencoe and winter climbing gave me moments of completeness. I will never forget them.

Though I still intended to pack it in after the Mustagh trip, it was hard to imagine what I did with myself before climbing came along. The company, the personal struggle and the intensity of sensation on the mountains are all highly addictive. And more than that, I found all my customary worries and concerns – money, love life, boredom, the future, the past, politics, whatever – ceased to weigh on me in Glencoe. Such things cease to matter. All that matters is this move, the next hold, keeping the rope running out, the approaching storm clouds and the beer at the end of the day. All other worries slip off one's shoulders and slide away into obscurity, like the sacks we sometimes sent off down a snow chute, to be picked up again on our way back down.

The weight one takes on in committing oneself to a mountain or a route is considerable, but it's nothing compared to the weight of the world one leaves behind.

It was at the Clachaig that I first met Jon Tinker, the third of our lead climbers. I knew he'd been out to the Himalayas once, on an unsuccessful but highly educational trip to Annapurna 3, and that he was beginning to make a name for himself with some bold Alpine ascents. 'A bit of a headbanger,' someone opined. 'I don't know,' Mal said, frowning, 'I thought he was pretty impressive when we did that new route on the Ben.' At twenty-four and a couple of months younger than Tony Brindle, he was the youngest of the team. I'd been forewarned that he'd be the most awkward and abrasive member, and that there could be some interesting strains between him and Tony.

'So you're the author chappie who wants to poke about inside our heads' were practically his first words to me. And then he laughed, just a shade too loudly. That was typical Jon: the remark that niggled, then the forced laugh that seemed to say he was just joking yet with just enough edge to make it stick. I was to see him do it many times with people he'd just met – with men, at least, for he was much more charming and at ease with women – and quite often with those he knew well. He seemed to always strive for the upper hand.

I considered him. A blue-eyed, fair-haired, compact, Anglo-Saxon boy. Prickly and intelligent. He lived in Bloomsbury – unlikely address for a climber – with his parents. His father was chaplain to the University of London; his mother had written several books on housing the aged. A very pleasant English upper-middle-class household, yet Jon spoke in a quasi-cockney accent and was the scruffiest of the bunch of scruffs we were. I wondered if his background was a reason for his defensive–offensive attitude.

He went on to tell me that in an expedition it's everyone for themselves. 'No one's going to look after you.' Though that was undoubtedly the bottom line, his attitude was so different from

Mal's that I wondered how much I was being told about expeditions and how much about Jon.

Over the next few days we relaxed with each other somewhat. In many ways I had more in common with him than any of the others; he had a degree in politics, made a point of having nonclimbing friends, and was strongly interested in books and modern music, the more obscure the better. When we got onto that common ground he was quite a different person, open and enthusiastic, one I liked and found interesting.

And then suddenly one would be back to first base with him. I'd see a hesitation come over him as he remembered that I was a writer, that I might be studying him, and his eyes would twinkle with malice as he prepared one of his remarks. His desire for privacy seemed strong and genuine. He said he liked London because of its anonymity, and mountaineering because of the private nature of the experience.

He struck me as a competitor who went to great lengths to show that he wasn't. I think of him always as lounging back, legs sprawled, hands stuffed in anorak pockets, a position of exaggerated indifference. He loved to accuse other climbers of 'secret training' and to protest how lazy and uncompetitive he was.

Maybe that was the basis of the antipathy that seemed to exist between him and Tony, for Tony was so openly intense and enthusiastic about climbing. He didn't brag, but saw no point in self-denigration and pretending to be less committed than he was. He loved climbing and didn't disguise it; he seemed to have no interests outside climbing. And Jon on the surface was exactly the opposite, yet I suspected that underneath he was the same, 'a real revver' as Mal said. Maybe that was why Tony seemed to irritate him.

I was there when they met at the Clachaig for the first time in a year. Yes, a definite tension there. Even Tony was less buoyant than usual, and Jon even more indifferent and uninterested. While Tony talked on about his latest doings to Mal, Jon lolled back as if oblivious and entered the conversation only to say 'I've got nothing to prove, mate,' with just sufficient emphasis on the 'I'. And when Tony asked him directly if he'd done anything recently, Jon answered, 'Don't try to wind me up, Brindle – you can't do it.'

I asked him later what bothered him about Tony. 'He's so

wound up and intense about it all. I just like climbing,' he replied. Which was exactly what Tony had said to me about Jon. I began to agree with the prediction that their relationship could be an interesting part of the Expedition.

We treated each other a lot less warily after I came into the chalet happily drunk in the early hours while he was dossing on the settee. 'Great to see you, Jon,' I bellowed, and proceeded to demolish his resting place and his Walkman set-up as I blundered about in the dark. I was being natural for once, and he responded.

Jon was as pessimistic as Mal was optimistic. He gave us a 5 per cent chance of climbing the Mustagh Tower, and less with Gasherbrum 2 – yet he was utterly determined to go and give them what he called 'maximum pastry'. The phrase quickly entered Expedition vocabulary, as did the 'shuffling dossers' coinage of a friend of his, which evokes perfectly the whole hand-to-mouth, day-to-day peripatetic lifestyle of so many climbers. Being free to do serious climbing tends to mean lacking visible means of support. Mal got by with guiding and the help of his wife Liz's job; Tony was at college on a student grant; Jon worked for little more than pocket money in a climbing shop between trips. Only Sandy Allan, who I hadn't yet met, made serious money during his spells on the oil rigs. Borrowing, cadging, hitching and sleeping on floors, spending what we had on drink and climbing, shuffling dossers is what we were. It indicated more than a lack of finance; shuffling dossing is a state of mind, unselfconscious existentialism.

But the phrase that really stuck to Jon came out of a heated argument one evening in the chalet between him and a climber who was going on what was reckoned to be a lightweight, no-hope Everest expedition. The climber in question had only a reasonable Alpine record, had never been higher than 19,000 feet, but was quite confident that with sheer determination and 'going for it' he had a good chance of making the summit.

'You'll die,' Jon said brusquely.

'I'm going to go for it.'

'It doesn't matter if you go for it – you're going to die with that attitude.'

'What's going to stop me?'

'Altitude. Weather. All-round deterioration. You don't know anything about it. If you're lucky, you'll all be driven off early. If not, you're going to die, old son,' Jon repeated with evident satisfaction.

'Well, I'm still going to go for it,' the climber replied defensively. 'I think I can do it.'

Jon, lounging back, flashed his most sardonic smile. 'It doesn't matter what you think. You've got a squaddie's mentality, mate.' The room seemed to quiver with hostility. Jon sprawled back even further and added the *coup de grâce*. 'You *deserve* to die.'

And since then 'You're going to DIE' became a chorused catch phrase, one he accepted with good grace. It was only later that I learned part of his vehemence stemmed from his experience on Annapurna 3, when one of the small team died during a five-day blizzard that drove them off the mountain. And it was a long time later that he confessed to me that on his return to Kathmandu he had stumbled round the town for a day, blinded by tears.

A complex character. Mal and Tony are just themselves, they don't change according to their company. But there are at least three Jons – the prickly, laughing, abrasive one, the casual, sardonic Jon among climbing friends, and the disarmingly enthusiastic, open and interesting Jon when relaxed and outside the climbing ethos.

'You really think I've got a chance?'

'Of making the Col on Mustagh? Should be no problem, if the weather behaves and you can take the altitude. You're not going to set the climbing world alight, but you seem to have taken to it well enough.' Pause. I consider Duff's perennial optimism. 'Your biggest problem may be the scale of things out there,' he continued thoughtfully. 'You haven't even been to the Alps, and Himalayan scale is a different thing again. It can be pretty daunting.'

This on a cloudy, wet day, sitting halfway up Dinnertime Buttress in Glencoe in late March, smoking cigarettes. The nicotine constricted the circulation at my fingertips and they felt cold. Himalayan scale . . . I shivered, certainly daunted already, yet a new composure made itself felt deeper down.

'See how it looks when I get there,' I replied. My voice sounded surprisingly matter-of-fact. I wondered if I was changing, and beginning to pick up as one might a disease, certain climbers' attitudes.

He nodded. 'You're going to spend a lot of time on this trip being totally hacked off. Headaches, sore throats, the cold, all that hanging around in the middle of nowhere, you'll think, "This is utterly pointless." And it is.' He seemed to be addressing himself as much as me. He was coming to the end of his winter guiding season and looked worn down. 'There's no reason for it at all,' he continued. 'Going up a mountain and coming back down again doesn't mean anything, it doesn't affect anything. Well, except you. It doesn't *do* anything.' He gazed gloomily down into the valley. 'At those times the only thing that keeps me going is the thought that I could be sitting on that 8.10 train with my eyes glazed over.'

We'd become close in the last six months, during days in the hills and evenings in the Clachaig or the pubs of South Queensferry with Kath and Liz. Because I was not a dedicated climber, he could air his doubts, worries and reservations with me. Malcolm had my father's fascination with information; his sober level-headedness was like my elder brother's, while his impetuous enthusiasm and fondness for flying a kite in argument reminded me of myself a few years back. He seemed at once older and younger than me, and our relationship oscillated between those two poles. Turning up at the foot of the north face of the Eiger, seventeen years old and fresh from his Edinburgh public school, with a sleeping bag, an ice dagger and a couple of screws, ready to do battle with the big one – that was pure Malcolm. (He got as far as 'the Difficult Crack' – some 2000 feet up – and had to turn back. 'I realized I wasn't quite ready for this.' 'You George Watson F.P.s are all the same,' I retorted, 'you think all you have to do is show up at the hill and it'll roll on its back and say, Walk up me!')

He passed over another cigarette and we lit up. Duff's diet is a dietician's nightmare, I reflected. He seemed to live entirely on coffee, white sugar and cigarettes by day, and lager and cigarettes by night. He avoided fresh fruit and raw vegetables like the plague. And he had the nerve to be healthy! I glanced at him: leaning forward elbows on his knees, chin resting on clasped hands, frowning thoughtfully at nothing in particular – this was the way I'd always think of him.

'Why did you really ask me on this trip?' I asked casually.

He grinned and snapped out of his mood as I'd intended. 'I'd never met one of you writer chappies before. I thought it might be interesting to see how you'd react if I actually put you on the spot.'

So that was it. I'm here and going to the Himalayas as the result of someone's whimsical curiosity. Not just anyone's – no one other than Duff would have come up with such a suggestion and carried it through. I laughed in delight at the absurdity of it all. Mal shook his head as if trying to shake the dust from his brains. 'You showed you had the right stuff. The trouble is,' and here he concluded the line of thought he'd been trudging down, 'by the time you get to climbing in the Himalayas, you've forgotten why you started in the first place.'

I was to think often of this conversation in the coming months. We went on to chat casually about Rocky Moss on Mount McKinley, the sex life of butterflies, suitable film, the origin of the Jesuits – and of the intriguing *ménage à trois* of the other three Americans on the trip. Burt Greenspan, Donna and Sybil lived together in a big house in Chicago, Burt and Donna downstairs and Sybil upstairs. It all sounded very decadent and American, and we were curious to see how it worked out in practice. Burt and Donna were coming to climb, while Sybil was part of the trekking party. Finally stiffening muscles, growing thirst and wet snow drifting out of the greyness sent us off downhill towards the lights of the Clachaig.

I felt strong, ready and willing. Next stop Islamabad.

Only it's never as simple as that.

I walked into the Clachaig the following Friday to find Mal leaning against the bar, looking pale and tired.

'Here, read this.' He thrust a newspaper at me.

British climber killed on Matterhorn, the paragraph was headed. I looked up, read on. It reported briefly that Mr Brian Sprunt had fallen to his death on the mountain, and his companions Charlie McLeod and Malcolm Duff had been taken off by helicopter. I glanced at Mal, he managed a rueful smile. 'I seem to be in two places at once. Trouble is, the rest of it is true.' Brian Sprunt . . . the name was familiar. Hadn't I met him, the first time I came up here? 'Yes, he was sitting at our table for a while.' I could picture him now, a face among many, drinking and laughing and planning the new season. And now a face among the many dead, written off in a brief, inaccurate newspaper paragraph.

'Did you know him well?'

'Well enough. We were together on the Nuptse trip. You get close to somebody . . .' He paused, looking into private memories. 'Hell of a good bloke. Bit upsetting, really.'

And with this massive understatement, so typical of Mal and climbers and Scots, he turned back to the bar. 'What you drinking, youth?'

But he was in low spirits all weekend, suddenly quiet and withdrawn, cracking a joke then forgetting to laugh and instead frowning into his lager, right knee jumping incessantly. His wife Liz was very protective, said nothing but quietly put her arm through his. Not for the first time I sensed how emotional he might be. Much of the joking, well-that's-life attitude was part of the necessary protective mechanism, as are the endless death stories and prophecies of doom that climbers love to tell.

And as we finally stumbled over to our chalet in the dark, he said quietly, 'Brian's the second person I had pencilled in for the Mustagh trip who's been blown away.' Pause. 'Makes you think.'

More typical of him and of mountaineers was the attitude he suddenly expressed a week later as we came off a route. 'After all, when you get serious about climbing, you accept there's a chance you'll get blown away. There's nothing tragic about getting killed doing what you want to do. Desperately sad, but not tragic.' Then he hurried off down the hill and I followed more circumspectly, considering him with new interest and sympathy.

A letter came from Sandy Allan who'd been with Brian on the Matterhorn. It was full of Sandy's och ayes and hey ho but that's life, but the pain behind it was evident through the brittle gaiety. He briefly mentioned what had happened. Brian had been belaying him and Charlie as they prepared to leave their bivouac that morning, on a ledge near the top of the face. He was clipped to an old peg left from an earlier climb. Then for some reason – the little, fatal action that always eludes explanation – he untied himself from the rope. Then the peg pulled. 'Oh God . . .' And that was that.

It set Mal back for a time. For me it was a sobering reminder of the seriousness of this game, and of the importance of maintaining concentration at all times. It made Mal seem a little older. 'It's a wonderful way of life,' he remarked once, 'but every so often you look around and realize how many of your friends aren't here any more.'

That's what gave the edge to the good company, to all the fine nights we had, the foolery and laughter, the meetings and partings. It was all precious because so fragile, like an eggshell-thin bowl. One night at the end of a rumbustious after-hours ceilidh in the Clachaig Snug, a straggly-haired northerner with round glasses sang an unaccompanied lament for lost good company, and touched something deep in everyone there. It was in the quality of the silence afterwards, and the stillness while he sang. When he finished we all dispersed unusually quietly to our bedrooms and chalets and tents, for there was nothing left to be said or done that night, and none of us wanted to spill the emotions we each carried inside ourselves, privately, like water brimming at the lip of the bowl.

Then my father died on 24 April, six weeks before we were due to leave. It is still bewildering and strange to write these words sitting at his desk, and know he'll never read them.

There are very real consolations. His life was as long, varied and productive as anyone's could be; he thought and felt himself extraordinarily fortunate; he died before his illness became more pain-filled and humiliating, and he had long accepted death in the dry manner of a Scottish atheistic doctor.

As with Brian, there is nothing tragic here. The shock, the numbness, this physical wrenching I feel in my chest, is for the living, for us who live on. It is for the half-remembered yarns I'll never be able to confirm, the humorous bloody-mindedness, the man himself.

There are more cells in the human brain than stars in our galaxy. When a person dies, a universe collapses into a black hole. I have no notion as to whether it reappears in another dimension. Personally, I doubt it. (I think this and smile, shake my head at my dad's picture, realizing where my scepticism came from.)

So I'd never be able to come back from Mustagh and tell him about it, to show the photos, to in some oblique way say thank you for the life I've inherited.

There's nothing to be done but swallow, shrug and get on with it. To try to live honestly, with appreciation and flair. And the living obscurely rejoice at the news of a death, in the knowledge that it's not us, that we're still in the game.

Kathleen came back for his funeral with news from Mal. Rocky had been struggling desperately on his McKinley warm-up climb, and finally gave up and went back to LA. There the doctors discovered his adrenal glands had packed in. Which meant he was simply not capable of doing two hard days back to back. Despite his quite phenomenal training, fitness and physical strength (we're talking about a fifty-four-year-old who cycled from San Francisco to LA, some 450 miles, in thirty-six hours), there was nothing he could do about it. There was no chance of him climbing Mustagh or Gasherbrum 2.

But he insisted we go ahead without him. He'd still back us.

My first reaction was relief. I hadn't realized till that moment how set I was on this adventure. I'd have been desperately disappointed had it been called off.

My second feeling was sympathy for Rocky. He'd been so keen, so dedicated, so wound up for this Expedition. He hated 'failure'. This happening just five weeks before departure would leave him devastated and disgusted.

Then I felt gratitude – no, more than gratitude, *respect* – at his insistence that we press on and he'd still fund us. The trekking party that were going to accompany us dropped out, but we were still in the game. Again that selfish joy, the relief.

Purely selfish too was the sense of loss for this book of one of its central, most colourful characters. How would I write about what we'd christened 'Rocky's Horror Show' without Rocky? I'd been interested to see how his earnest American 'there must be a solution' approach to the climb would play off against the more anarchic, stoic and improvisational attitudes of the British climbers. I'd been interested to find out why someone who had so much going for him should want to risk his neck doing something like this.

And I was all the more sorry now he couldn't come, because I was impressed by the magnanimity of his gesture. It indicated a sense of community, of joint purpose, a kind of honourable seriousness one doesn't associate with the 'me-centered' American ethos. He demonstrated as much of the Right Stuff in insisting the Expedition went ahead as he possibly could have on the climb itself.

So at the last minute we had to rethink the Expedition. Many of the problems that were to follow stemmed from this. We had to drop the Sherpas who had been going to assist Rocky, Burt and Donna, and without their support we could no longer think of fixing ropes most of the way up. This made our chances of success that bit more marginal.

What had at one point seemed something of a Himalayan circus had been whittled down to a more acceptable modern mountaineering team with a few extras. Much better style, but Burt, Donna and I were worried that with Rocky's absence the spotlight would switch to us, and that we might just be tiresome baggage that would slow the others up. We'd have to work harder, do better, push ourselves further. The Expedition's success might depend on how much support we could give the lead climbers. Were we up to it?

Our chances of success? Mal reckoned it 80 per cent likely that at least one of us would make the summit of Mustagh. Most people considered that wildly optimistic. Roughly one Himalayan expedition in ten succeeds. We counted on one hand the number of active British climbers who'd stood on a summit the height of Mustagh or Gasherbrum 2. The list of those who'd been killed on such peaks took both hands. That was an alarmingly high rate of attrition. Yet we had to start some time, and a new generation of British Himalayan climbers had to appear. If this trip went well, it would establish some new names.

All our lads swore blind that competition and ambition meant nothing to them, that they just liked climbing. Don't believe it for a moment. Duff, Brindle, Allan, Tinker – they were all revved up and hungry for success, for the Mustagh Tower and the further glittering prize of Gasherbrum 2.

*

So even before setting out, we had our losses and setbacks: Brian Sprunt, Rocky, my father. In a curious way they all seemed to connect. In each case there was much sadness, then the determination, almost the duty, to carry on. It's the best thing we can do, the only thing other than despair. Remember them when we're out there, remember what we owe them, then – Go for it, youth.

4

The Third-World Body-Swerve

In which we get all shook up
7–21 June 1984

Mal, Kathleen and I left South Queensferry by bus on a rare, perfect June evening. Blue sky, blue water, green fields. We sat in silence most of the way, each in our own thoughts. A 60-foot-long shark passed by on a flyover. It was no more surreal than sitting on a local bus en route to the Himalayas. Mal had spent the day fishing on some loch, quietly reflecting under his Indiana Jones bush hat. I'd sat on the rocks by the sea, noticing how beautiful my country was. When Kath found me and said suddenly, 'We will come back, won't we,' it seemed one third question, one third statement and one third expression of intent.

Mal tossed the *Daily Express* aside. 'That's the last paper I'll read for three months.' That suited me. I wanted to be away from the western world, from its self-absorbed trivia – and my own. The news increasingly left me stunned or indifferent or helplessly angry, diminished in any case. Now I wanted only our small travelling company and its vast stage, and the unscripted drama we were yet to play out.

At Waverley station Kath and I stood aside as Mal and Liz said their goodbyes. It was a tender, highly charged moment that they both tried to play down by being very matter-of-fact. Then she hugged us briefly, said 'Now make sure – no politics, no death talk!' and walked away.

A short silence, then we began loading our twenty-five items of baggage onto the train. We pulled out into the night. I sat by myself, looking out the window into the dark, feeling the cords that tie us to our everyday life stretch and snap one by one.

*

Next day we began assembling at the Tinkers' house in Bloomsbury. Jon and Sandy Allan were already there, joking and wearing identical T-shirts: a scruffy figure with a Rastafarian hat emerging from a dustbin, and the mysterious legend ALPINE BIN-MEN GO EAST/IN AN ALPINE STYLEE. Jon explained that through a friend of theirs he and Sandy had worked as bin-men in Chamonix to pay for their climbing. The Rasta hat was a nod in the direction of Jon's passion for obscure reggae records, some of which would carry an inscription regarding their style or *stylee* in Rasta-talk, e.g. *in a rubadub stylee*. Alpine style was the modern, lightweight manner in which they intended to climb Gasherbrum 2, carrying everything in one load on their backs, and hoped to use as much as possible on the Mustagh Tower. The *stylee* was to stick.

We sat and joked in the sunny garden. I'd been told that Sandy would be the most easy-going member of the team, with an impressive Alpine record. He'd also been with Mal and Adrian on the first Nuptse West Ridge trip. 'Sandy just grins – and climbs' was the general verdict. The grinning part seemed true enough.

Adrian Clifford arrived. Handshakes all round, and a clowning photo session. Like the rest of us, Adrian was high with adrenalin, but seemed distracted. He was irritated by the nonarrival of the rabies vaccine, and still brooding on how his wife Sue had been pressing him not to go on the Expedition up to the eve of his departure. 'Not too good for the old morale, old boy.'

We gathered for a Last Supper round the big dining-room table. A lot of food, more wine, laughter, politics, and all the old death-and-destruction yarns. Mrs Tinker listened and watched as she took in the sort of company Jon was committing himself to for three months.

Then down to the Lamb for the farewell booze-up with friends, girlfriends and acquaintances. We were all raised, eagerly taking in the last hours of ordinary life yet longing to be away, and after a few drinks everything seemed bright and loud and warm, laughter echoed round and round my head, mixed in with scraps of Adrian's argument with Mal about the value of work, Kath talking politics with Jon, Sandy mumbling amiably at the girl beside him.

After closing time we all reeled out into the warm London night. Jon and Sandy disappeared to say certain complex and personal goodbyes, Adrian grumbled about Sue, Mal lit another cigarette, looked up at the stars and nearly fell over, Kathleen hugged me and we tripped over each other. We finally got back to the house late, drunk and thoroughly dishevelled – totally the wrong way to set off on a big expedition early next morning, but all good stylee as Jon pointed out. I shut my eyes and my head swung its way dizzyingly down into sleep.

We step out of the plane at Islamabad into the Third World dawn: gunmetal grey shimmering heat, the thermic equivalent of a Ramones concert. Soldiers, policemen, porters, officials, all moving slowly as in a dream through the humid veil of the morning.

Miraculously, all our gear – some thirty items of baggage by now – is unloaded and released through customs in twenty minutes flat. Mal and Sandy regale us with yarns of week-long delays in India as we walk out of the terminus to meet the Americans.

I look at them curiously as we approach. Like us, they stand out by being white, soggy-looking and disorientated, i.e. not yet part of the Orient. A tall aristocratic figure stands like an eagle at bay surrounded by our blue Expedition barrels, children, beggars, taxi drivers and fruit sellers. His eyes are blue and wild. I assume this is Mr Burt Greenspan, because near him is a short, round, oddly froglike figure with popeyes, waving his hands and talking excitedly – the very model of the Comic Slave in classical comedy. This must be our American slave who's paid to be Base Camp manager, bring us tea at ridiculous hours of the morning, wash our feet and so on.

I'm quite wrong. The aquiline aristocrat leans down from his six foot four and drawls, 'I'm Alex Reid, your American slave.' His eyes are dancing, he looks extremely stoned. Burt Greenspan interrupts his rapid flat Chicago whine long enough to shake hands – he looks very pale, downright ill, is sweating profusely; one eye looks at me while the other swivels somewhere over my left shoulder. He's lamenting and cursing the nonarrival of one of the blue barrels from the States: customs problems, our schedule for today. 'No problem,' says Mal, 'we'll sort it out.' He says that about everything here. 'Stay cool in the Third World or you'll end up neck-deep in sweat.'

Kaleidoscopic jet-lagged impressions from the taxi window: oxen in the streets, ancient vans groaning with glittering charms, old men cycling slowly on antique black bicycles in the middle of the road with their knees sticking out, children darting and disappearing like minnows. A female beggar sits cross-legged on a blanket on a pavement in the middle of nowhere, no one passing by, her hand held out just the same. Very tall thin men with mournful faces drift like ghosts in pale grey pyjama suits; short men with cropped hair dyed ginger-red spit in the gutter. And everywhere people group, ungroup, cross the road, sit down, spit, stare – a slow mesmeric shifting of patterns whose shape and significance escape me. There is no obvious sense of purpose let alone urgency in their movements. Roadside stalls of watermelons, car tyres, butchers, bakeries, drapers, scooters. Shacks, houses, three-wheeled taxis, glittering buses ricochet past . . .

We gathered for lunch in the dining room of Flashman's. It turned out to be impressively opulent – and expensive. Cool white tablecloths, napkins, waiters, menus . . . Jon and Sandy especially were awed by this vision of luxury and ease. 'Not the kind of thing we shuffling dossers are used to.' Like Mal, their normal style is a sleeping bag in the corner of a doss with wall-to-wall cockroaches, a standpipe and a hole in the ground. Expeditions on a dozen freeze-dried packet meals and a few Mars Bars; like most Brit expeditions, the grimiest of the grimy and the lightest of the light. And here they were, as Sandy recorded in his diary, in what was more of a travelling circus than a modern Alpine-style trip, with trekkers (Kath and Sybil), clients (Burt and Donna), an American slave and – most dubious of all – a writer who would be poking his Walkman recorder and diary into their every conversation and inner life. 'I suppose it's good value, but find it hard to be so sure. A friend, an 8000 metre peak, that's all one needs really.'

We all felt unreal, I think, half of ourselves still back in London. We were staying in a class hotel, air conditioning and all, separate rooms, a swimming pool ('Death on a stick,' Adrian warned us immediately, assuming his medical role, 'once your lips touch that you can kiss goodbye to this expedition'). Everything was

paid for, other than drinks. And on the way out, PIA had given us
the full VIP treatment and a huge excess baggage allowance as if
we were something special, not just the bunch of scruffs which we
knew ourselves to be. We all felt that any moment the manager
was going to discover there had been a terrible mistake and we'd
be out on the street.

Bemused but thankful for our new-found luxury, we toasted
the absent Rocky Moss and vowed to repay him in the way he
wanted – with the summit of Mustagh Tower. A po-faced Alex
went round the table pouring our tea in the most dignified
manner.

'How long are we staying here?' I asked Mal.

'A week.'

'A week!' I'd expected a couple of days. 'Do we really need that
long?'

We did.

Mid-afternoon, 13 June, I lie on a sweat-soaked sheet in our room
in Flashman's Hotel while the air conditioner roars and falters
like an old VW engine, and consider my companions.

We've been here four days now while Mal and Burt go through
the necessary bureaucracy and we sort out and pack and weigh
our supplies. Time enough in the heat and the boredom and the
separation from friends and lovers for the shape of things to come
to gradually appear. We're all still weighing each other up rather
warily, still discovering our roles in the Expedition.

In fact, we're not yet an expedition at all. We're a bunch of
bemused individuals thrown together in Rawalpindi. The
Mustagh Tower seems a long way away, and we're a long way
from being ready to tackle it as a team. I hope that this frustrating
week here and the ten-day walk-in to the mountain will serve to
acclimatize us not only to this country and the altitude, but also to
each other.

As we sat for lunch that first day, we were all listening to and
watching each other, aware we would be stuck with each other
for three months. Will it work? Will I fit in? Can I stand his laugh
at 17,000 feet? It was like the first week at a new school for all of
us – the same anxiety and curiosity, the same little testing
confrontations and conversations, the same assigning of roles –

the Clown, the Straight Man, the Mother Figure, the Leader, the Rowdy ... Jon's eyes flicked across the table and caught me studying Adrian, our doctor, who was giving a short lecture on Third World hygiene ('Death on a stick, old boy, if in doubt – *don't*'). He winked. 'Being the author still, mate?' That assumed cockney drawl. The others looked at me. I shrugged. 'Always on duty, Jon,' I replied neutrally. One of a hundred moments of near-invisible testing out.

He's so variable. One moment acerbic and sarcastic, striving for what he seems to see as the upper hand, and the next remarking with simple frankness, 'I hope I grow up somewhat on this expedition.'

Another power cut. The air conditioner winds down and the humid heat of 'Pindi in midsummer pours through the window. Sweat is tickling my legs and chest. Why do hot hotel rooms – well, any hotel rooms, really – always make me randy? When will Kath come back from her shopping? The others feel it more, the separation from wives and girlfriends. Gusts of homesickness and sexual frustration blow through our company.

Jon in particular is very paranoid about my being here as a writer. He eyes my recorder as if it were a voodoo box about to snatch his soul from him. When I speak to him, I can sense he's ultra-aware that anything he says may be written up later. As indeed it might! He finds that very threatening, and said as much yesterday. His privacy is so important to him. I think Sandy Allan has similar reservations. I hope for the sake of the book-to-be and for myself that they will get used to me. Like Kath, I really feel out on a limb at times, with no real function here. Perhaps I'm making too much effort to fit in, and being too obtrusive with the recorder and notebook in an effort to demonstrate that I do in fact have a role.

Last night as we all sprawled stranded with a few beers in Room 45, Jon suddenly said, 'This trip is not a holiday for me.' Implying that it was for certain of us? 'And it's not really a job either. As far as I'm concerned it's a ... *vocation*, that's the nearest I can get to it.' He glanced over to Sandy who nodded and grinned his big Sandy grin. They often do this, seem to understand each other instinctively despite their differences. Then he added, suddenly the abrasive Jon again, 'So what's it for you then, Andy?'

Again I feel he's put me on the spot. I suppress my irritation, which may after all be the result of heat and indigestion and a longing for the coolness of home, and simply say, 'A bit of all three.'

Sandy. We're already falling into our natural groupings, and Jon and Sandy seem very much a pair. The Alpine Bin Men. They're totally unalike, but have shared times together in the Alps. With Mal away hassling bureaucracy much of the time and missing Liz the rest, they're together a lot. Tony's following us up the Baltoro in two weeks once he's finished his exams in Wales. They are both amused and bemused at the luxury of their surroundings and the troupe of semi-climbers, trekkers, bumblies and jesters they find themselves with.

Sandy just grins his big rubbery, lazy grin and shakes his head. He's from the Black Isle in the northeast of Scotland, an affable, taciturn Scot. Always relaxed yet busy, easy-going, in control. Yet something elusive behind that open countenance. Not that he's trying to protect something – unlike Jon – but as if a lot of him is elsewhere. Or is he just the cheerful chappie he presents?

He mentioned the other night that he lost all his hair in his mid-teens and was completely bald for a year. I tried to imagine how that would feel, what one would go through at that age . . . Is that part of the key to him? That red-blond hair has grown back and flops forward often over his eyes, hiding them.

Bulky and muscular, a sleepy bull, a honey bear, he gives the impression of having a great deal of solidity and strength in reserve. He's doing a lot of the sweaty, practical work here. He seems unflappable, extremely capable. That had been Mal's impression when Sandy first came on one of his Alpine guiding courses some years back. Sandy had done one Scottish route, then decided he'd like to learn something about Alpine climbing and signed up on the course. 'It was totally obvious,' Mal recalled, 'that though this youth didn't know much technically, he could become a star. He was immensely strong and persistent, learned fast, and had the right kind of temperament. You'll never see him lose the head. He was a natural.'

Sandy trained as a distillery manager. At twenty-five he remembered a promise he'd made himself at fifteen that if he didn't like what he was doing by then, he'd chuck it and do something else. So he did, and took up climbing seriously. He works as a roughneck on the oil rigs – 'Good jest that, gives me enough money and time to fly to Chamonix every few weeks and do some climbing.' On the rigs he picked up the Canadian 'Eh?' with which so many of his sentences end.

He jokes about everything. Listening to him, it's hard to imagine how recently he stood helplessly while a few yards away his friend Brian Sprunt fell to his death on the Matterhorn. If it affected him – as it must have – or his appetite for climbing, he shows no sign of it. The only serious remark I've heard from him yet came when I was saying what a relief it was to be away from First-World news and how I couldn't care less what happened there. 'That's not right, youth,' he said quite sharply. I looked at him, then nodded. Fair enough. Perhaps more to amiable Sandy Allan than meets the eye . . .

Kathleen's just wandered in. Her blue shawl points up the vivid colour of her eyes and her tanned face. She's soggy with sweat, but quite radiant. I watch idly as she peels off her damp clothes. She catches my eye and winks. 'I need a shower first,' she says and goes into the bathroom.

Back to work. Or vocation, as Jon would have it.

Adrian Clifford – Doc or Aido as we already call him. He's twenty-eight, got married just a few weeks back. Despite his natural Scottish accent, he's picked up the 'old boy' stuff from the RAF with whom he was a doctor for some five years. He's tall and lean, a naturally serious and conscientious person whose literal-mindedness is saved by his sudden schoolboy sense of humour. Very meticulous, likes everything just so, can get ratty if it isn't.

Medicine is the first thing in his life, and he takes his role as expedition doctor with us very seriously. He checks out the kitchens wherever we go, takes our blood pressure, gives us our rabies shots, advises us on altitude medicine. I casually mention the painful twinges in my knee from running and he immediately bombards me with questions followed by a full examination. He seems the very picture of a sober, dedicated young doctor.

As indeed he is. Yet against that he confesses that normal life isn't enough for him. That's why he didn't answer when his wife Sue asked him to give up climbing. He wants marriage, his work, financial security – he's the only Brit with any money, drives a red Porsche – but needs the opposite as well. He needs risk and excitement. He's very careful about his health, yet until recently was climbing, parachuting and driving a big motorbike. He doesn't like or approve of risk, yet courts it.

'I can relate to that, old boy,' I said, parodying him. He burst out laughing, and we've got on easily since then. He's done a solid amount of rock and ice climbing in Scotland and the Alps – he too met Mal on one of his Alpine guiding courses, and went with him on the Nuptse West Ridge trip. He doesn't count himself as one of the lead climbers but is certainly no bumblie either. I get the impression he'll fit halfway between the Four Aces and Burt and Donna.

Burt, Donna and Sybil . . . We were all intrigued to meet this strange *ménage à trois*. But if we were expecting three people who oozed libido and sexiness, we were quite wrong. Several people remarked on Burt's resemblance to a pallid frog, and he looks distinctly overweight for the walk-in. His main asset is verbal energy – a constant stream of yarns and wisecracks and comic routines, invective and wild exaggeration. He's the one who, along with Alex, entertains us when we're too hot or bored to speak. It's as if he thought the world would stop if his mouth did.

Talking and being plausible is his job as well as his nature. He was a professional hostage for a while, then became a minority rights job organizer, which means phoning people up and getting them to give work to Mexicans, Hispanics, blacks and so on. Trouble is he no longer seems to believe in it, and while some of his racist jokes are genuinely funny, he doesn't know where to stop and becomes offensive. The same goes for much of his male-oriented humour. There's bad taste that's funny and liberating, and there's simply bad taste. He doesn't – to my sensibility at least – know the difference, and I can frequently feel Jon's and Kathleen's hackles rise as he holds forth. I keep waiting for Donna, who seems a perfectly strong-minded and self-possessed woman, to slap him across the face or tell him to can it, but she doesn't. She just smiles.

As he says, 'I give good phone.' Kath heard that as 'good foam'. Well, there's possibly not that much difference, and certainly his foam down the phone has done wonders for the Expedition's sponsorship. He's drummed up veritable mountains of freeze-dried food and foil-pouched meals called retorts, Granola bars and Milk Duds, sun-block sticks that hang round your neck – a total success, these – decaffeinated coffee (groan!), tea, face wipes . . . An American candy maker asked him, 'What do I get out of this?'

'Only a picture of a box of your product on the roof of the world.'

'You've sold me!'

Yes, good phone, Burt. He's done a tremendous amount of good work on the American side, and is now once again with Mal at Karakoram Tours and the Ministry of Tourism, patiently working through Pakistani bureaucracy. Which is agreed to be quite on the ball – what would take an afternoon in Britain, an hour in the States and a week in India takes about two days here. The officials are polite, patient and don't expect to be bribed. It's just that they have a habit of saying what they think you want to hear. Like 'Yes' and 'No problem'. Trouble is, you come back the next day and they inform you, in the most roundabout and embarrassed way, that there is still this little problem, this unfortunate regulation. 'So you have to jump on their heads a while.'

He's irrepressible. He substitutes energy for dignity. Donna we all like; she's warm, sensible and self-contained. While Burt never asks us about ourselves – he talks about himself and he talks about people, but seldom *with* them – she always seems genuinely interested in others. It's hard to estimate their abilities as climbers – Burt talks a lot about 'when I was in Peru', 'when we were in Nepal', 'when we were on McKinley', 'when we were in the Alps'. Most of his stories are very funny and told against himself, about how gripped he was, how he hates climbing, how he got lost here and gibbered there. 'I don't know the meaning of fear,' he'd say in his nasal Chicago whine, 'I go straight to abject terror.'

The others might say that sort of thing for effect; I feel he partly means it – as indeed do I.

So he and Donna have been around a bit and obviously have more experience than I. On the other hand, Mal points out they've always been guided, and much of that guiding has been real kid-glove handling. (He was horrified to discover that Rocky, after a few seasons of guided climbing, wasn't sure how to put on his own harness and crampons.) It's generally agreed that Donna is the stronger of the two, mentally and physically. Good phone . . . but what will happen when the phone lines stop and there's no one left to persuade?

And then there's Sybil, who seems to revolve around Burt and Donna like a secondary planet, abused by the former, sympathized with by the latter. Sybil with her ever hopeful, eager, tired, bony face. She's put down and contradicted by Burt so often it embarrasses us, but she always comes back for more. Sybil who at breakfast today opined that President Reagan was the best thing that had happened to America and that Julio Iglesias was the finest singer in the world. Jon was left speechless, Kath raised her eyebrows in silent incredulity, I choked on my toast. We let it go. The night before an argument about politics had become heated and personal. For the sake of the trip, it had to become a nonsubject.

There's a ghekko hiding in the top corner of the room like a lurking thought. Every afternoon round 5.00 it moves out of the shadows and goes hunting. I've some thoughts lurking in the back of my mind but I can't bring them out and find the words. It's probably the heat, over 100°C every day, and feeling unsure and insecure about my place in this group. I'm no climber at all, what am I doing here? Yet apart from climbing, I've practically nothing in common with the others. Only with Kath and Jon can I talk about the things that really interest me. Climbing talk, death talk, climbing talk – the prospect of another three months of it is wearisome. I've nothing to contribute.

There goes my ghekko, stalking across the wall like a Japanese wrestler. Must be tea time soon. What on earth is Kathleen doing in the shower? If she doesn't come out soon, we won't have time . . . Oh, he's got his first fly of the evening. Perhaps everyone feels the way I do – a bit weary, restless, far away from home, unsure of where we stand. Certainly Mal and Adrian miss their wives, and even Sandy sometimes has that distant, abstracted expression. This vague sense of malaise warps these sketches of my companions. They're probably wildly inaccurate, the kind of thing one looks back on and laughs.

We know we'll know each other so much better in the next twelve weeks, but we don't know how. We know a lot will happen, but we don't know what. The ghekko is becoming active as the day cools down, and my thoughts are starting to disclose themselves . . .

But Kathleen's just stepped dripping into the room. She smiles and, wrapped demurely in a towel, sits on the side of the bed. 'Are you finished?' 'Yes.' My impressions of Alex will have to wait, here are matters more urgent.

Nothing became Rawalpindi more than the leaving of it.

It had begun to look as if we'd never get away. At the last minute we'd been assigned a new Liaison Officer. Fine. So all the gear we've bought for him is for a man four sizes bigger, but that's not our fault. Problem is, this new LO doesn't show up. And the country's having a three-day holiday, the Ministry of Tourism is closed, and no one knows where our LO is. The Ministry had been informed about it, not their problem, they're not part of the army . . . He'll turn up soon, *inshallah* . . . How often we were to hear that *inshallah* – 'God willing' or simply 'maybe'. But they were insistent on one thing: we could not leave 'Pindi without a Liaison Officer.

We pointed out that it wasn't our fault that he wasn't there; they smiled and agreed, agreed it was unfortunate, but these are the regulations. At this point we were all packed and ready to go. The nine blue barrels, more than forty cardboard packing cases, each meticulously weighed in at 55 pounds, and our rucksacks were all stacked in Room 45. We had been here seven days and we were desperate to leave. If we didn't get away that day, we couldn't go for another five days, because the road between 'Pindi and Skardu would be closed for repairs. We couldn't wait another five days, firstly because the Expedition simply could not afford it, and secondly because we knew inside ourselves that any longer here and we'd disintegrate. The Man-from-Lahore incident showed we were getting seriously out of hand.

Miracles. Our LO shows up, Captain Shokat Ali Bhatti. Let's go, for God's sake. But the Ministry gently inform us he has to be briefed. Okay, so let's have the briefing this afternoon. Ah, Sahib Greenspan, regrettably this is public holiday and briefing is not possible. Two days, *inshallah* . . .

At this point a silent scream rises in the throat and Burt feels like banging his or someone else's head against the wall – except that's exactly what he's been doing for seven days now. Sitting helplessly in the lobby of Flashman's, we're tense, silent, defeated.

The ever resourceful Mal and Burt try one more Third World body-swerve: Mal as Leader will stay behind with the LO for the briefing while the rest of us set off for Skardu by bus; they'll catch us up by plane.

They buy it.

For Christ's sake let's go before they change their minds.

We left in the charged twilight of a gathering thunderstorm. The sky was orange and greeny-grey, the clouds looked bruised. The banana trees hung like loose fists motionless against the swimming pool as we loaded the bus in the quivering humidity. Our bus! A travelling altar, a monument to the magpie instinct, a glitter grotto studded with tin, hung with charms and trinkets and glass and mirrors, decorated with coloured glass, paint, plastic, wood, raffia, it sat in front of the hotel as absurd and magnificent as a sultan's ceremonial elephant. But would it take the twenty-six hours' continual driving over 400 miles of some of the roughest road in the world?

Another last-minute crisis blows up as the sky grows dark. We've loaded the bus with our small mountain of gear, then our own packs, and found there's room left only for a small hard single seat each. Burt starts waving his arms around, his eyes swivelling, his legs quivering with rage, voice whining like a buzz saw – he's furious because this is not the size of bus he'd ordered and paid for. He for one is certainly not going to sit cramped shoulder to shoulder for twenty-six hours in that heap of shit!

Nazir, the helpful boss of Karakoram Tours who did much of our advance organization in Pakistan, is offended and embarrassed. He insists this is the size of bus ordered and, besides, a bigger one cannot be found at short notice. 'Forget it, Burt, it's no problem. We'll just go in this,' Mal says. Burt points out forcefully that Mal isn't going to travel in it, and no way is Burt going to be ripped off by these chiselling – !

'It just shows the difference between climbers and trekkers,' one of the Aces murmurs. 'Burt demands comfort and we're thankful not to have to walk it.' I immediately resolve not to whinge. A certain amount of suffering in life seems natural and inevitable to a Scot. Burt always hopes to get round discomfort with money, technology, training and pills. It can't be done.

Eventually, as always, a solution is found. We repack, stack the roof rack till it's practically as high as the bus, and create some twenty empty seats for the ten of us. And as we finally roll away from Flashman's, all our anxiety and tension are released in a soaring arrow of euphoric excitement. On the road again. 'In a bin-man stylee!' Jon exults.

We drove out of the city through the thunderous dark. Now the night had come, the day's fast that applies through the month of Ramadan had ended and all the pavement stalls and cafés were crowded with men. Round faces, angular faces, hands and eyes caught for a moment in the light of kerosene lamps as we ricocheted by. 'Forward going,' murmured Mohammed Ali, our Karakoram Tours guide, 'I am happy now.' He settled himself beside the driver and smiled into the night. Forward going . . .

We've been on the road six hours now. Our headlights flare through a night as dark and complete as our ignorance of what's up ahead. Certain members of our party have been indulging in illegal substances and the air in the bus is extremely potent. Perhaps that's why the music in my headphones is so intense and penetrating. Phrases I may or may not have heard aright tumble round my mind. I feel buoyant with amnesia, riddled as the times, going forward letting the past unwind behind.

Everyone is silent now, asleep or in reflective trance. I look round us all, one by one. Alex is sitting up front beside the driver, erect and motionless. He stares straight ahead, his bony face pale green and calm in the dashboard light. For all his bizarre humour and extrovert behaviour, it's hard to say what goes on in there. Raised in the Caribbean, he's by nature and instinct a Californian, i.e. laid back to the point of being horizontal. He's been a sculptor's model, sculpts and paints himself, is seriously involved in photography, has played in a rock band, and spent the last year climbing and guiding in the Cascades and Yosemite. For the last six months he's made a living humping other people's loads around between 10,000 and 14,000 feet, so for all his skeletal build he must be super-fit. 'Our dark horse,' Sandy commented. 'We expected a Base Camp Manager and we got an extra climber. That could make all the difference.'

Beside him, swaying easily as the bus jolts, is another unexpec-

ted plus. Mohammed Ali Changezi. Because Kathleen and Sybil
were down on a list as trekkers, not climbers, regulations insist
that they have a guide for going up the Baltoro Glacier to Base
Camp. It's a restricted zone, not surprisingly with China just a
few miles away. His services are costing us a lot of extra money,
but he's been an instant success. One of the most likable men you
could meet, adept at all forms of bargaining and body-swerving,
he's saved us a lot of money and hassle already. He's very good-
looking and knows it, with big observant brown eyes and black
hair always immaculately brushed back.

Adrian sits in front of me, staring determinedly forward as he
fights with motion sickness. Thinking of Sue and running over yet
again in his mind the contents of the medicine chest and the
possible side effects of drugs. He'd watched over everything we
ate and drank in 'Pindi, given us our rabies shots, passed out the
malaria tablets, sleeping pills and sun cream. Out of medical
curiosity, he decided to take our pulse rates and blood pressure.
Jon vehemently refused. Doctors or writers, he doesn't like
anyone monitoring him. Aido can quickly become irate at anything sloppy or casual, and so is probably the least sympathetic of
the Brits towards the Third World, but his meticulousness got us
all through a week in 'Pindi without any sickness, a minor
miracle. Getting to Base Camp acclimatized and in good shape is
half the battle.

Kath is sleeping on the seats behind me. Her face is relaxed and
soft. She looks very young. Behind her Jon is stretched out in the
nest he's made and clung to. He's got the best place on the bus and
simply doesn't hear suggestions that he might share it around. A
sharp operator. Donna and Sybil are asleep, propped against each
other like book ends.

Burt shifts and grunts in his sleep, still planning and hassling
even in his dreams. Looking back, I catch Sandy's eye. He's
surrounded by rucksacks, smoking quietly – something he only
does on expeditions, believing as does Mal that it helps
acclimatization. His head bobs to the unheard music of his
Walkman. His thoughts are not here but in Chamonix, thinking
of a golden earring and a sun-browned neck and the long black
hair of his girlfriend Dominique. He gives me a thumbs up, grins
lazily, perfectly poised and content.

My own ghostly reflection in the window looks suitably

mysterious and unfathomable. I can't see into myself at all. I scarcely know why I'm here, but it feels right. There's nowhere I'd rather be.

Precious human cargo in the grotto bus, cargo of hopes and fears, thoughts of home and girlfriends, of mountains and beer, insecurities and pride – I feel a warm swell of affection and tenderness towards us all as we bounce on through the night, our headlights skewing down the road ahead.

Next morning, one by one, we grope towards wakefulness. We're sweaty and uncomfortable and irritable. We drink warm water to rinse the staleness from our mouths. First cigarette and I start taking an interest in things. We're off the Karakoram Highway now, on a rapidly deteriorating track following the Indus river. It's a heaving, rolling, ferocious spate of glacier melt, more like grey liquid ice than water.

This bus trip is shaking us together. Through the day we swop places – except Jon, happily oblivious and dreaming in great detail of two naked Thai girls walking up and down his spine – and the conversation and shared discomfort is making us into something of a group. We're rubbing corners off each other – Jon's sweaty feet are in the small of my back, mine are behind his neck, Sybil's arms lie across my legs, Alex is asleep, his head resting on Mohammed's shoulder. It's a shake-down. We're grubby, disorganized, thirsty and bruised – but we're a group.

It's a long day, a long jolting grind uphill into the foothills. We stop for thick, sweet tea in a dusty village. We stare and are stared at. Mohammed bargains to reduce the price, we set off again. Jon is finally ousted from his cosy corner and starts chatting away about Thai girls and Chamonix and reggae music. We're lively for a while, joking and abusing and handing out stress to each other. As the 'road' winds higher and deeper into the Indus gorge, we gradually fall silent. Looking out the window is not pleasant. Our wheels are a foot or so from the crumbling edge of a rough track blasted into the side of the mountain. Above us, some 3000 feet of rock-fall-prone scree. And below us, a straight 800-foot drop into the glacier river.

'Fuckin' desperate,' Jon says quietly. No one disagrees. The driver's been at it sixteen hours straight now, and the bus suddenly slides out across the road. We all instinctively lean away from the edge, the front wheels grip again and we veer away from the lip. We feel totally helpless. There's nothing we can do. Watching is too much of a strain; I shut my eyes, turn up the volume on my Walkman and resign myself to the will of Allah. Wake me if I die.

When I open them two hours later the situation has if anything deteriorated. The road is a track of rubble, fit only for a Land-Rover. The drop on our right has doubled. We keep grinding past concrete stacks. 'What are those?' I ask Mohammed. 'Many men killed making road – these are monuments.' 'Do buses ever go off the road?' 'Sometimes.' He smiles warmly. 'Not this time, *inshallah*.' He instinctively fingers the travelling amulet he wears on his right upper arm.

'How can you know anything about me,' says Sandy, 'when I know damn all about myself?'

'You're not jolly Sandy Allan at all, are you?'

'Search me – how should I know?' He bursts out laughing. 'Borrow your Joan Armatrading cassette, youth?'

At the turn of the road, the first great mountains swing into view, Haramosh and its neighbours. 'Like a shield,' Kathleen thinks. She is stunned by their height, their white menace. 'Someone here could die on those.' She feels at first an instinctive revulsion. Even from 40 miles away, the Karakoram are more daunting than she'd ever imagined.

To me, the shattered, gleaming teeth are beautiful and terrible. Wondrous and an assault on the eye. Epic. My heart leaps out towards them. The Karakoram Himalayas.

Jon looks out the window. 'Foothills,' he says.

Another tea stop. Sweet relief of open air, free movement. We sit on benches round a wooden table in the dusk. A boy limps over and lights a kerosene lamp. He looks at us curiously, impassive, only his large eyes moving as they flick from one to another of us. His smile is swift and complete and decisive. He vanishes into the shadows. The cook is ringed with fire as he pulls chapati from an oven.

Adrian resolutely plunges into the 'kitchen' to check it out. He emerges shaking his head. 'Total death on a stick, old boy. You might survive the chapati and dal, but that's all.'

'Good stress,' says Jon, nodding vigorously, 'about bleedin' time. Too much luxury on this trip, not enough shuffling dossing. Great!'

The Man from Lahore, I think, as we settle back into the jolting forward motion of the bus, was the low and high point of our time in 'Pindi. He had picked us up in Flashman's dining room. His English was more than adequate, like his stomach and his purse. Both his money and his need for company were very evident. He insisted that we were his friends and that we should have a party with him. As a Pakistani, he couldn't buy alcohol, but we were infidels and we could . . . He'd pay for all the beer we could drink if he could drink with us.

It seemed too good to be true. We went back to Room 45 and ordered our first crate of beer.

We were in a bored, frustrated mood that night and needed to let off steam. The first crate was emptied as he rolled out his life in front of us like a carpet salesman. He was a rich man's son. He didn't work. Instead he drank with 'sweet friends' like us. His marriage was arranged, neither he nor his wife liked each other. She had a colour TV and a VCR, and he moved round the country from Lahore to 'Pindi to Peshawar to Murri to Lahore to 'Pindi . . . His allowance kept him on the leash; should he leave the country or find another woman, the money would stop.

A second crate arrived. He insisted we turn up the music and he expanded on friendship. 'When sweet friends drink together and are happy, then God is happy.' Well, fair enough, but we knew very well that we were not friends of this man, only drinking companions, and we were only drinking companions because he was buying the drinks.

He insisted we dance. Particularly the women. Dance, dance! Donna and Sybil got up and swayed about the room – which now seemed to be tilting and melting at the edges – while Alex did an extraordinary shuffle round an invisible totem pole. Sandy and Kathleen refused point blank. Why should they perform for the Man from Lahore?

'Because you're drinking his beer,' Mal murmured, leaning at an alarming angle on the couch as he opens another beer.

'That's no reason,' said Sandy curtly.

The Man from Lahore ordered more beer, more music, more ice, more food. The hotel waiters brought it, looking unhappy and sullen. To them he was a corrupt Muslim making a fool of himself with foreigners, bereft of dignity. He papered up the cracks by throwing money at them. They continued to serve us, with icy disapproval.

The Man from Lahore suggested a midnight coach ride to the hill station of Murree. He'd pay, of course – and he could promise to lay on some 'dancing girls'. Some of our company perked up at this, their sexual frustration now superheated by alcohol, their bodily loneliness exacerbated. There followed intricate manoeuvres to persuade the women that Murree would be boring and pointless, but that just to humour the Man from Lahore, some of the guys would go along.

In the end there proved to be no available coaches for hire. I felt drunk and uneasy. We'd started off going along with him for the ride, and were ending up being morally hijacked. Jon, who has a very definite cut-off point, abruptly left, followed by Adrian. The night degenerated further with the Man from Lahore sweating and cajoling from the couch as the girls danced for his pleasure. Alex crawled around the floor as a dog while Mal and the Man gave him orders. A hand-kissing routine started by the Man and the auctioning of Sybil were threatening to get completely out of hand.

Finally Alex disappeared and walked back in wearing a gorilla mask. He had become Robbie, the mute Himalayan chimpanzee. His way of standing and looking, everything about him had changed. It was a triumph of mime as he silently went up to the man from Lahore and poured him a beer.

I have never seen anyone so thunderstruck. His jaw dropped, he looked at Robbie, at us, at Robbie. He scowled. He tried to smile. He looked pale and ill. Then we roared with laughter. We laughed ourselves onto the floor. We laughed at him.

The Man from Lahore was angry, scared and insulted. 'Take bad man away!' he shouted. 'Make him go away!'

It was very funny and not very nice. But we're not very nice, are we? We're part good, part bad, and part easily led. Loneliness, frustration and boredom – that night they all came to the surface like salts left on the skin from a drunken sweat.

We left Mal, Burt, Alex and the Man from Lahore to drink themselves into helplessness. They finally slipped the Man a sleeping pill and poured him, half-conscious, into a taxi to Islamabad. That was the last we saw of our sweet friend.

Next morning we realized no one even knew his name.

And now at last we were nearing Skardu. The day had been long. We were beyond weariness. The things we'd seen were disconnected memories, like slides shot up on a screen. What lingered in my mind were the tiny irrigated villages we saw across the Braldu gorge. In the midst of that vast desolation of rock, that ultimate barrenness, they were little mirages of green. We'd rubbed our eyes and looked again. Yes, tall slender trees, little rock houses, green patchwork fields draped across the hill like a shimmering scarf. Below them, a 1000-foot drop to the river; thousands of feet of bare rock above. They were connected by barely discernible terrifying paths that snaked right across the face of the cliffs.

They were tiny islands of life, a few hundred feet across, where a handful of people lived their entire lives, knowing little and needing less. They were glimpses of a life we could scarcely imagine and certainly never know. They looked like torn-up scraps of an original paradise, saved from the ruins of the world around them.

We stared and stared in the fading light. We took our pictures, then turned up the cassette player and churned on towards the darkness, towards Skardu.

Our last pit stop was some three hours short of Skardu. Our driver's eyes were inflamed after twenty-four hours of heavy driving. While Adrian rummaged about in our medical kit for eye drops, we sat by lanternlight in the Baltistani equivalent of a truckers' drive-in. The night was cool and soft and black. A scent of thyme in the breeze. We drank water and sweet tea, lit up another cigarette, waited for the inevitable chapati and dal.

No one spoke much. The night was full of stars. We heard the piping cry of bats, were aware of sleeping forms shifting in the darkness around us. We were dreamlike and numb, yet oddly wide awake to the beauty and promise of that night. Nothing

particular was said or done in that half-hour, and yet our brief
supper has stayed with me as the distillation of the joy of travel in
company. Our silent closeness, our patient fatigue, and flickering
through the night the flame of adventure. I can still picture the
faces sculpted by the firelight from the chapati oven, see the
gestures and attitudes, and the vague glimmer of our Magic Bus
waiting to take us away.

We arrived in Skardu after midnight. Twenty-eight hours of
travelling had reduced us to the living dead. In the K2 motel we
found cool sheets, a bed that did not shake, and sleep within
minutes, dreamless sleep.

Skardu is the end of the road. The last telephone, last electricity,
last helicopter, last motor vehicles, last shops and banks are here
in this market town oasis, completely encircled by the mountains.
The air was wonderful after 'Pindi, cool and clean. And less of it;
already at something like 7800 feet we were having to move a
little slower, not get too excited. Otherwise, rapid shallow
breathing and slight dizziness.

Kath and I walked along the main street on our first morning
there, happy and elated and quite ignorant of the storm that was
brewing up back at the motel. 'Good ethnic action,' Jon had
remarked cryptically, and it was. Now we were in Baltistan, the
people looked quite different. Instead of the moon-faced,
frequently corpulent people of 'Pindi, the men here had strong
hooked noses, high cheekbones, a reddish rather than a brownish
skin. A few had blue eyes, that stood out startlingly. They looked
like mountain men, lean and stringy.

Kath stood out too, for in that busy little town there were no
women on the streets. None. Nor in any of the shops. Only men
and boys. It was oppressive, all that maleness. No wonder the
men tend to touch and hug each other a lot, and sometimes hold
hands, and gossip and carry on – they have to create in themselves
the whole missing female element. Which, ironically, can make
them very charming and less macho. They wear flowers behind
their ears and giggle and nudge each other like schoolgirls – then
abruptly revert to solemnity.

We could feel all eyes on us as we ambled down the street. I was overpoweringly aware of Kath's femaleness, of the softness of her contours, her light hair and blue eyes. So was she. And so, it felt, was the entire population of Skardu. She was deliberately dressed as unprovocatively as possible, baggy blue trousers, a blue scarf over her head and arms and round her throat. No one whistled or laughed or made any gesture – it was more of a falling silent, and the sensation of a hundred pairs of eyes silently swivelling as we walked by.

The difference between Pakistan and Baltistan was striking. They were Shiite Moslems here, followers of the Ayatollah Khomeini, whose portrait was in evidence in cafés and shops and houses. For all that, they seemed very gentle, though they looked fierce enough. They're largely Afghan by descent, with the occasional smaller, slightly slant-eyed man as witness to the Chinese and Tibetan strains in them. They spoke their own language, Balti, and wore distinctive woollen hats that looked like several chapati stacked on the head, then folded under like a French beret.

Baltistan is to Pakistan roughly what Scotland is to Britain – part of it but distinct. They too have what they consider to be effete southern neighbours. Their Hadrian's Wall is the 400-mile long road through the hills we'd just come off, and it quite effectively preserves their separate identity.

Would-be porters were assembling on the lawn of the hotel, dropping in and chattering like bedraggled swallows gathering for migration. They were a mixed bunch, but wiry and strong. Alex struggled with an endless list of contents of barrels as he tried to work out how many porter loads we had. It looked like an awful lot more than we'd expected.

Burt took me aside. He seemed hesitant. One eye was on my forehead, the other looking over my shoulder. 'How close a friend are you of Malcolm's?' he asked. 'I don't know how to tell you this, but he's really dropped you and Kathleen in the shit.'

In a show of frankness, Burt came clean. Mal had misled either Kathleen or the rest of the Expedition. As Kath was nominally a trekker, she had to stay on a highly specific route up and down the Baltoro Glacier – and that route did not include Mustagh Base Camp. Even accompanied by Mohammed as official guide, she was not allowed to go there. And she would have to share the

costs with Sybil of their porters and Mohammed's guiding fee to
Karakoram Tours.

We knew she didn't have anything like that kind of money.
And as for Mohammed's fees – well, it looked as if he was
working full time for the Expedition now. In fact he was doing
wonders in bargaining for us, arranging porters, tractors, jeeps,
haggling prices, securing permits. The man was priceless, was
practically the King of Skardu, was related to everybody up and
down the Baltoro – an asset to the Expedition. So why shouldn't
the Expedition pay for him?

'The Expedition hasn't enough money,' Burt said simply.
'Your friend Mal gave Rocky a hopelessly low budget. I'll show
you the figures if you like. There's not enough money – and you
and Kath are going to have to come up with some from
somewhere.'

Kath was bewildered, angry and tearful. We were sitting
talking in low voices like conspirators at one end of the corridor.
At the other end, Alex was going through his baggage lists again,
with Mohammed beside him looking very unhappy. I could hear
the angry voices of Sandy, Jon, Donna and Sybil from one of the
rooms. Something had definitely gone wrong.

Two expeditions turned up on their way back from the
mountains. We watched these worn and weathered veterans
jump down from their jeeps and saunter with just a hint of
swagger into the hotel. We started talking to the French team
who'd made the col on Broad Peak but were driven back by
sustained bad weather. Just like the Spanish group we'd met in
'Pindi, who'd spent twenty-one out of twenty-five possible climbing days stuck in their tents at Gasherbrum 2 Base Camp and
simply run out of food and enthusiasm. And it could just as easily
happen to us, for the weather is supposed to get worse as the
summer drifts on.

But at least they'd got out to their mountain. At least they'd
been there. They'd earned the right to their nonchalant ease, to
get stoned in the dining room and gaze at the flickering TV. The
way things were going, I was beginning to wonder if Kath and I
were ever going to get to Mustagh.

To save money, we were now doubling up on bedrooms and
paying for our own lunch. In fact we were feeling so mean we all
just settled for Coke and toast. Sandy and Burt calculated and

calculated, working out porter costs, walk-out costs, Mohammed's fees, walk-in provisions, insurance. Burt sweated and
yelled, his eyes popped and swivelled, he cursed Duff and the Paki
government and the hapless Sybil. Sandy scored out one row of
figures and started again.

Finally Burt announced, 'A crevasse of nonviability has opened
up beneath us.'

And as Sandy went over the figures, we saw that he was right.
Even leaving Mohammed out of it, we did not have enough
money to hire enough porters to carry our loads to Mustagh Base
Camp, then on to Gasherbrum 2, then back out again. We sat
there, slumped and defeated, while the newly arrived Swiss
expedition celebrated their success on Nanga Parbat.

'What if we forget about Gash 2?' someone suggested.

Jon sat bolt upright. 'There's no way we're going to forget
about Gash,' he said vehemently. His eyes were bright with anger.
Sandy nodded agreement and wondered to himself if Mal had
ever had any serious intention of going to Gasherbrum 2. Had he
only booked it to tempt Jon and Sandy out as cheap labour guides
for the Mustagh Tower bumblies? And that was another thing –
Burt and Donna had the impression they were support climbers,
while Sandy and Jon had been told that they were clients to be
guided up the hill. And Burt had hinted that Mal was being paid
a guiding fee by Rocky, so why had they heard no mention
of it?

Sandy tried to put these unproductive thoughts behind him
and, while argument raged on round about him, worked out how
much it would cost to carry their own gear to Gash 2.

No. Even that was impossible. He'd told Mal just a few weeks
ago that his estimate of sixty porters was way low. From Alex's
figures it looked like eighty-five loads. What if we dropped
Kathleen and her porters? No, even that won't get us through. Or
if we added, say, five pounds to each load, how many loads less
would we have? Not enough. What if . . . No.

It went on like that all afternoon. By the end of it we were
divided, suspicious, and very tired. We went round and round
trying to square the circle, to prove the impossible was possible.
But there was never quite enough; there was always something or
someone who was going to get dumped, and nobody wanted to
be the one.

I was alarmed at the way our cumulative disappointment, suspicion and hostility were being directed at the absent Mal. Yes, he had fucked up by seriously underestimating our costs in Pakistan, but the level of abuse and accusation was way beyond what the situation merited. Burt's spittle sprayed across the table with the violence of his denunciation. This wasn't a climbing expedition, this was a lynching party. I hoped that the weather would allow Mal's flight in tomorrow. Kath and I in particular needed him here – or would he leave us in the lurch, as some insinuated?

To save money, we decided we'd eat Expedition food on the grass outside the hotel. Somehow Mohammed persuaded the manager to allow us to do that. Sitting cross-legged in the brief twilight, we ate our first Expedition meal, rice and retorts. At least the retorts, being real food – stews, chilli con carne, steaks – without preservatives, not freeze-dried, were a success. With the last platinum-pale light hitting the highest peaks in the distance, and the porters gathering and singing quietly beside the river, it should have been a joyful, calm evening.

In the early hours of the morning, while some members of the party sat up frying their brains with best Paki black, Kathleen came to my single bed and lay sobbing with anger and disappointment. I held her but there was little I could say. It was difficult to see our way round this one. She fell asleep but I stayed awake a long time, scheming and worrying.

Next morning I woke feeling low and headachy. When I blew my nose, it began to bleed. This wasn't just stress, this was altitude. If I was reacting to it like this at 7800 feet, how would I handle Base Camp, let alone being on the mountain? Mal had mentioned that some people simply don't adjust to altitude. Maybe I was one of them.

Suitably depressed, I went in to breakfast, only to remember that it was being made by Alex on the lawn outside. We were all subdued and dispirited. In the middle of another pointless wrangle, I think it was Jon who finally announced, 'Look, we're all in this Expedition. We've got to pull together and solve these problems instead of arguing about them.'

Silence as we considered this. He was right. If we didn't work together, we were nothing. Mohammed then made an astonishing offer: he'd lend us 100,000 rupees of his own money (some £7500) to pay our porters, and we could repay it when we returned home. We were moved by his trust in us and his commitment to the Expedition – and shamed, for these were the qualities we'd so conspicuously lacked.

We couldn't accept his offer. It's pretty bad when you have to start borrowing off the locals – we were supposed to be endlessly wealthy westerners handing out money, not receiving it. Besides, we couldn't guarantee repaying him.

But his suggestion made us pull ourselves together. In a couple of minutes it was agreed that we'd all put in whatever personal money we had with us. In the case of Burt, Donna and Sybil, this was quite a large amount. We trusted each other to declare honestly our assets. Sandy did the sums. Yes, if we pooled all we had, there'd just be enough cash to get us to Base Camp and back. When Mal arrived he'd have to try to raise some 40,000 rupees to repay us and pay for Gash 2. If necessary, he'd have to fly back to 'Pindi to do it. That was up to him to sort out; for the time being we could at least guarantee getting ourselves to the Mustagh Tower. (Or so we thought!) That was all that counted when it came down to it, that someone at least got onto the mountain and had a chance of climbing it.

At last we were thinking and working as an expedition.

So we all set off to the bank, clutching our pounds and dollars and traveller's cheques to change them into rupees. A simple enough operation, you'd think.

A total epic.

The bank is a two-room shack with peeling plaster walls, a faded portrait of General Zia and two bare lightbulbs. Four battered desks and clustered round them, behind them, on them, a motley crew who might be tellers or janitors or friends or the local bin men. We are admitted by a cross-eyed guard with a shotgun and an enormous bandillero of cartridges looped across his shoulder.

By a process of elimination, we find the manager. Change traveller's cheques? Need passport. We produce our passports. Need photocopy. Why? Need photocopy. Oh, okay. Need traveller's cheque list, and photocopy. But why photocopy? And why the list of numbers? Some of us don't have our lists – you're always told not to keep them together. Burt left his in 'Pindi. Shrug. No photocopy, very sorry.

Look, we have our passports and our traveller's cheques, why do we need photocopies? Shrug. Follow man, he show you.

We're taken to a taxi that drives to the other end of town to a shack that supposedly has a photocopier. Closed. Cousin's funeral. Is there another photocopier in Skardu? Shrug, *inshallah*, a beaming smile. We go see.

We find another shack. Closed. Gone to see brother. Wait here. We wait in the blistering heat, resolution rapidly ebbing away. The sky's clear, will Mal and the LO fly in today? Will we ever get out of here? Man comes back, makes photocopies. Pay him, pay taxi, back to the bank.

We work through the crowd of leisurely gossiping bank employees, relatives, friends, farmers, priests, porters, brigands, goat herds, to the manager's desk. He gravely puts on his slippers and considers our documents, then reaches into a drawer and pulls out a wedge of forms. Answer here, please. We sigh and obediently fill them in. The manager considers them thoughtfully for five minutes, then hands them to a guard, who takes away passports, cheques, photocopies, everything. We wait. And wait. Forms appear on the desk, are signed or merely motioned away. None of them is ours. There's no sign of actual money anywhere. The manager eases off his slippers, smiles, indicates the bank is closing in five minutes. For how long? Three days. I take off my shoes and settle into the corner. No way we're leaving here without our rupees.

The guard returns. He's so cross-eyed he'd have problems deciding which barn door to try to hit with his shotgun. Another set of forms, sign here, please. The forms are taken away again by a shuffling janitor.

To pass the time, I decide to change my remaining dollars into rupees. I finally get to the counter and hand them over. Passport, please. Sorry, but that man took it away. Photocopy of passport. Why? What on earth? Do I need a passport to certify the mighty dollar? I dig out a second photocopy, and fill in more forms. Might as well help employ Skardu. Do the notes have to be consecutively numbered? He looks at me seriously, shakes his head regretfully.

Back to the manager's room. It's past closing time but no one's leaving. We're trying not to be tense or aggressive. It's counter-productive anyway, and too hot to hurry. The manager smiles suddenly, offers round a battered pack of K2 cigarettes. We light up. They make Gauloises seem like Silk Cut. Sandy cracks a joke, we laugh and relax. No hurry after all. We'll wait here for hours if necessary.

Hours is what it takes. One by one, our forms come back, the manager signs the magic chit and we go from desk to desk slowly tracking down our elusive rupees. The manager explains that a month ago someone cashed a large amount of stolen traveller's cheques, and thus all the precautions.

My traveller's cheques come back. The manager looks concerned. My countersignature is different. No, it's not. Signature different. But it's my signature, you saw me sign it. Not same, cannot accept. I try to explain that I cannot exactly duplicate my original signature, made light years ago with a ballpoint pen in the sane and respectable town of Edinburgh, with an italic dip pen in this sweating hole when I'm suffering from altitude. Cannot accept. Okay, I'll do it again. Okay.

Carefully as any forger, I try to duplicate my original signature. The manager looks at it critically while I idly picture him strung up by his necktie to the overhead fan. Okay, he says finally.

So once again I follow my forms as they move at a random and leisurely pace from desk to desk, are exclaimed over, chuckled over; heads shake in profound sorrow, eyes narrow suspiciously or widen in disbelief at such headstrong foolishness as trying to change money in a Skardu bank.

Till some three and a half hours later we emerge triumphantly into the blinding light, our pockets bulging with rupees. The Expedition is viable again.

We returned to the hotel for tea on the lawn, after which Mohammed led us forth for another shopping expedition, buying cake and tea and cooking stoves and kerosene, eighty pairs of sandals, eighty pairs of sunglasses, and a few hundred packets of throat-mangling K2 cigarettes – statutory provisions for the porters.

By evening we were exhausted but optimistic. Instead of seeing problems, we were solving them. We'd all put in our money and gained a certain solidarity. And the magic Mohammed had decided he might be able to body-swerve round the trekking problem and get the LO to agree to Kath and Sybil visiting Base Camp. Furthermore, Mohammed had been adopted as part of the climbing team. He wanted to help out by load-carrying from Base Camp further up the mountain. We were short on manpower and, though he'd never done any technical climbing before, his strength, agility and experience of altitude could make all the difference.

He was such a warm man. He would sometimes sit and watch us as we talked and argued, his observant brown eyes moving from one to another. Like a student, Jon thought – not judging, just taking in. For some reason, despite our money problems and disharmony, he seemed to trust us and identify with us. That in itself was a great boost, and with his cheerfulness and ability to fix anything from a discount on our hotel bill to a knackered starter motor, he was the biggest plus that had happened to us.

Kath and I were now quite cheery. We packed our blue barrel with climbing gear and clothes and books for Base Camp. Unlike the others, we had to share a barrel, and this meant we had a lot of extra gear, including our precious box of personal munchies, scattered about in the big standard cardboard boxes.

A lot of tactical cunning went into the packing of these loads. Everyone wanted to off-load as much as possible from his own rucksack to make the walk-in easier, yet because of our finances we had to impose a set number of porter loads per person. People were going round at the last minute slipping a sleeping bag in one load, cassettes or spare clothing in another, while still trying not to go over the 55-pound limit. The constant repacking and reallocation was driving Alex to distraction as he tried to keep up with his contents list.

Jon came up to me as I repacked my barrel for the last time. 'Ah mate, you seem to have some space left in there. Would you shove these in for me?' He handed over half a dozen books and walked away. A classic Jon manoeuvre, the same one he used to keep the best seats on the bus. I was suddenly fed up with it. I ran after and stopped in front of him. 'Look, Jon, if I can fit your books in, I will. But they're your responsibility, not mine. If they're too heavy, I'll leave them. Okay?'

He gave me what was intended to be a withering look,

shrugged and went into his room. But he'd heard me. If the books didn't turn up at Base, that was his problem. There were dozens of moments like that when one had to judge when to be helpful and put oneself out, and when to refuse. The balancing act between looking after one's own interests and those of the group is at the heart of a mountaineering expedition and determines its character. It's the same in 'ordinary life', of course, only less evidently so.

I looked at his books: some Russian novels and a history of the Spanish Armada. Very Jon. I found a space for them, wondering if I was an obliging fellow or a mug.

Now we were all packed up and ready to go. Our eighty-five porters were selected by Mohammed (who seemed to be related to most of them). They sang a prayer, a blessing on the Expedition, then they and our loads went off ahead by tractor through the desert and hills towards Dassu, where we hoped to follow them by jeep the next morning. But we couldn't leave till Mal and our LO showed up. The plane hadn't got through, and the road was still closed for repairs. Would they show up the next morning so we could get away? And how was Mal going to react to the coming confrontation?

In the evening, while the sky grew paler and paler above the mountains and darkness seeped up the valley towards us, Kath and I, Adrian and Jon took a walk through the miniature fields of Skardu. Potatoes, maize, wheat, a few cattle and goats, bordered by poplar trees hissing in the breeze against the darkening sky, crisscrossed by irrigation streams, dotted with rough stone houses crouched in the trees. It was deeply peaceful after the last two days' stress, and we were content to walk along in silence. The imam started calling the faithful to prayer and the streets were empty as we walked back in the soft half-light. The high-pitched sobbing yell trailed off into silence. We stood for a moment, each with our own thoughts of home, of tomorrow, each alone yet not alone.

'Good action,' Jon said quietly.

We were all gathered in the corridor of the K2 motel. It was time to go to bed but we were too wound up and anxious to leave. The hostility and suspicion against Mal were reaching a new crescendo, conducted by Burt, who was practically foaming at the mouth as he talked of the thousands of dollars he'd put into the trip. I thought how Kathleen's few hundred had been all she had. And just then, the man himself walked in with the LO. Big wave, big smile. Very muted 'Hi', curt nods in reply.

They were happy and pleased with themselves to have arrived. They'd enterprisingly flown to Gilgit, then commandeered a jeep on the road from there to Skardu. They were tired and wanted to eat and catch up on our news.

The reception was not friendly. Because of Shokat's presence, we couldn't launch straight into our cash crisis. We had to make conversation politely, while my heart for one was hammering with adrenalin. This moment of confrontation had been delayed so long, it had got out of all proportion. 'For God's sake, take Shokat aside,' Sandy whispered. So Kath and I had to chat to the good captain about the bus journey, the weather, weren't they clever flying to Gilgit, yes Baltistan is lovely, while all the time straining to make out the muffled voices from the room the others had taken Mal into. I felt that once again we'd been edged onto the periphery, and suspected that any further economizing would be at our expense.

We persuaded Shokat to go and eat, then hurried along to see how Mal was taking it. He looked dazed and baffled as he tried to take in in five minutes what we'd turned over for three days. But he soon saw the seriousness of our position, that we desperately needed money and that it was his responsibility to find it. That acceptance, together with his simply being there and obviously not a scheming monster, helped diffuse the situation, though the atmosphere was not exactly friendly.

So it was agreed then and there he'd have to go back to 'Pindi next morning and raise some 40,000 rupees (£2500). Somehow. Anyhow. By telexing Rocky, or getting an overdraft, or arranging a second mortgage through Liz and getting her to wire the money out. The message was clear: don't come back if you haven't got the money. If he managed to raise it, he'd probably wait in 'Pindi for Tony Brindle's arrival in another week, then they would follow us up to Mustagh Tower as quickly as possible.

Once the others had finished putting him through the wringer, I took him aside. I felt some sympathy for him as he sat, dazed, on the bed, hand on his forehead as he smoked and stared at the floor. I told him as much, that I still considered him my friend, and tried to explain how things had gone in his absence and why there was so much aggravation. He listened in silence, still trying to take it all in, still looking for solutions.

Then came the sticky part. I told him that we needed a clear statement of his and Rocky's commitment to our being part of the Expedition. I asked him to assure us that either he or the Expedition would pay some of the Karakoram Tours expenses since it was the Expedition, not Kathleen, who was benefiting from Mohammed.

And, being Malcolm and, despite what some of the others had said or feared about him, an honourable man, he said yes. We were part of the trip, Rocky wanted that, and somehow or other he'd find the money. I believed he was sincere. I just didn't know if he could do it. Like most serious climbers, he was broke most of the time. I felt acutely sorry for Liz at the prospect of his phoning her up and asking her to raise some £2500 of their money. Could they do it?

But there it was. We said good night. We hoped to meet again at Mustagh Base Camp in ten days or so – it seemed a long way off and fairly unlikely. Then I took three aspirin, my Streptotriad, my Stressguard and a sleeping pill, checked my pack for tomorrow – and fell asleep, grey and blank as an old blackboard, face down on the bed.

5

Living on Balti Time

In which we get a little higher

22–24 June 1984

That day was raised.

For us all it was one long sustained high note of joy. The joy of forward movement, of companionship, of scene after scene flicking by as we revved and jolted up into the mountains. The further on and up we got, the further we were from civilization, from officialdom and its pratfalls. Every mile left us lighter and freer.

We had bundled our rucksacks into the jeep in the cool early morning sunshine, grabbed our water bottles, cameras and sunglasses, and swung up into the open back of the Suzuki. For the first hour we bounced along the remains or the beginning of a road with the wind in our faces and the sun jumping in and out of the poplar trees. All the jokes and repartee started to flow for the first time in days. 'Let's not use Duff any more as the needle to thread our jokes on,' Alex murmured as he clung to a crossbar, his elongated legs dangling over the side. We nodded. Point taken. The past was behind us. We were living on amnesia once again.

Mohammed turned to me. 'Forward going,' he said, his brown eyes shining. 'This is my home.' And he stood up in the jeep, swung his cowboy hat above his head and let out a rodeo whoop of pure joy.

Then we entered the desert, and the jeep slithered along old tracks through the soft sand. None of us had expected this, a desert at 8000 feet, stretching away for miles on all sides. Over a stomach-lurching Third-World bridge across the Braldu river, then a first-gear haul up a pass through the foothills. The scenery was growing wilder and more desolate all the time, with range

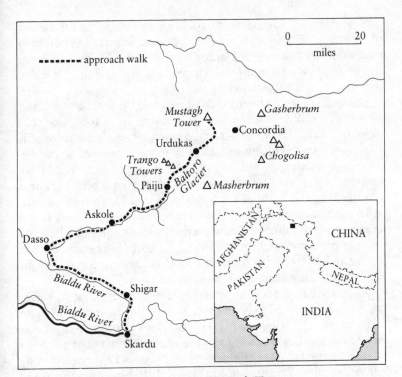

The Walk–in to Mustagh Tower

after range of 'foothills' – between 12,000 and 15,000 feet high – opening up more sand and shattered rock and granite peaks than I'd ever imagined existed. The scale of it all and the sheer desolation were a shock to the mind and body. It scooped us out of ourselves like the stars do. It left us feeling tiny and liberated, finally jolted us free from the shell of our supposed importance.

Then we came on small villages, little miracles of fertility in the wilderness. I'd look up and see a straight green line slashed as if by a razor, slanting down across the cliffs, and know that it bled water and round the next bend would be human habitation, made possible by that lifeline of water channelled off a melting snowfield. The villages grew more grubby and more lovely as we drove hour after hour deeper into the mountains.

Maybe I'm drowning and this is my life, Kathleen thought as one scene tumbled after another before her eyes, vivid and joyous.

Tall poplars, broad-leaved apricot branches whipping off the top of the jeep. Bright fields of wheat and lentils, shimmerimg irrigation streams running along their margins. A herd of goats shepherded by a beaming dwarf, chickens zigzagging in front of our wheels, magpies clattering out of a tree.

Sun in our eyes and our heads turned and turned, but we could never take it all in. Only a few images remain to set beside that richest of days. An old gap-toothed man carrying branches on his back looked up at us, his mouth open in astonishment or a smile. A young woman pulled her red shawl across her face as we approached; others stood motionless. A boy with blue eyes held out his arm, the palm of his hand facing us. He stood like that, grave and still, till we were 100 yards down the road. Was it a greeting or a warding off? And there was a man squatting beside a stream, his arms outstretched, watching glittering beads of water shiver and fall from his fingertips. Lost in some distant trance, he never turned his head as we went by.

As the villages became poorer, we began stopping in them. Mohammed seemed to be the best known and most popular man in Baltistan. Old friends and relatives clustered round him, shook his hand as they exchanged favours, made arrangements or merely chatted. In five minutes our jeep would be surrounded by an extraordinary variety of humanity. Tall, lean Afghans, small Tibetan-looking women with slanting eyes, village idiots with wide eyes and open smiles, children in bare feet and layers of sacklike shifts. Alex was clicking picture after picture in the most unobtrusive way, with a compact camera held casually in the hand that dangled by his side; no one was aware he was taking them. 'The way I figure it,' he drawled, 'why drop a stone into the lake and make interference when you can place it on the surface and let it sink?'

That's how we'd like to move through this country.

In the heat of the day, we stopped in a dusty village called Kashmal and were led to the headman's house. There Adrian was asked to look at a few people with cuts, bad eyes, bad chests. While he had his surgery, we sat in a cool, dim room and waited for tea. It was very simple: a couch, a bed, a framed photo of the Ayatollah Khomeini, a table, a copy of the Koran. The walls were roughly plastered, there were fading rugs on the floor.

It was deeply relaxing. No clutter of possessions, no radio, no telephone, no newspaper. The only sounds were the murmur of voices outside and the wind in the trees. We were quite content to sit and smoke and wait, while the bars of sunlight flickered on the opposite wall. Chat ran its leisurely course till the luckless Sybil came out with one of her Profound Remarks: 'Well, nobody has to like what they don't like.' A pause while we considered this pearl. Then she added defensively, 'That's what I think, anyway.'

Alex uncoiled himself from the far corner. 'W-e-l-l, that's a sane concept, but – we can still put it on THE CHOPPING BLOCK!' He brought the edge of his hand crashing down onto the table in front of him. Jon laughed in pure delight. It was typical Alex – quite bizarre, perfectly timed. And maybe just a little cruel.

Adrian came in, looking at once amused and harassed. Would Kath come and help him? He had a female patient; the problem was he was not allowed to examine her. He had to stand outside a door while Kath relayed the symptoms from inside and he directed her what to look for. Eventually he diagnosed a bad case of worms for mother and child, dug out some pills from our medicine chest and with Mohammed's help explained the course of treatment.

'I've heard of examinations done through a hole in a sheet, old boy, but this is the first time I've examined anyone through a door!' Mohammed explained that medical help for women in the remoter villages was a problem. There was a doctor and dispensary in every second village – which was typical of the impressive degree of organization we found in Baltistan – but often female patients were not allowed to see a male doctor. This also was typical. They could see a female doctor, but they were few and far between, and neither the men nor the women were keen on the men being examined by a female.

We took our tea, exchanged handshakes and smiles and clambered back up onto the jeep. 'Trouble is,' Adrian brooded, 'anything I do here is just a drop in the ocean.'

Sandy was talking about climbing in Chamonix. 'When you're up on the crag, you want to be lying on your back in the valley, eh? And when you're in the valley, you wish you were up on the crag.'

'Yeh,' Burt added, 'people only want what's impossible.'

But that ain't necessarily so. All that day I'd wanted what was not only possible but also present and actual. I wanted what I got. That was happiness, and more. It was Mohammed's hat swung aloft in the glittering air.

Travel-weary and jubilant, we arrived in Dassu at sunset. The road ended abruptly in the village square. From now on we walk. We shouldered our packs, took the track through the village, past the dusty trees and mud houses, teetered across a log over a stream and came to a military-looking compound where we were to spend the night.

Miraculously, our blue barrels and the already battered card-board boxes were waiting for us, all present and correct. So too were our porters, who squatted in the yard like a flock of chaffinches, all motley and chattering. The air was sweet with the woodsmoke from their fires as they brewed up *chai*. While Mohammed and Captain Shokat hassled for a reduction in our camp fees and negotiated a body-swerve round the regulation that we eat and pay for the food provided, we went inside.

A concrete floor, one trestle bed, a hurricane lamp. 'Shuffling dossing at last – *great*!' Jon enthused. We all acted in character. He lay on his Karrimat with the headphones, arms folded and staring at the ceiling like the effigy of a medieval knight. Adrian fussed about cleaning his corner and sorting through the medical gear. Kath went outside to watch the last mauve light drift up the highest slopes. I lit the lamp and hunched making notes in its smoky, yellow light. Burt and Sandy muttered over financial calculations in the room next door, Shokat like a good Muslim went for his evening wash, and Alex simultaneously got wrecked and got supper together.

We were all in a mellow mood that night as we talked quietly and ate in the half-dark. The room was lit by the fitful glare of a chapati oven outside, where dim figures moved in and out of the glow, leaving a brief vivid image of deep-set eyes, high cheek-bones, white teeth. We wondered how Mal was doing in 'Pindi, discussed his chances of raising the money. Our Expedition would be in desperate shape without it – but tonight all that counted was that we had finally come to the walk-in, and nothing could stop us short of Mustagh Base Camp.

I went outside to look at the moon. It was low and white,

casting enormous mountain shadows across the valley. The air
was cold and thin. The stars were smeared all across the sky –
how odd and reassuring it was to see the Plough still up there,
making its slow eternal furrow through the dark. And us – where
will our trail end? Will Kath and I be able to keep up and not
make fools of ourselves? Will we acclimatize? Just how hard is it
going to be?

I shivered in my Thermafleece, drew the zip up to my throat.
Kath came out to join me and we stood beside each other in
silence as the oven glowed, the porters murmured in their
blankets, and the stars tracked silently across the indifferent sky.

I hum a Chuck Berry anthem to decadent, innocent, rebellious
western youth as I slither out of my sleeping bag. The Karrimat
didn't soften that floor much. I'm bruised all over. There's going
to be another two months of sleeping on the ground. Suppose I'll
get used to it, just have to. Well, you don't come up here for
comfort, do you?

Hard to know what to wear. It's cold now, but by 10.00 it'll be
pushing 100°F in the shade. It stands to reason the first couple of
days will be the hottest, so I'd better wear the pajamas. I pulled on
the old yellow Marks & Spencer pajamas, feeling faintly ridiculous. Hell, what's good enough for Don Whillans is good enough
for me. But nobody laughs at Whillans. No, the pajamas make
sense – they're the lightest men's clothing one can buy. Then a
light sweater and the Thermafleece, can carry them in my pack
later. Got to keep the weight down – dump this sleeping bag in
one of the boxes, maybe get rid of a few cassettes too, if no one's
looking.

The Nike boots. They've been ace so far, no breaking in at all,
no blisters. Now we'll find out what they're up to. Foreign Legion
hat, ridiculous but effective. Umbrella, ridiculous and ineffective.
Too late to dump it now. Sun cream, water bottle, Milk Duds,
rolling tobacco, aspirin, notebook, Walkman, spare socks . . . I'll
never know how the weight adds up. Sandy must be carrying a
good 40 pounds, he's even got his axes. He's a bull. I've got
maybe 25 pounds, and that's enough for seven hours' yomp-

ing . . . Ready as I'll ever be, get a decent breakfast in, hey ho
let's go –

– *UP in the morning and out to school –*

'Oh God, you're not one of those cheerful sods in the morning,
are you?'

Our porters gather to receive a military-style briefing from
Captain Shokat – which leaves them amused and bemused – and
a more direct pep-talk from Mohammed. The basic message:
don't steal, don't lift, be nice to foreigners, money at Base Camp,
sorry no sunglasses.

Adrian gives them the statutory medical inspection. This is
something of a farce: he looks them in the eye, squeezes the odd
bicep, and asks if they feel okay. Naturally they grin and say
'Okay!' There's a good living in portering. They're a very motley
crew, aged from sixteen to mid-fifties, all lean and wiry. One or
two look slightly shifty, the rest look you in the eye and smile or
nod: nothing servile, just hello. We've heard stories of sit-down
strikes, of pilfering on a massive scale. The Spanish expedition we
met in Flashman's used sealed and locked barrels for their gear;
the ingenious porters removed the labels, cut into the barrels and
removed what they wanted, then replaced the labels over the
opening . . . By the time the Spanish discovered this, they'd lost
several thousand dollars' worth of gear, and the porters were
back in their mountain villages.

But they look trustworthy enough to us. As with anybody, it
probably depends how you treat them. Treat them as a lazy,
shiftless bunch of thieves and, insulted, they'll act like that. And
we've got Mohammed who knows personally every man there,
who they know will be back year after year looking for porters;
he's made it clear he'll not be amused if anything goes missing.
Only the ever cautious Adrian has festooned his pack with little
Chinese locks, which only serve to suggest there might be something inside worth breaking in for.

It's 7.30, the air is not so cool any more. Mohammed's
promised us a six-hour trek today, to the village of Chaqpo. That
will take us through the heat of the day. We're impatient to be
away, but now each load has to be assigned to a porter and noted
– he'll have that load and be responsible for it all the way to Base

Camp. The first porters rope up their boxes, strap them across their shoulders and backs, and stagger to their feet, steadying themselves with the stave each carries. In a biblical gesture, suggestive of Moses pointing the way forward into the Promised Land, the oldest extends his stick down the trail ahead, and now finally, on 23 June, we start walking to the Tower. This is the one big adventure I've always wanted; it's happening now as I put one foot after another down this dusty track, following a flock of porters into the mountains. I glance at Kath. She looks well. She says nothing but looks and looks around her, living her dream.

'Maybe I'm drowning and this is my life . . .'

Our walk-in would follow the Braldu river for several days to its source in the Baltoro glacier, then we'd trek up the glacier for another five days or so. At the top of the glacier is the greatest concentration of high mountains in the world: K2, Broad Peak, the four Gasherbrums, Masherbrum. To find the Mustagh Tower you turn left three days from the end.

None of us had done this walk-in before, but many mountaineers have come this way and it's agreed to be one of the most extended, arduous and occasionally dangerous walk-ins in the world. Joe Tasker in his classic book, *The Savage Arena*, described it as the hardest thing short of actual climbing he'd ever done. He was not a man given to overstatement. Tasker, Boardman, Haston, Bonington, Messner, Herman Buhl – all the heroes and companions of my armchair climbing had come this way, forded the same rivers, stayed at the same camp sites, been filled with the same dream as we had.

From the accounts we'd read, the main ingredients of hardship seemed to be the heat, the shortage of good water, and long stretches where the path skirted dangerously above the Braldu. 'If we get everyone to Base Camp in good shape, it'll be a minor miracle – and half the battle,' Mal had said in 'Pindi. I wondered where he was now, in what sort of mood, and if he'd managed to raise the money. The more pessimistic Jon, probably trying to wind us up, had added, 'You've probably got as good a chance of being crippled on the walk-in as on the mountain.' I was beginning to appreciate there was more to Himalayan climbing than just stepping onto the mountain and giving it Jon's 'maximum

pastry' for a few days. The climb had started when we stepped off
the plane in 'Pindi – it had started long before that – and we had
to gear ourselves to three months of concentration, stamina and
vigilance. As Aido pointed out, it was as important not to eat
death-on-a-stick cream cakes and to add iodine to every water-
bottle as it was to strap your crampons on super-tight and test
every piton before clipping into it.

We were soon to find out what the path by the river was like.
After an hour or so, the trail was forced down to the river by cliffs
on the left. 'Be careful,' Mohammed had told us that morning. 'Is
no problem, but very careful not to slip.' I could see why. The trail
was a foot's width of loose sand or grit or dried mud running
across the steep slopes that ran straight down into the river. It
looked very insecure. At times the trail was only a foot or so
above the water, at others a couple of hundred feet up, but in
either case if you slipped or the path gave way, you'd almost
certainly end up in the river. And if you ended up in the river . . .

The river was scary. You could feel great wafts of cold blowing
off it, as if someone had just opened a fridge door. The water was
a thick, impenetrable grey, solid with silt – and inconceivably
violent. It didn't flow, it hurled itself through the gorge. Bits of it
would suddenly leap into the air, or spit as you hurried by. All the
time there was a deep rumbling of boulders being savaged below
the surface. It was deep, fast, freezing, and desperately hostile. If
you ended up in the river you'd be drowned, knocked out or
frozen to death – either way, you'd probably be dead.

We plugged on for a couple of hours like this, concentrating on
every step. Only concentration can displace fear. I reasoned that
if our porters could do this with 55-pound loads and smooth-
soled sandals, so could we. It was not so much scary as a challenge
that made the heart beat a little faster.

Finally the trail broke away from the river and zigzagged up the
hill on the left. We began to fall into our natural order. Jon
striding out in front with his headphones on, head nodding in his
own world. He liked to be alone up front, possibly competitive-
ness, probably a desire for privacy. Sandy ambled along in the
rear, the amiable Honey Bear, chatting with Mohammed and
Alex. He had all the time and energy in the world. If only, he
thought, I could stop worrying about our finances . . .

Adrian moved up and down the long straggly line of porters

and climbers. He talked about home, about the Tower, dispensed pills and medical advice. He took all our little complaints – a sore knee, a rough throat – quite seriously, knowing they could well develop into problems. We were learning to monitor ourselves and become highly aware of our bodies. How strong am I today, have I drunk enough water, what's my pulse rate, what's causing this headache – the light or the altitude? It's like driving a car with a broken petrol gauge: we nurse ourselves along and try to estimate how much we've left inside. We chatted a while, then, still clutching his striped golf umbrella, he dropped back down the line.

Most of that day I spent some distance behind Jon, keeping him in sight. I am mildly competitive, I wanted to test myself. Kath and I were content to walk separately much of the time, then we'd meet for a short break and swig from our water bottles and talk over our experiences. For this trip we were intimate friends, not lovers. That would have shut the others out.

She took off her boots. Her heels were blistered and beginning to bleed. She was the only one without the sponsored Nike boots. It was not a good sign. She took a couple of aspirin and fitted some of Adrian's moleskin round her heels. 'You be all right?' She shrugs. 'I'll just have to be. There's no way I'm going to let that creep beat me to Chaqpo.' I smiled, knowing whom she meant and enjoying her spirit. I was pretty sure now she'd make it. When strength gives out, there's always pride.

Burt, Donna and Sybil trekked along as a group. He was talking less now and sweating more. Donna looked strong and at ease, working well within herself. Sybil trailed along awkwardly, cheerfully, doing her best, asking innocent questions and suffering Burt's scornful replies.

As we slogged slowly on the long uphill, Captain Shokat caught up with me. None of us had had much time to get to know him, just the odd chat in Skardu or during the jeep ride. He was immaculate in a tan suede shirt and new black cord trousers – I felt very conscious of my grubby yellow pyjamas but couldn't help thinking that tight black cords were hardly the thing to wear in this heat. He was like that – very smart and attentive to detail, keen and out of place. Unadapted. It was his first trip as a Liaison Officer and he was finding it hard to grapple with the gap between his image of what it would be like and how it actually was. He'd turned up with pages of regulations looking for a military-style organized expedition, and instead found a bunch of shuffling dossers with no obvious leader and not enough money.

Where, he wanted to know, was the solar shower Malcolm had told him about? And in future he wanted a cooked breakfast each morning. Why did we carry our own packs when he had given his to the cook to carry? Because we can't afford more porters, I said – it was easier than trying to explain that carrying at least some of your own gear was good Brit stylee. He asked me about Kathleen who he was obviously rather taken with and I took the opportunity to explain how upset she was about this piddling regulation that prevented her from going to Base Camp with us . . . He agreed it was unfortunate, but that was the regulation.

We all hoped that a few days on the trail would take some of the starch out of his new cords and his military mind. Then perhaps he would be amenable to sweet pastry and persuasion.

It was now approaching noon. Energy suddenly drained away and vanished like water down a plug hole. Every day was like that – the first couple of hours you'd feel good and strong, a little stiff maybe, and then for no apparent reason you were suddenly really struggling. Time for another water break. The disgusting pink juice from my bottle tasted good, so I must have been dehydrated.

I got to my feet and stumbled down a long precipitous path towards the distant river. When I arrived there, the first porters were lighting their fires and Jon was sprawled at ease in the shadow of a cave. 'All right, mate?' 'Aye. Interesting section that by the river.' 'Impressive,' he drawled, 'very impressive.'

I took off my boots, washed socks and feet in the river. It was numbingly cold and solid with silt. Shokat turned up, then Kath, limping with her blisters. It was good to stretch out in the shade, feeling tired enough to be pleased with ourselves. The others showed up but lunch didn't, due to several failures of communication. The porters eventually took pity on us and offered us some of their tea and chapatis. The tea was very sweet, very milky and very wonderful; I liked the porters too, they had a cheerful directness, a casual dignity about them, were neither ingratiating nor standoffish.

It was absurd to be by the river yet have no water. The glacier melt was solid with silt and almost certainly infected from the villages further up. We'd brought several thousand coffee filters with us but they didn't really work. Still, Mohammed cheerfully promised us clean water in Chaqpo, just an hour or two further on.

Mohammed had no sense of time. The second half of the day was the heartbreaker. Always expecting to arrive, never arriving. We plugged on and on, up and down, long awkward traverses by the river then trudging through soft sandy areas then jumping or wading across streams. All I wanted was to keep Jon in sight and lie by clear water in the village of Chaqpo. In the heat of the day my thoughts became confused, then vague, then virtually stopped altogether. There were long periods of blank absence, then I'd come back and notice my tan boots were still moving over the dirt and the pack still dragged on my back.

The trance state was all right. Each moment was all right – uncomfortable perhaps, but not unbearable. What is hard to bear is when one thinks ahead and imagines another two hours of this, another eight days of this. Then one feels doubly fatigued because one is carrying two burdens, that of the present and that of the future. The future – or the past, come to that – is much the heavier. The present moment is seldom unbearable. I must cultivate this living on amnesia – amnesia towards the future as well as the past. It's the only way to hump this load . . .

It was with these simple reflections that hours later I rounded a bend and saw Chaqpo ahead. The razor slash of green across the mountain, then the village cupped in the green palm of its trees and fields. If it had good water, it was the Promised Land. I met Jon lounging ultra-casually under a rock as he changed cassettes on his player. 'Joy Division,' he gloated, 'pure death and destruction – great!'

In the shade of the apricot trees the first porters shrugged off their loads and smiled. 'Okay, sahib?' '*Salam*. Okay.' One offered me a K2. '*Shukria*,' I said, carefully trying out the first of the Urdu words Shokat had written down for me. It seemed to work, he nodded and smiled again.

I lay back against a tree and luxuriated in that cigarette. Already the memory of the day was fading. It wasn't so hard, was it? Piece of cake, old boy, I'd say to Aido when he arrived. Soon I'd go to find this clean water, but for now there was the pure pleasure of not moving, and the thin blue smoke filtering up through the branches of the apricot tree.

By the time we'd put up our tents – Kath and I casually watching how the others did it, then imitating them, trying not to appear total bumblies – it was time to eat. By the time we ate – our now standard meal of chapati, dal and retorts – it was dark. By the time it was dark – a cool, brown, Asiatic, soft darkness – it was time to sleep.

I could see it was going to be a simple life.

We sat up a little late – that is, after 8.00 p.m. – round a porter's fire, chatting idly of the days ahead, the day gone by, wondering how Mal was doing in 'Pindi. Burt had heatstroke and was lying pale and shivering, drinking pint after pint of water. My knee that I'd damaged while training was painful; Kath's blisters were oozy with blood; various porters had headaches, blisters and cuts. Adrian attended to us all and when I crawled into my sleeping bag he was the last of us still up, with a line of patients between him and sleep.

I woke to the porters' laughter and the smell of woodsmoke from their fires. Breakfast was the usual scramble: where's the oatmeal, who took the last biscuit, Alex, where's the electrolytic drink powder, get an extra Granola bar, lighten my pack by stuffing a jacket and some cassettes in the sleeping bag and putting it in a porter load. The usual little tensions and self-serving. Only Alex and Sandy are generous and unruffled at these times; the rest of us are out for ourselves.

We set off too late on another cloudless morning. My pack felt awkward and painful on yesterday's shoulders, and my right knee was weak. Kath admitted she'd scarcely slept and felt dizzy this morning. Her face was swollen with water retention, and her fingers were too fat to take her rings off. People seem to react to the effects of altitude at different heights; I'd felt lousy in Skardu and was fine now, she was coming up against her first barrier. There was none of yesterday's exuberance and novelty. The Americans were ahead of us. Time for some head-down-no-nonsense mindless trekking. We'll see who's ahead at the end of the day.

Mohammed had warned us this would be a long day to Chongpo. He was right about that. We spent the cool of the day on a long, slow trudge uphill. Already it was noticeable how as soon as one got off the level onto the slightest gradient, the pace slowed. It had to. We breathed heavily through our mouths, trying to suck in air that wasn't there. Then a long and slightly hairy section above the river, traversing on dust and loose rock. Most worrying were the bizarre mud towers overshadowing us on the left. They were up to 200 feet high and studded with boulders. Between the towers and the river, this section is a death trap when it rains. Mohammed said several trekkers and porters had been killed or injured along here, and now they refuse to set out from Chaqpo during or after heavy rain. There was no sign of rain now, not even a cloud, but we were still glad to leave that area behind. The porters move very quickly when they need to, almost skipping along with their loads.

After four and a half hours' heavy-duty trekking we came to a valley shimmering with heat. But there was good water; we slung down our packs, refilled our bottles and drank and drank. There must be a tremendous water loss: I'd had three pints of fluid at breakfast, two more on the trail, three more here – it all went in and nothing came out.

'Take picture,' Captain Shokat demanded in his peremptory way, and carefully arranged himself in the shade of his umbrella, combed his hair and looked at the camera with such a smirk of self-satisfaction it was hard not to laugh. With his spotless attire, the umbrella, and the service he demanded from the porters, he was ten times more Raj than we could ever be.

He demanded hot showers, special food, juice from our water bottles if he didn't like his own, considered the porters at his disposal. They didn't like it but went along with putting up his tent, fetching him water, airing his sleeping bag. We made it very clear that we were not part of this.

When he was tired or querulous, we handled him by playing on his considerable vanity. We told him how fit, strong and tough he must be from the army – he smirked, pulled in his stomach, and tried to live up to the image we'd given him. And in fact he was doing all right. He was quite fit and tried to be part of the Expedition. He was beginning to realize that Mohammed was not a hired man to be talked down to, and the unspoken trade-off was that we'd do things to help him if he helped us. Kathleen had been putting in a lot of sweet pastry with him, working round to asking to be allowed to stay at Base Camp.

He'd settle in. This was a big change for him from the ordered army life with two showers a day, the officers' mess and attentive servants.

As we sat having lunch in the nonexistent shade, we could see the afternoon's task ahead of us: a 1500-foot shoulder of a mountain. It dropped sheer into the river, so we had to go over it. No wonder we were in no hurry to set off. I hoped that the exposure wouldn't freak me out. Still, what Burt could do, I could do.

I mentioned to Sandy that I was feeling the lack of air – which at round 9500 feet seemed a bit premature. 'That's all right, youth.' He grinned. 'I'm feeling it too.' He said the secret was to begin slowing everything down, make no sudden movements, don't get in a flap. Until you're acclimatized to each new level, even three quick steps will leave you weak. He said he concentrated on the habit of breathing slow and deep, rather than the snatched, shallow breaths I'd noticed in myself.

With that in mind, we set foot on the crumbling zigzag path that crawled up the cliff. Sandy went very slowly indeed, a steady slow-motion plod, never hurrying, never faltering. I took my pace from him and was pleased to feel I could keep it up for hours. And hours was what it felt like, with the noonday sun hammering down and the energy plughole wide open. I was aware of nothing but this step and the next, the heat shimmering off the rocks, the sudden unexpected wild flower. It was all vivid and simple. I felt very happy.

We finally came out on top of the hill and took a breather. Now I had time to look around, I could see how steeply this promontory fell away on three sides, and immediately felt uneasy. I was at least six feet from the nearest edge, but was still gripped. I was alarmed and angry at my own weakness. Sandy gave me a reassuring grin, shouldered his pack, and together we set off along the ridge rising to our left, further up into the mountain. Some of it was very exposed. I kept my eyes down, focusing only on Sandy's tan bootheels.

That uphill went on and on. At the top, we seemed to have reached quite alarming heights. It was not imagination that made the air seem thinner; it was quite noticeably so. It's not just thinner in the lungs, it's somehow thinner in the mind. My mental and emotional processes seemed to be becoming stripped, slower, simpler. One feels one can see for great distances, outside and within.

Mohammed appeared from nowhere and pointed out a distant white peak up ahead: Masherbrum. The name meant nothing to me but it looked vicious, even some 40 miles off, much higher than all the hills round about us. They were still below the snow line so probably under 15,000 feet; Masherbrum stood across the top of the valley like a lighthouse and had several thousand feet of snow on it.

'Now I see why it was called K1,' Jon enthused, 'it's the first major peak you see coming up this way. Fucking great, isn't it?' He and Sandy stared at it hungrily, pointing out various possible and impossible lines on it. Mountaineers are not monogamous by nature – even while obsessed with one mountain, they note the potential of every other one they come across, and file it away in the little black book of memory and desire. Even while passionately engaged with one mountain, they are planning how to woo the next, and dreaming of the one after that.

I decided they were promiscuous and crazy. I could understand the impulse, but it seemed obvious what they were really flirting with. I was different. The Mustagh Tower was my one and only, my first and last. After this, my probing ice axe was going where it belonged: in the attic. There would be only one mountain in the photos on my desk . . .

With these self-righteous and self-deceiving thoughts, I picked my way carefully after Mohammed.

Mid-afternoon of that seemingly endless day found Kath, myself, Alex, Adrian and Sandy lying in the shade of a great overhang beside the trail, some 2000 feet above the Braldu river. In the back of the cave where the sun never shone, it was blessedly cool. Jon had gone on; Burt, Donna and Sybil were nowhere in sight. We were in no hurry now, it was all downhill from here.

So we had a smoke and some peaceful, desultory conversation. We shared a sense of godlike detachment as we looked out over the river, the endless ranges of hills, the little green villages across the valley and the distant band of snow-capped mountains. Only the desire to get the day's trekking over with finally made me get up and leave that place. Only an hour, Mohammed had said.

Mind you, he'd said only two hours from our lunch spot, and that was at least three hours ago . . .

Should you ever have the good fortune to come this way and engage Mohammed Ali Changezi as your guide, remember this: he is a wonderful man, but he has no sense of distance or of time. He has this in common with all the mountain people in Baltistan. Balti time is elastic; it has nothing to do with watches. It is quite inscrutable, and has something to do with one's state of mind and the amount of effort it takes to go from one place to another.

In Baltistan the question 'When?' is a waste of valuable breath.

I wasted my valuable breath cursing Mohammed as that descent went on and on through the blistering afternoon. Again and again I had to clamber down into the gorge of a river, then scramble up the other side. These rivers were swollen now with the full melt from their invisible sources, and a couple of them necessitated hazardous jumps to the tip of a rock in the middle, then continuing across. Through a daze of heat, tiredness and dehydration I remember a bizarre traverse across and down a slope of fine, shifting sand: down was easy, but if you failed in the across you were into a chute that ended in the refrigerated Braldu. During my semicontrolled slide I heard a shout, looked up and saw Mohammed on solid ground, holding out his ski pole; I grabbed it and pulled myself across to him.

'I thought you said it was an hour from the cave,' I protested, ungrateful to the last.

He shrugged, smiled. 'Is not far. Maybe one hour.'

I made a face and scrambled on, muttering over and over under my breath, 'Living on Balti time, living on Balti time . . .'

It comes to an end, as it always does, quite suddenly. There are the fields, the trees and their leaves clattering in the late afternoon breeze, the mud and stone huts. Chongpo is the poorest village yet, a lot of goitre swelling out of the necks of adults and children, several village idiots, a couple of dwarves. Yet they don't seem to view it as tragedy. The same with age and death. Rightly or wrongly, for them it's just something that happens. I find Jon sitting with some porters, laughing and teaching them 'London Bridge Is Falling Down'. I lower my face into the nearby stream and let the water flush the day away, treasuring this long-awaited moment, the coolness, the sensuous fading ache of muscles finally at rest.

Kath limps in, pale but still on her feet. Then the others trail in. We're all rather wasted, it's been a big day. We put up our tents, it gets dark, we eat, it's time to sleep. My knee's aching, but there's Mohammed's solemn promise of a short day tomorrow to Askole, the last village in Baltistan. I look at the stars last thing. They're still there. Jon stands beside me.

'Sweet as a nut,' he says cryptically, 'sweet as a nut.'

I don't know what he's talking about, yet I know what he means.

It's the oddest feeling. I'm sitting naked in hot sulphurated water in the middle of a valley of stone. It's early still, and the cool morning breeze raises goose pimples along my arms. Ten minutes of pure happiness at 10,000 feet, till Jon suggests I get a move on and let him wash his sweaty body in the famous sulphur pool between Chongpo and Askole.

I reluctantly make way for him. Sandy ambles up and asks where the girls are. In the pool round the corner, I say. 'Good value, eh?' He grins and goes off to join them.

Good value indeed. Two hours later, we were all smiling as we walked into Askole. Pete Thexton had written that the Askole chicken is probably the most unfortunate life form on earth, so we were expecting the pits. Instead, bubbling irrigation streams of clear water running under the tall trees, fields of young wheat spread out like green plates of a banquet beneath the blue sky, sweet-smelling shrubs, little round stone mills powered by sparkling sprays of water rushing down hollowed-out logs . . . Askole is paradise simple but visible, a balm to tired eyes.

The houses and people looked distinctly less desperate than those in the tiny villages we'd left behind. We were formally introduced to Haji Mahdi, the head of the village, and pitched our tents in the village square. We were finished for the day, and had the prospect of a rest day after that while we bought final provisions and kerosene and engaged more porters. Joy, joy, joy.

I spent the most unflawed hour of my life washing socks in the clear spring high above Askole. Warm sun, ice-cold water, the shade of trees; the green fields stacked below, the barren hills all round, the snowbound peaks floating off into another world. A slow purification of the senses, a cleansing of the mind along with the socks. Completely on my own, completely happy.

As I finally pick up my things and saunter down the paths towards the village, I feel born again into the world. No doubt about it – altitude affects the mind. Hang on to that scepticism, son, it's the best inheritance your father left you.

That night, as the moon rose and its pale waters flooded the valley, I sat in front of my tent in an F.S. Smythe stylee, smoking my pipe. Trouble and activity all around me – Adrian was painstakingly cleaning and stitching a gash on a boy's foot ('next time tell him *not* to cover it in mud, old boy'), Alex stormed about looking for a lost sleeping bag, the others were locked in yet another urgent conference about money.

The Expedition has changed so much from its original conception. Gone are Rocky Moss, the four Sherpas, half a dozen trekkers and an awful lot of fixed rope. Mal and Tony aren't here, and there's no guarantee they ever will be, if Mal doesn't find the money. Discussing it earlier this evening, we realized our cutting edge was reduced to just Sandy and Jon, and Jon's feeling sick. The edge isn't so much blunter as thinner, too thin probably to hammer home any advantage good weather might give us. There's just not enough skilled support, not enough manpower, no margin. The only chance we have left is to attempt an Alpine-style ascent from the Col. Alex, Adrian, Mohammed, myself, Burt and Donna are here to set up that attempt by carrying loads to the Col, if possible.

I don't mind, I don't think anyone does. 'Shit or bust' was Jon's comment, and Sandy nodded. It's better this way, less of a circus and more of a modern climbing expedition. It would be an insult to a great mountain to put clients on the top of it, using Sherpas and fixed rope throughout.

It made me think of Hartog's comment about the first Mustagh ascent: 'Now we knew it might be too hard for us, morale went up enormously.'

6

Stranded in Askole

*In which we fall apart and wait
for deliverance*
25 June–5 July

On Sunday 25 June, in Askole, the Joint Anglo-American–Nepali Karakoram Expedition finally fell apart. The inner cabal – Sandy, Jon, Burt – had been up half the night doing their sums, and whichever way they added it, the answer was always the same: NO MONEY. Not enough money to take all our loads to Mustagh Base Camp and still have a reserve to pay for the walk-out.

The instant porridge was thick and tasteless in my mouth. Kath was silent, resigned or angry, I couldn't tell. My heart was fluttering at the slightest provocation. I could see what was coming next. Either the Expedition was going to have to wait here in Askole – which would cost, and eat into our valuable time and provisions – in the hope of Mal turning up in ten days with some cash, or else something, *someone*, would have to be jettisoned. For the good of the Expedition, the least essential members and their loads would have to be left behind, enabling the others to go on.

A long, tense silence as we sat on our boxes in the village square. Shokat looked bemused, Mohammed looked very unhappy; the rest of us didn't look at each other at all. A moment of truth that many expeditions have to face eventually: who is least important here?

We did it the easy way: who is most important? Sandy and Jon, no one else has any chance of climbing the Tower. Adrian as the doc and support, Alex as support and camp manager. Mohammed, if we can persuade Shokat into letting him go without the trekkers.

So, asked Sandy, who would 'volunteer' to stay behind? Sybil, well prepared for this kind of situation by life with Burt, immediately said she would. Which was pretty decent, seeing she'd put her spare cash into the general funds and still had to pay half of Mohammed's fees, all for a trek that looked like ending in Askole. Then Kath said okay, she would stay. She was already fascinated by Askole.

Sandy said he couldn't be sure till they'd repacked the loads, but more of us would have to wait in Askole if the 'sharp edge' was going to make it to Base Camp. 'And have enough to get to Gash 2,' Jon added swiftly.

I wasn't too keen on that. Were the lads sacrificing us to have an outside chance of Gasherbrum 2? While our argument flared, Sandy and Alex were hastily conferring. Then Sandy interrupted us: 'Look, I'm sorry about this but all of you are going to have to stay. We've eighty-five loads here and we can only pay for fifty. That means only the absolute minimum of people and supplies can go to Base Camp.'

After a pause, Burt accepted he and Donna would have to stay. So I accepted Kath and I would too. It seems childish, doesn't it? But the truth was that all of us were prepared to do the right thing to save the Expedition, but none of us wanted to be a mug.

Thus ended our breakfast conference. I decided to leave the pressure cooker of the camp behind and trek up to the high spring. I took soap, a towel, and half a dozen water bottles but that was just an excuse. I needed out for a while.

I was feeling breathless and headachy as I followed the paths that looped round one field after another, stacked in layers back up towards the spring. It was irritating, having to walk so slowly on that mild uphill. A lot of things were irritating that morning. But after ten minutes, a couple of hundred feet above the village, I began to gain enough perspective to see how much of that aggravation came from me and how much from what was happening round about. I'd been ratty and paranoid and it was partly from altitude. The effects of altitude seem to make themselves felt not at the time but the morning after you've slept at a higher level than before.

I cooled my thoughts and slowed my steps.

The path I was following snaked up near the boundary wall of Askole which was some six feet high, made of boulders and topped with thorns. To keep out predators, I supposed – snow leopards? The division the wall marked was startling and absolute: on this side, lush green fields of young wheat and lentils; on the other, barren red rock, scree, desolation, the wilderness.

The path looped along by the irrigation channels. Some were clear, some muddy, some had no water in, only damp silt. I began to appreciate the extreme simplicity and complexity of the system that allowed the villagers to flood, moisten and let dry out, according to daily need, what was probably over a hundred fields spread out over an area of hillside roughly a mile and a half wide and the same in length. It was a network as complex and organic as the circulation of the blood, divided similarly into main arteries, veins, capillaries. I saw the sun flash on the spade of a villager half a mile up the hill; three minutes later the channel at my feet filled with muddy, silt-laden water. I stood and watched the life force of Askole snake its way downhill, branching out, flooding out across some fields and passing others by. An aged man below who appeared to be passing by chance bent down and removed a small stone from a junction of two channels, and the water took off on an entirely new tack across the fields. The gap-toothed peasant carefully placed the stone on the bank and walked on. The man up the hill and the old one below hadn't even looked at each other, let alone shouted instructions.

It was as subtle and simple as water itself.

Two round black boulders in the fields beside me stirred, then straightened up . . . Two Askole women, patiently weeding. They wore thick, coarse black cloth woven from goat and yak hair, offset with a bright scarf and plastic beads, zips sewn around the rim of their flat caps. They saw me but did not turn away and hide their faces. Instead they stood and had a good stare. '*Asalam o aleikum*,' I called. After a pause and a giggle, '*Salam*.' Then they bent again to their work and all I could see were two black, rounded backs.

The women in Askole seemed to be more independent and visible than in other parts of Baltistan and Pakistan, certainly more so than in Skardu. Perhaps this is because the Askole economy so clearly needs them to be out and working in the fields – mostly weeding and planting. The men spend their time digging and directing, repairing irrigation ditches, ploughing the fields with a wooden plough and two oxen, cutting and carrying loads of firewood. Little children carry weeds in tiny wicker baskets; the weeds are spread out to dry and used as animal feed through the five-month winter. Old men carry loads of dried yak dung for fuel, or sit in the shade of the school in the village square, chewing a green tobacco substance and shooting the breeze with Haji Mahdi and the young schoolteacher. Boys herd yaks, goats and the miniature sheep. Girls work in the fields, giggle when you pass, their decorated hats jingling as they move. Old women cook and look after babies. Young men hope to be porters. The harvest involves everyone.

Everything is used, everyone has a role, everything fits. Askole life is as unbroken, unforced and interconnected as the irrigation channels that sustain the village.

I came to the high spring, to the cool willow trees and the green grass beneath them. Once again it was a balm to the mind and all its fretting. I knelt down and began filling the water bottles.

Returning to camp was walking back into the pressure cooker. Our boxes were strewn about the courtyard as we feverishly sorted out and argued over the essential and the nonessential gear. Alex was wild-eyed, constantly bombarded with 'Where is?', 'How many?', 'How much?', irritable and worn out. Jon and Sandy were grim and determined. For the first time I saw some of the self-centredness that made them mountaineers: they'd sacrifice anything and anyone to get to the Mustagh Tower.

Burt emerged from his tent, walked over to Sandy and started waving his arms about. We could hear snatches about the money he'd put in, how he should go on, how Duff had fucked up. Mohammed squatted beside me looking very distressed, running his hand through his thick black hair. 'Anger,' he said slowly, 'is glass in my heart.' I looked at him closely. He put his hand on his chest and made little clawing gestures. 'It cuts *me*. You understand?'

Our eyes met. I felt I understood him perfectly. I'd understood it at the spring, that nursed anger wounded mostly oneself. I nodded, and our glance seemed to leap across the gap between our cultures.

'All men,' he continued hesitantly, 'the same. But different. Anger . . .' He spread his fingers in the dust. 'See, five fingers. All different length, different shape. But all fingers, all my hand. All *this* finger, not *that* finger. When I see this about men – no more anger.'

He looked up questioningly. I spread my hand, looked at it, let his words sink in. There was nothing more to say.

Then Sandy called him over; he clasped his hand round my forearm, got up and walked across the compound. He was being asked to give our LO 'sweet pastry'; Shokat was getting more and more unhappy at the prospect of the Expedition splitting. It was against regulations. We each took turns to talk with him, soothe him, flatter him, anything to stop him blowing the whistle on us. Burt played poker with him, but unfortunately won. Kath put on her blue headscarf, looked into his eyes and asked him to escort her round Askole and interpret for her. As an officer and a gentleman (though unfortunately not a Balti speaker, so he couldn't understand most of what the locals were saying) he was delighted, combed back his lick of black hair, shook some imaginary dust from his black cords, and set off with her into the maze of mud and boulder houses. She had strict instructions to keep him away for as long as possible while we attended to a few other minor body-swerves.

The highlight of the day: midafternoon, when we were at our most fraught and exhausted, there was a hissing from one of our boxes in the middle of the square. One of our two oxygen cylinders had been left out in the sun. Everyone scattered as if from a bomb; the safety valve blew and with a great WHUMPH the cylinder blew out.

As silence and dust settled again, there was scattered applause. Someone laughed. Then we all started laughing, laughter to the point of pain in our unacclimatized lungs. All the tension went out of us, all the pressure blew out into the mountain air.

Adrian spent much of the time treating local people for everything from conjunctivitis to TB. The prevalence of goitrous swellings and the simplicity of eliminating them – iodine for pregnant mothers and occasionally through childhood – upset him a lot. When he said, 'Give me a year here and I could halve infant mortality', it was a simple statement of fact. He tried to persuade them that covering wounds and sores with mud or yak dung was not a particularly good idea, that pills were to be swallowed, not kept as talismans to ward off sickness, that aspirin might cure headaches but not epilepsy.

Finally, waiting in line, was a yak. His jaw dropped. Was this an Askole joke? No, Haji Mahdi explained, it had been mauled by a snow leopard, but it was a strong yak and had escaped. We were astonished, because we'd thought snow leopards were near-mythical, elusive creatures that never came near human habitation. But there were great chunks torn from the animal's back. Keeping a very wary eye on the unhappy animal's great horns, Adrian cleaned out the bleeding wounds with antiseptic, took a guess at the yak's body weight and shot it full of penicillin.

Haji and the yak's owner were delighted. That evening, a dozen fresh eggs were quietly delivered to our camp.

Evening. A last supper together round the fire. The light flickered on our faces, the muezzin wailed into the dusk. All our possessions were split into two piles. It was like the break-up of a marriage, and no one was sure how amicable it was. I alternated between acute anxiety and calm indifference to our plight. The drive to scheme, work and manoeuvre to secure what we want, and the ability to accept what is and will be – as the last brews went round, those conflicting impulses flickered in me like the light and shadow cast by the lamps.

At least some of our Expedition was still going forward. Mohammed had managed to persuade Captain Shokat that the guide should go on to Base Camp while the Liaison Officer would stay in more comfortable Askole and wait for our honoured leader and his 40,000 rupees. And Shokat had quite casually agreed to letting Kathleen visit Base Camp, assuming she ever got there.

Even Sybil had had a good break. A couple of English climbers that Sandy knew had turned up in Askole; they were going down the valley, then turning off to trek elsewhere in Baltistan. Yes, they'd be delighted to have Sybil with them. Even now they were all getting wrecked round a camp fire in the upper camp site and, judging by her high-pitched, delighted laughter, she was having a wonderful time. Burt scowled and looked uneasy, Jon caught my eye and winked.

As I drifted off to sleep I could hear Sybil giggling as she stumbled about among the guy ropes, and Burt hissing in the next tent as he cursed 'Duff – and that pair of fucking liberal cocksuckers'. It's always interesting hearing oneself talked about. Apparently Kath and I were personally responsible for his plight.

It was hard luck on Burt. He'd met a problem that couldn't be solved by phone.

So that morning Sandy (now by general consent the acting leader), Jon, Adrian, Alex and Mohammed set off on the five-day trek to Base Camp with forty porters. In addition to us, they left behind our barrels, kerosene, most of the Gasherbrum boxes, books, the expired oxygen cylinder, and some provisions. They took with them a mild sense of guilt, two goats and three chickens – the first in their hearts, the second on a lead, the third squawking indignantly from a box on a porter's back.

Kath and I walked with them for the first couple of hours. We parted from them at a bend in the trail, shook hands. 'Good luck, youth', 'See you at Base Camp', 'Go for it' – the usual. Sandy apologized for the situation. 'But you see how it is,' he said and shrugged. Adrian took us aside. 'If I was you, old boy, I'd take one porter between you and follow us up.'

It had occurred to me. It had certainly also occurred to Burt. I could see us sneaking away separately before dawn and Captain Shokat waking up to find himself abandoned. An entertaining prospect, but not on.

We waved goodbye and turned away rather than watch them dwindle into the distance.

Jon (26 June): And so we left like naughty schoolboys allowed out on an undeserved treat. A retreat from Moscow in reverse. Mohammed in flowing white robes, ski stick and red rucksack looks like a latter-day Moses leading the damned/chosen through the wilderness. He's a man desperately trying to remain an individual under a stifling culture, regime and religion. We do like him.

Jon (27 June): Delicate purple and yellow blooms behind porters' ears – a gesture against their harsh physical lives? The way they crowd together, Balti hugs at seeing a friend again.

Me and Sandy feel the responsibility and our lack of experience, but still in good heart.

Where to begin when talking about Askole? It's all so interconnected, I find it hard to talk about one aspect without talking about every other.

Here's a beginning: Askole has no shops. Haji Mahdi has a parlour where he has cigarettes, sometimes cheese, tea, sugar, tins left from other expeditions, which he will sell to climbers and trekkers passing through, but that's a service to westerners, not inside the village. No one there lives by buying things at one price and selling them at another. No one lives by employing other people to work for them. There is private property, but a house or field or mill doesn't seem really to be owned by an individual, more by an extended family.

Askole has a schoolteacher, paid by Haji, a policeman (though he looks like a porter and seems to spend his time portering, and never seems to do any policing), and a priest. It is not a cash economy. Unemployment does not exist; more importantly, it is a concept which would be incomprehensible in these mountain villages. The smallest child, the oldest man, the most cretinous half-wit, all have their roles (carrying tiny baskets of weeds, collecting dried yak dung, herding goats, respectively).

As a way of life it is not so much medieval as neolithic. The only metal tool I've seen there is the blade of their irrigation spades. Even the ploughs, a single prong pulled through the soil by two oxen, are entirely wooden. The baskets are woven from branches. I presume there must be an axe to chop down wood, but I never saw one, and I have seen porters chop wood by bashing it with a sharp stone, crouched in the same attitude as our earliest ancestors.

Their houses are like a Scottish croft or but-and-ben built of rocks, except the one room is stacked on top of the other. The ground floor – often dug down into the earth is for the animals and grain, the first floor is for people, where they eat, sleep, gossip, feed babies, giggle and stare at the curious westerner who has many rupees but no land or family or permanent home. The Baltis have not yet invented the chimney; instead they have a square hole in the roof and a room thick with smoke (hence the conjunctivitis).

Often on the roof is a woven tentlike structure for sleeping in during summer. In the winter, everyone moves downstairs with the animals for warmth. In winter there is snow on the ground for some five months, and there is nothing to do but sleep, eat a little, talk a little, keep the animals going.

'But surely,' I insisted to Haji as he explained aspects of Askole life to us in his quiet, mild murmur, 'you must do *something* in winter.'

He looked up slowly at me, then Kathleen, then down at his feet with a smile of recollection or perhaps anticipation.

'Also,' he added when we stopped laughing, 'perhaps we make hats.'

We'd seen the hats. They are the chief and characteristic ornamentation of the mountain women, made of stiff black cloth, then fringed and hung with beads, glass, plastic, expedition tags, ring-pulls from cans, anything bright that came to hand.

'To sell?' Kathleen asked, sensing a cottage industry.

'If too many hats, we sell.'

Then he smiled mildly and head down, hands clasped behind his back in a Duke of Edinburgh stylee, shuffled down the mud alleyway of the main street, trailing us in his wake like bewildered, enchanted satellites.

The more we saw of Haji Mahdi over the following days, the more impressed we were. He has more natural dignity than anyone I've ever met. It is a dignity that has nothing to do with a straight backbone or any kind of aloofness. It is a dignity that one senses comes from deep inner tranquillity, from being completely at home with who and what he is. It is a dignity that needs no assertion.

He always wears a grey Pakistani-style pajama suit with a tan waistcoat. He never hurries any movement, word or gesture. His eyes are brown, mild, intelligent, at once amused, absent-minded, and alert. He drifted round Askole in what looked like carpet slippers, his eyes to the ground, his hands precisely so behind his back: right hand clasped loosely round his left wrist, left fingers hanging down relaxed. I spent a lot of time following him on the single-track paths between the fields, and I never saw those fingers ball up or clench. He seemed incapable of tension. He'd pause to murmur a word here, an instruction there. He'd spend an hour in the shade of the schoolroom with the old gap-toothed men of the village, watching the children chanting through their lessons, chatting over this and that. Then he'd pad up through the fields, or watch someone weaving, or joke with the old women squatting at their doors. I'd come upon him in the street, mildly contemplating a scrawny goat that stared back at him from its crazed yellow eyes.

He is responsible for the overall pattern of Askole. He channels its resources in the same unobtrusive way the villagers direct the water that makes their lives possible. A rock lifted, a cut with a spade, a word, a nod, a joke – all part of the same activity.

His position as the headman of Askole is not conferred by the state or the law. Nor by election, heredity, or the amount of land he owns. In a tiny, organic society like Askole where everyone is related, where three or four hundred people know each other from cradle to grave, there is no need to count hands to know the village's will.

His authority seems to have two sources. The first is religious: he is a haji, he has made the pilgrimage to Mecca and gone through the statutory processes of instruction, prayer and reflection. In fact, he's been there twice, he admitted with a shy smile. I found it hard to imagine this man flying to Mecca on a jet plane, catching a taxi, dodging traffic, changing money – and yet, of course, he would do it patiently, calmly, humorously, as he does everything else.

And that's the second source of his authority: the man he is. His humility, natural intelligence and self-possession allow him to direct and represent the village. He deals with the climbing and trekking parties that pass through Askole – a considerable number, perhaps forty to fifty a season, each with from four to 200 porters. We were never alone on our camp site the whole time we were there. At times it was like Piccadilly Circus. Putting them up, selling them flour, lentils, tea, fresh meat or livestock if necessary, supervising the hiring of local porters in accordance with government regulations, requires a considerable amount of bargaining and organization.

He showed me a fat, battered notebook full of spidery moon-writing Urdu script with notes, recommendations, autographs in English, Japanese, German, Swedish, French, Italian. He pointed out the signatures of Messner, Bonington, Pete Boardman, and seemed to have a fair idea of who was who in the Himalayan climbing world. In that notebook were listed all the parties expected through Askole that season, how big they were, how many porters they might require.

Surely this influx of foreigners with their needs, their money, their attitudes and possessions, would damage the economy and social structure of Askole? Kath saw the effect of climbing parties epitomized in the locals walking round with climbing rope holding up their trousers, or slings used as leads on sheep, or the expedition tags on the women's hats. What comes from outside is used and incorporated, but does not dominate. Not yet.

The culture of Baltistan is very resilient. It is sustained by its religion – Shiite Moslem, rather than the Sunni Moslem of Pakistan – and by the inevitable nature of its agriculture. Not only is Askole too remote to be mechanized, there is little room for mechanization in the irrigation system. You cannot plough stacked paddy fields with a tractor.

Trekking and climbing have brought money into Askole but not yet turned it into an acquisitive society. The people have, to our eyes, astoundingly few possessions – little more than the clothes they stand up in. The schoolmaster has a cassette player, two old Rolling Stones tapes and one of Indian warbling. They have no radios, books other than the Koran, magazines, alcohol.

So where does the money from portering (a highly paid job in Pakistani terms) and selling provisions go? The porters don't spend it on good gear for their job, that's for sure. They wear little rubber boots, smooth-soled sandals, disintegrating gym shoes, all without socks. Not surprisingly, they suffer a lot from cuts and blisters. If regulations force expeditions to outfit them with, say, shoes and dark glasses, they never use them but sell them again in Skardu.

I think porter money goes towards supporting relatives, some of them as far away as Iran or Saudi Arabia. One of the attractive aspects of the Moslem religion is the in-built social security system prescribed in the Koran, where one has a clear responsibility to provide not only for immediate and distant family, but also for the poor and unsupported (usually through the mosques). This is why there are few beggars or complete destitutes in Pakistan; though many are poor, and the village children barefoot, ragged and grubby, no one seems to be starving. And the Baltis are very affectionate towards their children.

The village cash, together with any surplus wheat or lentils they grow (their only crops), allows them to buy and carry from Skardu tea, sugar, salt, rice, and cigarettes. Like many far-flung peoples, they have enthusiastically taken up cigarettes at the very time the self-absorbed western world is giving them up. I asked Haji if many local people died of lung cancer. He shook his head. 'Cancer very not often. One man, I think, in village near here, but not lungs.' We were sitting in the shade of the schoolhouse, watching the children hand back their slates to the teacher. I offered him a K2, he smiled but waved a refusal. 'Later.' I remembered it was still the fast of Ramadan and felt embarrassed at my clumsiness.

'You smoke,' he murmured, 'the smell is good. Smelling is not prohibited!' He repeated the remark in Balti and the old men rocked in silent laughter. It was wonderfully easeful being in their company. They seemed to draw from me any tension or anxiety without taking any stain of it on themselves.

The porter's dream is to save enough money to open a little stall in Skardu where he can drink endless cups of tea, develop a paunch and wear a hat like a pile of chapatis, and where he will buy back unused gear from other porters and sell it back to the expeditions who give it to porters who bring it back to him again. Balti wisdom! The man who sells the same pair of shoes five times over has found a way to deal with the world.

Askole people don't die of heart disease or cancer or automobile accidents. They die from infectious diseases and slightly premature old age. They are buried in little plots between the fields, on pathways, near walls, on the edge of the village square. There are no names or headstones, they are content to sink back into the vast anonymity of the earth under the sky. All that marks their final resting place are small rectangular wooden slats with little posts or sometimes white stones at each corner. They look for all the world like old bottomless seed boxes.

Is Askole a pit or a paradise? It is desperately poor, the animals are scrawny, the children dress in ragged sacks, their houses are full of smoke, their lives confined to this one valley, their thoughts to village thoughts . . . Most people who pass through just see the pit aspect. I watched a bunch of Askole chickens scratching in the dirt and remembered Pete Boardman's remark that they must be the most unfortunate form of life on earth.

No. Being an Askole chicken is better than being a battery hen. And, for me, that goes for the people. Better, far better, to live like this, scraggy, tatty, scraping out a living yet free, without bars, without crowds. Me, I'm glad to be here, free-ranging in the Himalayas, scratching through life.

We're a bunch of shuffling dossers. We're renegade roosters, run away from the comforts of the battery farm. And though there are things one often misses — the security, the central heating, the low red lighting — none of us is going back.

So, just to set the record straight, there are many worse fates than being an Askole chicken.

Every day seemed the same in Askole. I was brought up in the country and have always found rural rhythms deeply satisfying. Before dawn, the sobbing, ecstatic cry of the muezzin. At dawn, the clink of a spade, squish of boots as the men set off into the network of irrigation channels. The animals are let loose, the mill is opened up, the oxen are harnessed to the plough. Groups of women and girls shoulder their baskets and disperse into the fields to weed.

The school children gather under the tree in the square; yawning, the teacher carries the blackboard out of the school-house. As they sing the national anthem, the funny foreigners are drinking cocoa and looking at the clouds motoring up the valley, wondering when help will come. Haji shuffles into the square, ducks his head in greeting to the foreigners, contemplates the children, then joins the old cronies in the shade.

A flock of empty porters pass through on their way down the valley. They're paid off so are in a hurry to get back to their wives and the bright lights of Skardu. They pass on the latest news of the expeditions up the Baltoro. One of them hands a note to the American who looks like a frog. They collect the mail and hurry away.

Paiju, 26 June

Hello, how goes it there in Askole? I cut my heel wading a stream so had to get some attention from Aido. The rest of the team are going really well. Alex seems to sleep quite a bit. Aido has been busy doctoring folks. He had a bad head yesterday, but is going well today.

I hope you folks are OK down there. We've talked a lot about your situation, we appreciate being up here, but really wish you were here too.

So do something about that, eh!

All the best,
Sandy

That was the big event of the day. The lunchtime fires are lit and the air is full of woodsmoke. The children say a short prayer and run home. The women and the men drift in from the fields, the oxen are unyoked and tethered. Everyone has tea and chapatis, unless of course it's Ramadan in which case only the very young and the sick partake.

The heat of the day. Askole sizzles like a brown frying pan, surrounded by green salad fields. The miller falls asleep in the dim mill. A foreigner, entering from the dazzle outside, fails to see him at first, is aware only of a bundle of rags in the corner. What the foreigner sees is the white flash of the water rushing down the hollow log, hitting the blades that turn the wheel which spins round and round, grinding nothing. A circle of husks surrounds the grindstone, three goat-skins full of wheat flour are stacked beside it, next to a pile of unground wheat. The foreigner feels the cool waft of air from the water, hears the water and the creak of the rolling wheel.

'A husk, a prayer of wheat.' The phrase speaks quietly in the mind of the foreigner as he stands in the doorway, strangely moved. Then the bundle of rags in the corner stirs in its dreams, and the foreigner realizes with a shock that he is in a painting. It is probably of the Dutch school, brown, domestic and dim; it is called 'The Sleeping Miller'.

The foreigner leaves, quietly closing the door behind him.

Askole sleeps or merely waits.

Later in the afternoon, the men and women return to the fields. They do not hurry, their work is steady but not hard. The women go in groups and talk, the men set off alone or in pairs. A pair of trekkers with four porters come up the valley from Chaqpo; they are tired and thankful to arrive, and set off in search of Haji Mahdi who of course knows they are coming through the mysterious valley telegraph and is even now quietly leaving his house and heading for the village square.

The blue-eyed British memsahib is in the fields with a group of girls. They are laughing and communicating in sign language and her halting Urdu. The memsahib hands her camera to Kali, the most intelligent and independent of the girls. One may not take pictures of Balti women – but no one said they cannot take pictures of each other, which Kali proceeds to do, amid much laughter.

The memsahib is happy. Happiness is in the air and in their laughter. She is thinking she would be happy never to leave. She is planning how she could train as a nurse and return here.

The sick American, suffering once again from heatstroke and diarrhoea, totters across the square to the village latrine, much to the quiet amusement of the old men, then totters back groaning to the oven of his tent. His memsahib turns another page of her book about the Ninja of Japan. It is set in America; it is largely about people shoving themselves into each other and chopping each other into little bits.

Late afternoon. The Pakistani officer returns spick and span from the high spring, his moustache combed, his oiled quiff perfectly in place. He is holding his radio close to his ear and listening to the ball-by-ball commentary of the test match between England and the West Indies on the BBC World Service. The West Indies are chopping England into little bits while the commentators chat about cream cakes and the clouds gather over the gasometers.

With a sigh, Abdul the cook rouses himself and lights the fire. He stares into it and rubs his beard thoughtfully while he thinks of his wife in Skardu expecting their first baby in two weeks. Will the leader arrive in time to let him get back before it is born? Naturally, he hopes it is a boy. He sees the Liaison Officer approaching, and sighs. More orders.

The people return from the fields. The cooking fires are lit. Dusk starts to silt up the valley below while the foreigners sit on cardboard boxes round Abdul and eat their strange food from silver pouches. Above, the sky turns platinum, mauve, pale silver, and the snow summits catch the last light and seem to abstract themselves from everything below and drift away into a dream of their own, delicate as thoughts of home.

Finally, when it is judged to be dark enough, the muezzin cries out the end of the day. His long sobbing call trails into silence. It is time to face Mecca and pray, time at last to eat and drink and replace the sweat of the day.

The trekkers exchange news with the stranded climbers. The villagers talk over the events of the day by firelight, or by the glow of the few lanterns in Askole. It is time to have a last K2 cigarette, to soothe the last baby. The voices fade, the fires burn down, the day is ended.

Each day is the same. Yet each is subtly different, each is today not yesterday, though they seem a seamless garment. Everything is moving forward, the wheat and lentils and apricots inch towards harvest. When the climbers finally leave the mountains, it will be autumn. Then winter. Then spring. Then summer again, sure as water flows downhill, without pause or hesitation.

Kathleen and I had decided to do some walking most days. It kept us fit, helped acclimatization – and got us out of the camp site, which became at times claustrophobic. We were on reasonable terms with Burt and Donna – that is to say, Burt told us endlessly about how he'd assembled our American gear, their battery of drugs, their first trip to Nepal, their second trip to Nepal, their time in Peru, on Mount McKinley, in the Alps. We didn't have to ask for advice, it was showered upon us.

In that time, he never once asked anything about us, what we did, liked, thought, felt, family, anything.

We studiously avoided politics. We got on, though we had nothing in common but our predicament.

We are running into a new crisis: shortage of food and fuel. We had weeks of food in the Expedition boxes, but Burt didn't want to start on them, nor spend the remaining Expedition money that he had on buying food in Askole. Still ill and overweight, he didn't have much interest in food. Fit and underweight, I did. We were running low on kerosene, didn't want to buy more firewood. So we took out one of the Expedition Gaz stoves and tried to assemble it. Burt and I wrestled with it, and I ended up getting liquid gas over the back of my knuckles, which burned the skin and killed it off. Only later did it strike me as odd that the veteran of expeditions to Nepal, Peru, McKinley etc. did not know how to assemble a standard camping gas stove.

As Burt sounded off about the iniquities of the fiend Duff, I managed to extract from him the figures for the Expedition's assets, the costs of porterage, of Mohammed, of camp sites, jeeps, further provisions. I wanted to be able to do my own calculations, and work out our options myself.

'I've done the honourable thing once – I'm not going to do it a second time,' Burt asserted. I knew very well what that meant. If anyone, or anyone's gear, was going to be left behind, it wasn't going to be he or his. I was equally determined it wasn't going to be me. I wanted to get on the hill; I owed Rocky a book, and I couldn't write it in Askole.

So I just nodded uncommittally. 'The first thing I do when that fucker Duff arrives,' he went on, 'is get the money from him. Then we decide what to do with it.'

I determined on one thing: Kath and I had to get to Malcolm first. From the earliest possible day of his arrival, we'd have to be in position to intercept him before Burt.

But till then we were free to explore. One day we set off early in the direction the others had gone, followed the trail on till we could see the dark snout of the rock-strewn glacier in the distance. It felt wonderful to be out on our own, with no packs, no LO, no guide. Even more exhilarating was seeing a great wall of pinnacles and towers open out ahead. I thought I recognized Cathedral Spire, the Trango Tower and Mount Paiju. I'd seen the photos often enough, yet was somehow astonished to see they really existed. I had to get up there, at any cost.

Another day we went back to the hot springs. I'd picked up a flea that seemed determined to play join-the-dots across my body, so I spent a considerable time submerged in the hot sulphurated water to drown it. I washed all my clothes, changed sleeping bags – to no effect. That flea, along with its friends and relatives who'd come along for the ride, plagued me for the rest of our time in Askole.

Burt and Donna came later to the hot springs; that day Burt got heatstroke again, and spent the next three days moaning and shitting. After that, he and Donna attempted no more exercise. They read, sat in their tent, played cards with Shokat, and went up to the spring every second day. They visited nobody and saw nothing.

Their choice. But Mal had stressed the beneficial effect of spending time above the altitude you slept at. We might as well be as completely acclimatized as possible by the time he and Tony arrived. So we went on a long scramble up the hill behind Askole, gained 1500 feet, felt breathless and distinctly light-headed, hung about, then came down again.

We certainly slept better for it. No laboured breathing, no headache, no sleeping pills.

Lilligo, 27 June

A nice camp site, but very prone to stone fall which is not quite so great I suppose . . . Porters moving slowly, some of them have blisters . . . The glacier is not too difficult, the path is hard to trace here and there, but much better than I was led to believe previously.

The 'Team' are all in good spirits, getting on well together in fact and are looking forward to seeing Mustagh tomorrow if the clouds rise.

My heel is mending slowly, it's sore, but Aido gives it a lot of attention. We all wonder how you folks are getting along down there, and hope that you are perhaps a little bit happier now.

Last night we spoke to a Pole who thought the route was a hard one. That worried me, but today I'm full of respect yet confident also. Jon feels the same.

Sandy

We're sitting cross-legged on a blanket on the roof of Haji's other house, the one in the village across the gorge from Askole. The morning is cool, damp and fragrant. We sit with the elders of the village, surrounded by curious children, and wait for the inevitable cup of tea. The fat, white clouds slowly rotate and snag on the upper ridges of the mountains, then break free and drift on. Must be bad weather further up the glacier; if the lads have reached Base Camp, it's probably snowing.

Still, who cares? It's stunningly peaceful up here, looking back over towards Askole, smoking the first K2 of the day and listening idly to the elders' chat. The only worry at the back of my mind was the prospect of having to cross that death-on-a-stick bridge again . . .

Haji had come for us early that morning. Wrapped in a brown cloak, he looked part wandering monk and part wizard. The light flashed on his blue and silver haji ring.

'*Assalam o aleikum*,' he greeted us.

'*Aleikum salam*,' we responded.

'I over river going. You would wish to come?'

We grabbed our water bottles, sun cream, shades and hats, and followed him on his slow, stately wander down through the fields. He explained that his second wife lived in the village across the river. The Koran allows for a man having more than one household, but insists he spend equal time at each of them. So every day Haji crosses the Braldu river, and back again . . .

Pure Indiana Jones, that bridge. It sagged across the gorge, above the hurtling, spitting, glacier-grey river, some 300 feet across. It had a single rope for one's feet, and a rope for one's hands at shoulder height. It dropped steeply at our end, and rose steeply at the other. And on closer inspection it wasn't made of rope at all, but of thousands of twigs and little branches woven and twisted together. It takes two months to make, and they make a new one every year. This one, trailing broken lines along its length, looked on its last legs.

We'd picked up a group of Askolites by this time. We all sat down at the end of the bridge and contemplated it for a few minutes. I tried to breathe deeply and slow my heart rate. Maybe it was easier than it looked.

Haji murmured a few words, and three locals started the crossing, by way of demonstration. They seemed to do it slowly and carefully, so I attended. The problem was that as one got further out on the bridge, it began to sway and twist. In addition, the two handrails tended to close up, and one was higher than the other, so one was in a seriously unstable situation with little lateral support, on the edge of being pushed over sideways into the river. And the river shouted, with all the relish of Jon Tinker, 'You're going to die.'

So the locals had evolved a technique whereby they crossed in small groups. One would go ahead for 30 feet while the others tried to hold the rails apart. Then he would stop and, leaning back on one rail, push the other out with his foot while the rest picked their way towards him. This made my stomach turn just watching. In the middle, where the bridge was at its lowest, narrowest,

and most wobbly, the front man took up his position and the
others all came up to him, stepped awkwardly over his upraised
leg, and continued on. That was the bit I fancied least. From then
on the front man brought up the rear, holding the rails apart and
having them held for him.

Eventually they were across. Our turn. Haji looked at us with a
ghost of a smile. Damned if we're going to be wobbly westerners.
'Is no problem,' he murmured, 'but slowly, slowly.' We got to our
feet, a little pale, hearts thudding in our ears. I took a last drag,
threw away the cigarette in a Humphrey Bogart stylee, and
followed him onto the bridge.

This is really horrible. And exciting. Nowadays Kath and I
seem to enjoy testing ourselves. It's the company we keep.

Only concentration keeps fear at arm's length, and this one
demands total concentration. Each shuffling step, each movement of the hand along the 'rail'. Resist the urge to hurry and get
it over with. The bridge starts rhythmically swaying. The handrails close up, one above my right shoulder, the other below my
left armpit. I feel I'm being toppled to the left. The rails are too
thick to get a hand round, all I can do is try to clench a strand.
Each strand is clear, red-brown twigs, I can see each broken end.
Out in the middle the grey water hurtles hypnotically past my
feet, completely disorientating me. But I can't look away, because
I have to place each foot across a few inches of rope. I feel
suddenly as though the water is still and the bridge and I are
whizzing sideways downstream. I shake my head, blink, but the
movement beneath my feet still throws me. Take your time.
Concentrate. This is fun. Oh yes? Here's the middle, now I've to
step over his leg. Alfie Noakes . . . That was hairy. How's Kath
doing? Working at it. Bugger, my hand's bleeding. It gets better
from now on, must do. But I've still to come back . . .

Kath and I finally stepped off the far end, jittery with adrenalin,
pleased with ourselves. It felt damn good to be standing on solid
ground, breathing the shrub sweet air of Askole's sister village.

'If I lived here,' I said to Haji, 'I'd rather have one wife than
have two and have to cross that every day.' He laughed, put a
hand gently on our backs and guided us onto the path up to the
village.

Where we're now sitting taking our ease, on the rooftop of
Haji's second household. No rush, no hurry. The tea finally

Top: Jolla Bridge – Mal and Kathleen in
orange crate (photo Andrew Greig)
Above: Uli Bahl – reflection in glacier pool
(photo Tony Brindle)
Left: Tony bouldering at Urdukas,
Mustagh Tower behind (photo
Andrew Greig)

Above: Sandy going through bat wing – and smiling (photo Andrew Greig)
Top: Mustagh Tower and Icefall end of Ibex Trail (photo Mal Duff)

Above: Author in Icefall (photo Alex Reid)
Opposite above: The author and Jon in the Icefall (photo Sandy Allan)
Opposite below: Base Camp (photo Mal Duff)

Above: Mal traversing on rock wall (photo Tony Brindle)
Below: Tony traversing loose rock below camp 4 (photo Mal Duff)

Above: Jon on the summit of Mustagh (photo Sandy Allan)
Below: Weather-beaten Camp 3, tent lashed down (photo Mal Duff)

Bottom: Mal Duff and Burt Greenspan (photo Jon Tinker)
Below: Tony Brindle (photo Mal Duff)
Left: Jon Tinker (photo Alex Reid)

Top: Sandy Allan (photo Andrew Greig)
Above: Alex Reid (photo Jon Tinker)
Right: Adrian Clifford (photo Kathleen Jamie)

Top: Mohammed Ali (photo Jon Tinker)
Above: Captain Shokat Ali Batti (photo Jon Tinker)
Left: The Magic Bus (photo Mal Duff)

Above: Askole House (photo Kathleen Jamie)
Right: Kathleen on 'rope' bridge (photo Andrew Greig)
Below: Paradise above Askole (photo Andrew Greig)

arrives. All my senses seem sharp today, the tea is wonderful, the air sweet, the trees and fields are shimmering bright.

At length Kath and I set off up the hill for more acclimatization exercise. It's slow, steep going. A thousand feet up and we're definitely feeling the lack of air. We're light-headed, a little weak, but not headachy. We drink several pints of water, trying to thin our blood which is thick with red blood corpuscles that are frantically multiplying in an effort to catch and hold what oxygen there is.

An hour or two later we set off back down. We meet a group of villagers who escort us to where Haji is. They're in no hurry, and eventually stop awhile by a clear stream. Two young men are sprawled on the bank, talking and giggling, another lies on his back, sucking a straw and looking up at the sky. The old man chews and spits a kind of green tobacco that they get high on – the Balti equivalent of chewing betel nuts. He looks like a grizzly old Fife trawler skipper. As we lie taking our ease, I have a sense of *déjà vu*. Sunlight, water, trees, the lazy Edenic innocence ... Then I have it: '*Déjeuner sur l'herbe*', except that Kathleen is fully dressed.

Eden in Askole! I'd expected diarrhoea. Instead – Balti time, amnesiac mountain time, full of the present and of timelessness. Vast external spaciousness gradually mirrored inside.

On the hill, washing socks by the spring, drinking tea with Haji – something is happening to us here. I can feel a shift inside me. I feel an emptying out as if years of inner clutter was dissolving into the thin, cool air.

After reading Peter Matthiessen's *The Snow Leopard*, I was determined to keep all meditation, all philosophy and the Meaning of Life out of this book. Too much thinking, not enough climbing, was my reaction. But dammit, it's happening. I came here to climb, to take a closer look at Death and Destruction, not to think. If you can't think well in the valley, why expect to think well in the mountains?

Yet something is happening, and we're not even on the hill.

We'll move on, of course, being restless westerners. But something of this will remain with us.

(As I type this from my journals, Askole will be under several feet of snow. They'll be digging in for winter, half-hibernating, huddled for days on end in with the animals in their rock houses.

They'll be sleeping, feeding the animals, making hats, perhaps telling the children bits of the Kayser Saga, a folk epic about a humorous conqueror that exists in Balti, Afghani, Chinese and Tibetan. The rain spatters on my window. I wish I was there, as one aches to be with an absent lover, on a grey November afternoon.)

We crossed the bridge safely. At the other side I casually asked Haji if anyone had ever fallen off. 'Eight . . . perhaps ten . . . two memsahibs fell on the stones, they did not die.' 'Good value, eh?' Kath murmurs, mimicking Sandy.

We returned to the camp site mid-afternoon, straight back into stress again. Shokat was sulking that we'd gone off without informing him. He pointed out he could restrict us from moving outside the bounds of Askole at all, both for our own safety and because we might be photographing military installations, viz. the rope bridge.

There was another note from Sandy, dated 30 June, to announce they'd all arrived safely at Base Camp. He'd cut his heel crossing a river and Aido and Alex were suffering a bit from altitude. The weather was poor, but they hoped to start recon-noitering the Tower – which they hadn't as yet seen for cloud – in the next day or so. They thought about us, and hoped we'd be able to join them.

Which was fine, but like his other notes this one was addressed only to Burt and Donna. To my highly tuned paranoia, this was upsetting and alarming. Had we simply been cut out of the Expedition? What agreement had Sandy and Burt made between them when the others left? Were we to be left behind if Mal came with insufficient money?

Kath was upset too. She loved Askole, but was determined to get to Base Camp. Anyway, it wasn't up to Burt who went on, it was up to Mal. Which made it all the more important we get to him first.

That afternoon, on the other side of the world, Tony Brindle was applying himself to the last question of his exam paper. "Outline the main principles of the Treaty of Rome". He looked at the clock. An hour to go.

It is hard to concentrate on the Treaty of Rome when you're

about to rush off to the Himalayas. His bicycle was outside. In an hour's time he would jump onto it, hurry back to his digs, pick up a haul sack and rucksack bulging with clothes and climbing gear, rush with them to the station, catch the train to London, get out to Heathrow and board the PIA flight to Islamabad. And then, finally, the mountain . . .

It was a tight schedule. He sat in his chair, revving like a little sports car waiting for the lights to change. And then there was that mysterious phone call he'd had the night before, telling him to look out for a friend at the PIA desk at Heathrow . . .

Fifty-five minutes to go. He sighed and wrenched his mind back to the Treaty of Rome.

On the same afternoon, while Tony tried not to think of mountains and Kath and I worried and plotted, Jon and Sandy strolled down into Mustagh Base Camp with shit-eating grins all over their faces.

'What's up then, anyway?' Adrian asked, still nursing his sore head.

'We've been scampering about and found this amazing ibex trail that cuts out the whole of the lower icefall.'

They went into the Mess Tent to explain and have a well-earned brew.

Jon (1 July): Woke up feeling as good as after a route. Aido like death all day. Me and Sandy went for a look at the hill. First sight of Mustagh – big, black, beastly. Sobering.

The joy of making things – slings etc., all part of the tactile turning-into the work ahead.

Sandy with the iron close to his surface.

Jon (2 July) Work today. Me, Sandy, Mohammed and Alex up the Ibex Trail to the glacier. Me and Sandy don crampons. The route becomes more tottering . . . incipient headaches . . . still problems with crevasses. We set up the Camp 1 tent on a moraine bank far too far left. Some bickering, but all at a civilized level. Looks like we'll need another camp before the ice slope to the Col.

We go back down the right bank of the glacier, trying to find a better way. Gradually becomes even worse than on the way up. Both of us relieved to get out . . .

A brutal, typically thuggish Himalayan day. Cool down at Base with Alex's pancakes and reggae music.

Jon(4 July): A festerday today. Cancelled due to rain.

Scene in the Mess Tent: Sandy's gasping laughter, his whole face wrinkling up. Alex's off-the-wall Americanisms. Western music from the Walkman speakers, the purr of the paraffin stove. Jhaved crouched by it, watching the cabaret. Adrian delighting in puncturing his own seriousness with a schoolboy joke. Mohammed quietly watching and curling his moustaches.

I appreciate the feelings the city suppresses – the easy friendship, the tolerance, the quick forgiveness. When Mohammed said there were a lot of people praying for us – Skardu porters – I was moved entirely uncynically.

Wishing everyone else was here.

After a week, it felt as if we'd been in Askole for a year. Various expeditions passed through on their way up or down. I'd never expected the Baltoro to be so busy. At this point we'd met ten expeditions, only one of which – the Swiss on Nanga Parbat – had been successful. That seems to be the average Himalayan success rate, and it gave me a far more realistic notion of our likelihood of success on Mustagh. The commonest causes of failure were bad weather, loss of strength or resolution, and death or injury to members of the party.

A Scottish lad from the Brit Trango Tower team turned up. He looked very thin, very tanned; the backs of his hands were cut all over from hand-jamming. What was most striking was how they hadn't healed at all – the body's capacity for self-healing breaks down at altitude. The peak had been practically all rock climbing, despite its being over 20,000 feet. They'd gone at it for a week on the face, done thirty-odd rope lengths, then been driven back just two pitches from the final snow field up to the top.

Was he disappointed? Yes, but also in a way pleased and relieved to be done with it. They'd gone at it too fast and hard, hadn't acclimatized properly, burned themselves out.

It was good to have another Scot to talk with, someone who could share our warped Scottish humour of sarcasm and under-statement. I was made even more nostalgic by waking to the sound of rain pattering on our tent next morning. I looked out and the air was thick and mild with drizzle. Lovely stuff. Bad news for Base Camp, though.

That evening, the village elders sat outside, waiting to see if the moon would appear to signal the end of Ramadan. There was poor weather across Pakistan, but somewhere or other an official observer saw the moon, and the feast of Eid was declared across the country for the next day. Even Skardu accepted the official proclamation. But not Askole. In Askole, if they don't see it, it doesn't count.

So the scrawny goats and chickens were unslaughtered, the sweet pastries remained unbaked, and the people of Askole went round looking hungry all the next day, anxiously watching the sky. The muezzin's call to prayer that morning seemed more keening and sobbing than before. Shokat and Abdul, not being from Askole, gorged happily all day.

There was an expectancy, a curious silence in the village. The rain stopped in the afternoon, the sky partially cleared.

Dusk. The Askolites gathered outside their houses. The elders, Haji and the priest went to the raised patch of ground from which the moon had to be sighted. A hush settled over the village.

Then the moon tore itself clear from cloud and briefly shone bright and clear over the whole valley. The muezzin's triumphant call went on and on, was picked up and echoed by the entire village, like a pack of musical wolves. Haji came by and presented us with a basket of eggs and one of his rare smiles; I returned his Eid present with a tin of Parkinson's Old-Fashioned Humbugs from my precious personal stash of goodies.

Little work was done in Askole next day.

But we still had planning and plotting to do. We got up early next morning and walked up to where the trail entered the outskirts of the village. We sat on a rock outcrop and scanned the barren waste for any sign of Mal and Tony, like beleaguered settlers waiting for the arrival of the US Cavalry. We waited three hours. They didn't show.

I went up to the spring above Askole in yet another attempt to rid myself of the fleas that were joyously celebrating Eid up and down my body. Perhaps because of the mild, drizzly weather I took a cassette of Scottish folk music with me. Perhaps that was a mistake.

The first verse of the first song, Archie Fisher singing 'The Grey Silkie', made my heart suddenly turn over. A flood of memories washed over me. The song was sung in the ceilidh scene of 'Local

Hero', one of its heart-stopping moments, a jumbled, mysterious, tragic lament. I terribly wanted to know my own culture again. What am I doing here in this alien land? My country is in that music, in turn stately, blithe, death-obsessed, bawdy, sentimental, grim, realistic, hopelessly romantic, inconsolable, sardonic. I know all those conflicting impulses, know them from inside.

'We're aa' going East and West,
We're aften guy aglee . . .'

Heart heavy, eyes prickling, singing over the Walkman the song I'd always wanted Dad to hear but never got round to playing him. Remembering singing in the early hours at the Clachaig, and that unknown climber's lament for good company that hushed and touched us all. All the sweetness in us, and the loss, distilled in a particular voice at a particular time, opening our hearts – I bawled over the Walkman in the fields above Askole, tears running down my face till my heart was lightened.

I woke to hear Burt instructing Abdul.

'Me leader. No breakfast. Hot water only. No lunch. Understand? No chapatis, no lunch. Cook only when I say. Okay?'

I lay there, heart pounding with anger. I wanted food, I needed food. Since when had Burt been elected leader? When I crawled out of the tent, he beckoned me over. We looked at each other.

'Did you hear what I said?'

'Yes. I thought it was a bit autocratic.'

'Well, I am the leader.'

'Yeah – and the Lord High Executioner. Come off it, Burt.'

Kathleen came over. She said she thought it was a bit much. Burt cut her off and reminded her that she was in effect a nonperson on this Expedition.

'I'm the leader. I don't mind being unpopular.'

'Look. In the first place, you're not the leader. You couldn't lead a poodle down the street. And as a decision, it was autocratic, unnecessary, silly and selfish.'

He launched into a tirade about the burdens of leadership, the amount of money he'd put into the trip, how Mal had screwed it up, how Kath and I were a drain on the Expedition's resources.

Finally he sneered, 'You should thank me. Your four British friends wanted you two sent back. I said no.'

'I don't believe you.' We glared at each other.

That hurt. That cut to the quick of our uncertainty. Was it true? Surely they wouldn't have said that. And yet . . .

We walked away. Back in our tent, Kathleen burst into tears of anger and helplessness. It was the third time he'd brought her to tears. I couldn't forgive him that.

Breakfast – hot water and oatmeal – was a family sulk. No one spoke. We didn't even look at each other. It was the bottom.

Angry and sick at heart, we followed the path again up through the fields to the beginning of Askole, and waited at our look-out point. And finally, we saw two specks in the distance, coming fast our way.

Not ours. Two Askole porters hurrying home. They had no news of two Brits coming up the valley. We sat a while longer, not wanting to go back to the camp. It was our eleventh day in Askole. Already I couldn't separate one from another. They'd melted together like our paraffin-flavoured Milk Duds inside their packets. Such mood swings from Olympian calm to seething anger and back again. It must be connected to the altitude – and to the intensity generated inside an expedition.

To calm down, we decided to walk on to the next village down the valley. There we met a porter we knew from the walk-in. He invited us to his house for chicken and chapati. Lunch! We cheered up.

We sat on his roof, surrounded by ragged Dickensian children and would-be porters pressing their scrap-paper recommendations on us. We explained we had no money and weren't going anywhere. 'But when Leader come with rupees . . .' The whole valley seemed to know our predicament. A porter came into the village and spoke with our host. He turned to us and said, 'Leader coming – Mustagh Tower – rupees.'

We looked at each other. When? Today. How long? Shrug. An hour, *inshallah*. Me good porter, very strong.

I'll believe it when I see it. Still, our pulse rates went shooting up.

An hour later, climbing over the stile with ski poles and huge packs, came the long and the short of it: Malcolm and Tony. We waved from the roof. We could have hugged them. I think we did.

But had they got the money?

Mal shrugged, enjoying the moment. 'Yes, but I had to go back to Scotland for it.' What?! He'd flown back home, met an astonished Liz, sold and borrowed and overdrawn to raise 40,000 rupees, gone to the new Indiana Jones film, picked up a flabbergasted Tony at Heathrow, and revved up the valley.

I had to break the bad news to him. Burt and Sandy had miscalculated. We needed another 30,000 rupees to get everything to Base Camp. 'I know,' he said casually, 'we met Sybil in Skardu.' But did he manage to get it? 'Yeah, no problem. But we're fucked. Let's get on to Askole. 'Oh, and I've some mail for you two.'

Kath impulsively hugged him again. He did his best to look embarrassed. He'd played a blinder, and he knew it. I filled him in on the details of the costs ahead, and the situation back in Askole, and that the lads had made Base Camp. And whatever he did, not to hand the money over to Burt Greenspan.

He looked tired and a bit grim. He'd been rushing around like a blue-arsed fly, then shot up the valley with Tony. He'd left Liz and himself some £4000 poorer. The reaction was beginning to set in. We finished eating and set off for Askole, followed by half a dozen porters we'd promised to take on. Mal trudged along thoughtfully, while Tony prattled away with his customary energy and enthusiasm. It was his first time in the Third World. He loved it. His eyes were lit with excitement as he asked about the trek ahead, and tried to glean every scrap of news about the lads at Base Camp. He was panting to get on the hill. He never learns it's uncool to display such enthusiasm. He was just what we needed, a new input of energy.

And so we led Mal and Tony into Askole. The despair of the morning seemed weeks ago. No doubt we did look smug. Burt scowled as the four of us walked into camp, and I laughed out loud, remembering the I Ching hexagram Mal had thrown before leaving:

DELIVERANCE.

We spent the rest of the day making up porter loads, calculating costs, buying further provisions. We had enough money to take everything we needed up to Base. Burt and I went to Haji's and bargained, pulling together at last. Haji asked me to write him a reference; this was absurd, he had more dignity and stature than I ever would. We shook hands, looked forward to seeing him on the way back.

'Mustagh summit, *inshallah.*'

'*Inshallah*, Haji.'

When darkness fell, we had our twenty-nine loads and twenty-nine porters. Askole was packed that night with no less than seven expeditions, four of them heading up with us the next day. We decided to get to Jolla Bridge – which we'd been told was a bottleneck – before the others, so set our alarms for 3.15. We had a big meal, ate some personal goodies, pored over letters from home.

Our last night in Askole. Moon bright over the valley, the clouds like milk on a drunk man's floor. It was hard to sleep for excitement, and Mal's worrying, racking cough.

7

The End of the Beginning

*In which the Brits pull a fast one,
the weak fall by the way, and the Bin-Men
make heavy pastry*

6–11 July 1984

The race for Jolla Bridge starts at 3.15 a.m. Angora blackness as we silently take down our tents. The only hint of dawn is in the wind. The seven of us slip away from Askole, following our porters into the half-light.

Forward going, leaving more and more behind, walking at last into the savage arena. The frustrations and reversals of the past two weeks made it all the sweeter. We passed the turn in the trail where we parted with the lads twelve days before. This time we went on.

Midmorning we hit the glacier for the first time. It was nothing like I'd expected. I was looking for gleaming blue and white; the reality was the biggest quarryload of rubble in the world that entirely smothered the ice beneath. We picked our way up and down and round endless shifting heaps of boulders, rocks, stones, pebbles, grit – the chaotic smithereens of the world's greatest mountains. The rock under my feet could have been the summit of one of those peaks I watched through the mist up the valley. So walk with some care and respect.

The glacier moraine was hard going. Very demanding on knees and ankles, it took total concentration, perpetually stepping from one rock to another, most of them sharp edge up, many of them insecurely stuck to the ice beneath. There was no time to look up or around; a twisted ankle could happen in a second and spell the end of the adventure. 'Switch to endurance,' Tony said stoically, as he bobbed along under his huge pack.

We met the British Trango Towers team on their way down. We exchanged cigarettes and news. They seemed pleased to be on their way back, philosophical about their bad luck with the weather. A down-going party always slightly patronizes the one on the way up; they've been there, they're veterans.

We reluctantly parted from them and plugged on, thankful for the grey skies. A man wearing a green hat with a light pack and two ski sticks passed us, heading down. 'Hello,' he said. 'Hello,' I replied. We kept on walking. 'That was Rheinhold Messner,' Mal said casually.

So one of the gods had just passed by. He looked an ordinary sort of bloke. Except this ordinary bloke had just come from adding another extraordinary success to his curriculum vitae – a traverse of Gasherbrums 1 and 2, solo of course. I looked back thoughtfully as the green hat bobbed into the distance.

We finally crossed the glacier and stopped for a brew. Mal had withdrawn into himself, was quiet and looked distinctly grey. He lit a cigarette and frowned at the ground. 'Actually, I've been feeling bloody depressed today.'

The sky cleared and the temperature soared while we spent what felt like hours plodding through soft sand by an old river bed. With the sun hammering down from above, and bouncing back up from below, energy drained away down the plughole. I'd felt that a ski pole was sissy and unnecessary, but at times it seemed to be the one thing pushing me forward. Up ahead I saw Tony's figure shimmering through the heat wave. Kath was going well, sometimes in front of me, sometimes behind. I plugged on, suffering, annoyed at myself.

Early afternoon we reached Jolla Bridge – a grand name for a single cable strung across the bucking Braldu. We were practically the first there. Tony babbled away about how wonderful it was to be here, wonderful to be climbing soon etc etc, then added, 'But that was hard going through that sand, I thought it would never end.' That was reassuring. You tend to forget that when you're really feeling it, the odds are the others do too. The difference between climbers and trekkers is not that the former are so fit and strong that they don't feel fatigue and altitude and pain. They do. The difference is climbers' capacity to endure, to accept and keep going without complaint.

After the Askole rope bridge, Jolla Bridge was a pushover. You sat in an orange box hanging from a pulley on the metal cable and were pulled across by a cord attached to the pulley. It was fun, but slow and cumbersome. We'd got there before the other expeditions, but our porters hadn't. We found the camp site half a mile beyond Jolla Bridge, unrolled our Karrimats, propped up our brollies and settled down to read.

Some three hours later I emerged from the mellow world of Blandings Castle to notice that practically none of our loads had arrived. Most important, there was no food and no tentage. The schoolmaster, who was acting as sirdar and so giving the Askole kids a week's holiday, showed up very agitated, explaining that the bridge was broken and we had to do something or other. Mal and Tony were shagged out and pretended to be deaf. Kath had had to double back for an extra couple of miles to look for a ring that had slid off her finger, and she'd had enough for the day. Burt was groaning quietly and fingering his knee. Oh well . . .

A huge queue of porters and loads had built up at the far side of the bridge. The rope for pulling the box across had broken. After a long delay someone had somehow connected up a much thinner cord, so now only half-loads were coming across and very slowly at that. On our side of the river were most of the climbers from four expeditions, plus a dozen of our porters with nothing to port – their loads were on the far side. I could see our blue barrels and make out some of our boxes, scattered all the way down what I estimated to be a five-hour queue.

But we had an edge. Captain Shokat was in charge at the far side. I dropped a note for him in the empty box going back: PRIORITY BLUE BARRELS. BOXES 17, 22.

The Captain played a blinder. I could see him waving his stick, threatening and cajoling and organizing porters and loads, waving his arms, striding up and down in his best white pajama suit. This was an army-style operation; he was loving it.

On our bank, each nationality was behaving wonderfully true to character. The Italians were waving their arms and fighting with each other; the French elaborated bizarrely logical and totally unworkable schemes for speeding up the bridge; the Scandinavians slumped and looked at the ground and contemplated suicide; the Pakistanis all spoke at the same time, making quite sensible suggestions that no one listened to. Meanwhile perfidious Albion was watching the Brit barrels and boxes unobtrusively leapfrog up towards the head of the traffic jam on the far side.

An hour later I'd secured all our essential loads, rounded up the necessary porters and walked back to camp. I was feeling weak and drawn and slightly dizzy, but it had been great fun. It was good to make a contribution.

I got Abdul going on the evening meal. The camp site gradually filled up. Naturally we'd taken the best places. Two hours later Captain Shokat appeared through the gathering dusk, pale and hoarse. We gave him a round of applause. Here's your food, here's your brew, have a cigarette, you did great. Like most LOs, when it really mattered he was right behind us.

We were about to turn in when the French finally arrived with their gear. They went to lodge an official complaint over the way the Brits had been given preferential treatment. Unfortunately Shokat was the senior LO there and they had to present their complaint to him. He rose to the occasion superbly, was so full of wounded dignity, of sheer incredulity at this suggestion of jiggery-pokery, that the French leader ended up apologizing to *him* for such an insulting accusation.

From then on Shokat was one of the team.

Next morning, up and on the trail again. I'd picked up a cold, was running a temperature and my nose and throat burned. Nothing for it but keep taking the aspirin. It seemed a long day, following the river, climbing up away from it, descending again, sometimes on a track, sometimes boulder-hopping. It was overcast and windy, quite cold.

After a couple of hours I went into a hermetic trance, living entirely inside myself. I threw my mind sticks and watched it chase after them: the past, the future, home, Askole, Liz waving us goodbye, the lads on the hill.

We stopped for lunch in the windswept middle of nowhere and sat shivering behind rocks till the kettle boiled. Nobody said much. There was nothing to say.

Off again, back into the dreamworld. The scenery was nothing to look at, and there was no time to look at it. A couple of steep sections above the river, including a slightly awkward chimney, got the adrenalin going. After that I set myself to reciting from memory the whole of my *Men On Ice*, the narrative poems about three crazed climbers that had got me into this mess in the first place. That passed an hour or so. Then I chatted with the French party on their way to Gasherbrum 4, then back to solitude again.

And suddenly we were there. Paiju – a narrow strip of trees, shrubs, wild roses and long grass, running down the hill beside a stream. It looks like Paradise but it smells mostly of shit and Expedition rubbish. Tony and Mal, looking much better today, had already set themselves up; Kath and I found a ledge beside the stream, put up the tent, got the sleeping bags and toys out.

Burt arrived a couple of hours later, helped along by Donna and Shokat. He was absolutely white, apart from a hectic red spot on either cheek. He looked like a tuberculosis victim in the terminal stage. His knee had apparently completely seized up and he'd had to be half-carried over the last awkward miles.

The French doctor diagnosed tendonitis. Treatment? No movement for a week.

So we had a new crisis on our hands. We joked about helicopters, or being carried in a throne to Base Camp, but Burt was very subdued. He knew this could be the end for him. Despite our differences and antagonisms, I felt very sorry for him. We've already shared a lot. If I hadn't been lucky – and made the effort to keep fit – it could as easily have been me.

We decided to take a rest day at Paiju, to give Burt a chance to recover and decide what to do, and let Mal and Tony acclimatize. They were both desperate to get to the mountain, but knew there was no point arriving there in bad shape.

Waiting for lunch under Abdul's tarpaulin, listening to the rain and the subdued murmur of porters. Tony and Mal hunch over a chess game, Kath writes her journal, Abdul's hands flip out one chapati after another, but his eyes are distant. 'Skardu?' I ask. He nods, thinking about his wife and the baby due next week. Burt and Donna have been closeted in their tent all morning.

After lunch, a conference at Burt's tent. We all feel awkward and overcast as the weather while Mal outlines Burt's options. He can wait at Paiju while we send a porter back with a request for a helicopter; they're expensive, but luckily the insurance to pay for one is compulsory. He could be carried out. He could wait here and go back with Adrian, who'll have to leave Base Camp in eight days to get back to Scotland to start work. He could wait here and come on up after us if his knee improves.

I glance at Burt as Mal talks in his matter-of-fact way. He seems subdued, defeated, resigned. It's clear he'd dropped any idea of going on. After waiting eleven days in Askole, it's bad luck. The question of Donna remained; she's perfectly well, and the lads have agreed she might go quite well on the hill, could be a positive asset.

They ask for an hour to decide. We brood in silence under the tarpaulin. These developments happen so fast. One moment you're going fine, the next you're stranded in Askole or crippled with tendonitis and you're out.

Donna comes up and announces they've decided to summon a helicopter and both leave for Skardu in it. She's admirably composed and stoic. No complaining about her sacrifice, the money gone for nothing, the sheer bad luck of it. She's the strong one; all the more pity that she'll not be on the hill with us.

We commiserate, quite genuinely, with her and Burt. He doesn't complain either, he's just had enough. Shokat writes a line for the army helicopter, instructs a fast and intelligent porter and sends him off; he's a real asset at times.

As always – like at a death, even my father's – the relief that it's not you, that you're still in the game. With stirrings of pride and thankfulness and apprehension, Kath and I look at each other and realize we're the only bumblies left.

'That's how it is on these trips,' Mal reflected later. 'The weak – and the unlucky – fall by the wayside.'

'That's a bit cruel,' Kath said.

'I suppose it is.' He shrugged. 'But it's what happens.'

A very typical climber's attitude. The gentler emotions may arise – Mal is as sentimental a man as I know – but are always followed by a hard matter-of-fact realism.

As we sat under the tarp after tea, we heard a distant rumble. It got louder. It seemed to be coming our way. Then WHOOSH and the stream beside us was in spate, overflowing its banks and rattling stones down before it. The tent! We hurried down in the dark, found the head torches and discovered our ledge had turned into a paddy field in its irrigation phase. As the rain bucketed down, we dammed off the new tributary flowing through the tent, sorted out the damp, dry and soaking clothes and sleeping bags, quite elated by the simple struggle to preserve a small dry space to lie out in.

Finally we lay back and looked at the roof while listening to the river and the rain battering down outside. It felt very secure. I was about to doze off when I put my hand on the floor of the tent and discovered I was lying on a water bed. I looked out; the river had brushed away our little dam and was flowing energetically under the tent.

We scrambled out, pulled up the remaining stakes and lifted the tent bodily to higher ground. Abdul passed with a lantern, doing his impression of Christ in 'The Light of The World'. We retrieved various bits of gear from the flood, dragged everything inside and sorted it all out again. Now we had no dry clothes and no dry sleeping bags. There was nothing to be done about it tonight. We took a sleeping pill and left the world to get on with it.

It was a subdued, late rising in Paiju camp next morning. Bedraggled porters, everyone bleary-eyed, damp and stiff. We all said our brief goodbyes to Burt and Donna, crouching at the door of their tent. I envied them for a moment, soon to be on their effortless way home.

Three hours later, picking a way over the vast boulder moraine of the Baltoro glacier, the sun out again, I wouldn't have changed places with anyone in the world. We were finally starting to get among the great mountains. Every hour revealed something new. That 5000-foot phallus must be Trango Tower, those crazy gleaming wigwams will be Paiju Peak, that's Cathedral . . . Shit, surely that's the Lobsang Spire that was on the cover of the last *Mountain* magazine! It's all real, it's all true.

Kath caught up with me and we stood grinning wildly, riding a wave of euphoria. The Karakoram at last. What can you say about them?

'They're so . . . fucking . . . BIG.'

All you can do is stand and shake your head while your eye is drawn up one Tolkienesque fantasy after another. On both sides of the glacier, soaring spears of granite, spindrift pouring from the tip as if white blood were streaming out of a rent in the sky. The tortured pyramid of Masherbrum, dripping miles of snow ridges down into the valley. Trango Peak for all the world like a vast, ornate Victorian jelly.

We've finally been admitted into their austere, crazed, magnificently indifferent presence. Their attraction is in their repulsion, their manifest impossibility. They knock your eyes back, you feel them as a blow to the chest. They shrug and an avalanche that would wipe out an entire expedition smoulders down a slope. They don't give a damn.

They are killers, heartbreakers, the lovers you can never possess and never forget.

We trudged on.

Jon (6 July): Me, Sandy and Mohammed up to Camp 2, pitched four-man tent. Next day me and Sandy up to Camp 2, defeated about an hour from site by soft snow.

(7 July) Sandy levers me out of bed, feeling awful, get to Camp 2, pitch tent, back to Base Camp. Long day.

(8 July) Rest day for me and Sandy. Evening terrible, snow at Base Camp, gusting winds. Tied down Mess Tent, all gathered round candle and lanterns, singing, laughing, beating percussion on water containers and boxes, western dancing to Paki love songs . . .
Happy with having put up Camp 2, now need a couple of sustained good spells. Sandy doing really well. Only one argument so far, about the position of Camp 2 – a summer storm. Getting on well, considering the pressure we could put ourselves under.
Sandy a compulsive engineer, physically and mentally. Very strong, lots of stamina, a scribbler of plans and lists and sums on boxes, paper, tents. An all-round star.

You'd think a long walk-in would be a very communal affair, but most of the time we live privately, inside ourselves. We've only a finite amount to say, so after the initial flurry of getting to know each other, we begin to space out our conversations. We know we'll have another six weeks together. Pacing, I begin to see that a lot of it is about pacing yourself physically and mentally. This is not an Alpine three-day trip, this is a three-month expedition and

I have to be alert to my body, money, the mountain, weather, other people for that entire period, or I'll blow it.

So though we spend day after day in close proximity, much of the time we live in our own worlds. My world is becoming more uncluttered, simplified to motion, to one foot after another, to one day after another. The past, home, have become more and more unreal and dim. They have no hold on me. I am forward going.

Now – picking our way through the 50-mile quarry of the Baltoro glacier in the heat of the day – my world is a clear daze. It is my feet choosing between rock and rock. It is wisps of thoughts drifting across my mind like the clouds that play games of now-you-see-it-now-you-don't across Mount Paiju. It is wind and sunlight drying sweat from the skin. It is this little band of porters and climbers, for all the world like motley pilgrims, picking our way across the threshold of the throne room of the gods.

The Baltoro is rock around the clock, endless rock, rock without end, amen . . . Left foot, right foot . . . knee's getting stiff again – tendonitis? – only two days from Mustagh, I'll get there if I have to fucking crawl . . . wonder how they're doing up there, are they getting all the bad weather, could set us back a week, that . . . I'm the only bumbly climber left. Is there room for me? Wish Kath didn't have to leave with Adrian, I'll miss her support . . . She'll meet me at Edinburgh Airport, we'll go out for a meal . . . or a beer . . . Hope Mum's all right . . . Mustagh in two days, then we'll see . . .

And so trekking thoughts form and drift as trekking hours pass. Emptiness filled and emptied again, inner conversations with silence in the wilderness.

The sword of Damocles was nothing to the rocks of Lilligo. Our camp site that evening was below sheer walls of mud studded with boulders roughly the size and shape of television sets. I was too tired to worry much about sitting with Abdul round the fire he'd lit directly at the base of them – until there was a slithering, a clattering, a shout, and we scattered like crows from a shotgun as a rock slide ploughed into the packed earth where we'd been sitting.

We rebuilt Abdul's fire a safe distance away.

That night I was lethargic yet restless and jumpy. The shit, the flies, even Kathleen's proximity irritated me. Altitude gain. The mind can recognize the symptoms but not prevent them.

Then next morning was pure joy. I set off early on the rising track that snaked across the hillside above the glacier. It was clear and cold, the rising sun levelled mile-long shadows across the valley, the great peaks stood frozen to attention against the high-altitude dark-blue sky. I was out in front, the only living being in sight. I felt like an arrow, moving further and further away from the tension that set me going, getting nearer and nearer to my destination. After the uncertainties and setbacks of the last weeks, nothing could stop me getting there now.

Oh, yes? I looked at the mud pinnacles above me. They were studded with rocks between the size of cricket balls and semidetached villas. The trail was in their direct line of fire for a full hour or more Any one of those missiles could stop me from the Mustagh Tower – from meeting any future appointments at all for that matter, other than the one my father had now kept.

But I was alive. I put Bob Marley on the Walkman and carried on singing, trusting my fate. This blue flower my boot brushes past, the grey glacier river below, the chough drifting soundlessly by, the early sun lighting up the pinnacles one after another like a row of flares – they all happen once only, but that once is perfection enough. Inside and outside, the world is one rarefied upthrust of joy.

(Mal told me later that that section was probably the most dangerous of the entire walk-in. He had heard a whirring above him, ducked instinctively behind a ledge, a boulder crashed down 15 feet away from him. It is not a good place to put on headphones.)

I came down to a glacier river where the trail ended. There I sat and waited for the others to catch up. Our next move was to wade across the river. It was stunningly cold and painful. We staggered carefully across, the water up to our thighs. Watching Shokat cross was our biggest laugh since the oxygen cylinder blew up in Askole. Abdul was red in the face trying to hold back his giggling; this was one unpleasant task Shokat couldn't hand to someone else.

We set off again, suffering shooting pains as the circulation came back to our feet. As always, when the day started to heat up, the early elation wore off. I was getting better at slipping into the trance state required for endurance. My mind obediently chased and retrieved the sticks I threw it as the hours went by. Kath caught my eye and smiled. Every step was one step nearer to our goal. We were going to make it.

Finally, in the early afternoon, I climbed the last 400 feet up to the camp site at Urdukas, feeling breathless and sick. A big height gain today. Mansion-sized boulders, grass, flowers, shit, tent ledges cut out by the Duke of Abruzzi's party a hundred years before. I slung down my pack and emptied the last of my water down my throat.

Tony comes up to me, bright-eyed with excitement. 'Have you seen the Tower?' I stand up beside him, sight along his pointing arm. And there it is, across the glacier, ten miles away: journey's end. The Mustagh Tower.

First reaction one of relief. The left hand ridge running up from Col to Summit is less desperate than imagined, can't see much below the Col. It's big, beastly and fucking impressive – but feasible, to my unpractised eye.

It's a classic triangular pyramid. The Brown–Patey ridge on the left, the French ridge on the right, an unclimbed ridge in the middle. The ridges are white, the face between looks sheer granite. It's stunningly impressive, but not impossible – the perfect mountain.

Tony rabbits on, so revving with anticipation I half expect him just to start running towards the Tower. 'It'll be great . . . It's such a fantastic mountain . . . It'll be fantastic if I get to the summit, but that's not the main thing.'

'What is the main thing, Tony?'

'For me it's just being here, getting some climbing in.'

Mal comes up. He's thrown off the clouds that have hung over him the last few days, but as always he controls his delight. 'Looks as though I'm going to get some climbing, youth.'

'Might have to do some myself.'

We stand and look and look. That mountain over there has dominated our lives for six months. For the next weeks it'll be our entire world. Kath comes up, tired but still game. We point it out to her and stand and look some more.

We're brimming with excitement. Tony in particular is like a child on the eve of its birthday. 'We'll be at Base Camp tomorrow!' We put up our tents, take pictures, discuss our chances on the mountain. Our eyes return again and again like a compass needle to the magnetic Tower. How much will Jon and Sandy have done? Will the weather have kept them back? Mal hopes that they'll have crossed the approach glacier and built up a good stash of food, tents and gear below the Col. They don't have enough rope to fix the Col; all we can ask is that they've done the essential groundwork and are in good shape.

Listening to Mal and Tony talk over their hopes and plans for the future – Nepal, Kenya, Peru, Alaska, maybe K2 somewhere down the line – I'm staggered again by the strength of their obsession. Nothing is ever enough to satisfy their hunger. As Jon said in 'Pindi, it is a vocation. Their lives are climbing or preparing to climb.

I can relate to this only in terms of what writing is to me: the essential function of my being alive. Looking at the Tower, I realize there's no way I want climbing that badly. For me it's an enthralling secondary activity, something to do and get away with. It's the same for Adrian. After Mustagh, if I get away with it, I go home and hang up my crampons and axes.

The night before, as we lay in our bags before sleep – the only time of the day we're intimate – Kath asked me again to promise not to go up to the Col.

She seldom asks anything like that. I was touched and a little worried that she was worried enough to mention it. And I lay and asked myself again: have I the right balance of caution and drive? Why take the risk? I don't need to, no one's asking me to. Can it be worth it? There's so many other things I want to do and be and live for – why gamble on Mustagh? To impress whom, to convince whom? Climbing's not the biggest thing in my life, so why push my luck?

The same questions have occurred, disappeared, resurfaced ever since Mal offered me this trip. Perhaps one never stops asking them. But sitting on top of the huge split rock that gives Urdukas its name, looking at Mustagh, I wanted to go as far as I possibly could on that mountain. My commitment felt stronger than ever. I desperately wanted to climb on the Tower, though I was no nearer to understanding why. And for no reason I thought of Jon on the way back from his Annapurna 3 trip, walking weeping through the streets of Kathmandu.

'Mr Andrew!' I stuck my head out of our tent and there, improbably, delightfully, was Mohammed Ali. Smiles, hugs and handshakes. It was wonderful to see him again, I felt a rush of affection. Typically, he'd brought some sweet pastries with him, in case he bumped into us. We wolfed them down while he gave us the news.

It was good, much better than we could have possibly expected. The lads had Camp 1 loaded up, and Camp 2 had been established a few days before. Camp 2! Had Jon and Sandy got up the Col already? There was delight mingled, if I was not mistaken, with some consternation on Mal and Tony's faces. They didn't want to arrive at the Tower to find most of the climbing already done. Then Mohammed explained that the glacier running down from Mustagh had been much longer and harder than expected, so Camp 2 was at the bottom of the South-East face, not on the Col.

I'm sure I read relief in Mal and Tony. And in myself. If the lads had really moved that fast, and were going for an ascent in an Alpine stylee, there'd be little room or time for me to do anything on the hill.

For the first time since his hurried departure from Skardu, Mal felt a surge of confidence. Four strong climbers in good nick and with enough food to sit out bad weather should have a very good chance on any mountain in the world. Everything was finally coming right. The lads on the hill had obviously worked their guts out, laid the foundations. Now he and Tony were arriving with fresh energy at just the right time. All right, so he'd dropped £4000 of his and Liz's money, the deposit for a house, on the trip. There was only one way to justify that: climb the fucker.

He looked thoughtfully at the ground while Tony babbled out his enthusiasm. Kathleen and Andrew looked strong enough still. If the lads still agree we need fixed ropes to the Col, he'll have a chance to do something on the hill. Does he realize that he'll be asked to carry loads? When Aido and Mohammed leave, he and Alex will be the only support climbers left. Is Alex up to leading? Is Andy up to following? Find out soon enough . . .

Mohammed had one of our two-way Motorola radios with him. To our surprise it worked clear across 10 miles, and we were able to chat to Adrian. He sounded pleased and relieved we were on our way, and quite proud of their progress so far. Then we listened in on his call to Jon and Sandy up at Camp 2.

Jon's cockney drawl bounced through the static. He went straight to the heart of the matter: '*But have they got the bleedin' money?*' Aido said he wasn't sure, but Burt and Donna hadn't made it. No one seemed very surprised by this, perhaps it had always been on the cards and the old hands had recognized it quicker than I had.

We couldn't get through to Jon and Sandy direct so decided to keep our good news till we saw them. Let them wait and wonder.

The sun went down. We were now at roughly 14,500 feet and it got cold quickly. Last mug of cocoa, early bed. I took a sleeping pill, but was too excited to sleep. Like a child waiting for Christmas, all I wanted was the next morning.

I woke round 2.00. My pulse was hammering, I was gasping for breath. Unpleasant sensation. I went outside to breathe deeply and calm down. Moonlight mined silver on the ridges opposite, and on the Mustagh Col. That's where I wanted to be. Soon, *inshallah*. The air itself seemed to have a fuzz of light hanging in it – alpenglow, they told me later, caused by charged particles at altitude. Everything was frozen, no wind. I stood awed and elated in the absolute silence at the heart of the world's greatest mountain range.

This was it. The last day. We set off to cross the Baltoro and get onto the Mustagh glacier that met it at right angles. The day began blue and cold, but quickly grew hot. Breathing was unpleasantly ineffectual, too light and fast, and the going was very rough. Only once in a while was there time to look up at Mustagh.

I kept up with Mal and Tony till 'lunch'. They were desperately keen to press on and revved into the distance. Kath was suffering from her blisters and the altitude. I waited for her and she was in tears of frustration and anger at her inability to keep up. Abdul volunteered to stay with her, and I slogged on with Mohammed. It was good to be with him again and enjoy his optimism, energy and friendliness. But even he had found load-carrying on the hill exhausting, which made me doubt my own capacity to help the lads much.

The Mustagh glacier was no improvement. The rocks were loose underfoot, and every so often one would slide wildly on grit over black ice. I was in a thoroughly bad temper. Up front I could see that our porters had cut off the glacier and were toiling up a steep slope of eroded mud and boulders. I picked my way carefully up – and there was Jhaved, our Base Camp cook. He grinned, hugged me, insisted on taking my pack. I didn't feel like being proud, so surrendered it gratefully. Another 20 feet up onto a plateau and there it was. Base Camp.

Rough grass, a loose cluster of tents, smell of flowers with just a hint of slaughtered goat, cardboard boxes and jerry cans – home for the next few weeks. A cliff behind it, the Tower just out of sight round the corner, colossal Masherbrum with spindrift trailing from its nose cone back across the Baltoro, Lobsang Spire like the spike of a sundial across the Mustagh glacier – the camp was a veranda at 15,000 feet, with one of the world's finer views. On the entrance flap to the Mess Tent, someone had scrawled BREW ME CRAZY. I smiled and walked in.

Aido grinned and passed me a mug of cocoa. 'So you made it, old boy.' He seemed to have changed. Still laconic, earnest and schoolboyish – but now he had the Look. The Look that every party we met on their way down had. At once worn and fit, alert and withdrawn; the weathered skin, the eyes not so much distant as self-absorbed, relaxed yet revving . . . The on-the-hill look, the early stages of summit fever.

As he filled me in on their progress, I looked around. This was a five-star hotel compared to Askole or the walk-in sites. Jhaved turned out pastries, brews and goat's liver. There were even boxes to sit on. It was littered with books, opened boxes, cassettes, lanterns, stoves, clothes. Could have some good nights in here, I thought.

I went back to meet Kath. She toiled up the hill to the plateau with painful slowness and utter determination. She came over the crest, saw Base Camp – and burst into tears. Tears of relief, of exhaustion, of pride and pleasure. Her summit, her journey's end. She held on to me, laughing and crying at the same time. 'I can't let them see me like this, they'll think I'm a right bumblie.'

She rubbed her face, took a deep breath and walked with me to the Mess Tent, a little unsteady but very upright.

I watched the tiny figures of Sandy and Jon bob improbably across the face of the cliff behind Base Camp, some 500 feet up. They were on the Ibex Trail running right across the rock face and round the corner out of sight, towards the Tower. It looked very exposed.

We shook hands warmly; Kath hugged Jon. They seemed genuinely pleased to see us – particularly when they discovered we had the money. When I mentioned to Sandy that Kath and I had been hurt by his addressing his notes only to Burt and Donna and what did this mean, he was quite taken aback. It obviously didn't mean anything, other than our insecurity. And he categorically denied that he or the others had suggested sending us back from Askole.

Just back down from stocking Camp 2, they very much had that Look. Weathered, tired yet full of energy, eager for news and precious letters yet all their inner resources tuned to one thing: the hill. In shorts, Yeti gaiters, glacier goggles, Sandy with his Peruvian and Jon with his Rasta hat, dangling slings and krabs, sun cream and axes, they looked a total shambles. Yet they looked absolutely right and at ease. For the first time I was seeing them in their natural environment. They made much more sense here.

The porters squatted in double lines like primary school children, waiting to be paid off. They pocketed their handfuls of 100-rupee notes, receipted with a thumb print, and literally ran off down the hill to the glacier, whooping and laughing as if the summer holidays had just begun. We said a regretful goodbye to Abdul and arranged to see him in Skardu. He hurried away towards his wife and any-day-now baby, looked back once, waved, and was gone.

When I asked Adrian how the going looked up to the Col, he was serious and discouraging. 'Forget about getting to the Col. The Icefall below Camp 1 is not like anything you've done before. You'll have to have a considerable amount of glacier training before you can even set foot on it. You'll do well just to get to Camp 1, let alone 2.'

Sandy looked up from his conference with Mal. 'That's right, youth. The Icefall is death on a stick.' I just nodded. Being told I can't do things makes me all the more determined. He grinned and added, 'No problem. You'll be all right – but you will have to learn how to move on a glacier quickly and safely, without belays.'

'Like shit off a hot shovel, by the sound of it,' Mal added. 'This Icefall could be a real problem.'

'It is.' Adrian winced at some private memory.

'It's a piece of piss,' Jon said. 'They're just winding you up.'

'I'll take him up and we can romp around on the bitch.' This was Alex, slumped back on some boxes with his ostrich legs propped on his pack. He looked tired and out of sorts; both he and Aido had suffered from altitude headaches, and he was not fully acclimatized yet.

I resolved then and there to make Camp 2 at least. If Aido was frankly unsure of my ability to do so, I had something to prove. There was more than a heavy-duty trudge ahead. Kath looked over at me, raised an eyebrow. She knew very well what I was thinking.

We walked – painfully slowly, like deep-sea divers – up a bank and round the corner till we could see Mustagh. It looked brutal and unrelenting, but not outwith the bounds of possibility. As the last light hit its upper ridges, the Tower briefly mellowed, looked almost beautiful. It stood planted squarely across the top of the valley down which the glacier and Icefall tumbled, at once defiant and indifferent.

It was good to eat all together for the first time since leaving 'Pindi, a lifetime ago. We talked a while in the yellow lanternlight, catching up on each other's news, making plans, getting used to each other again. When I went outside, the air was full of moonlight and alpenglow. As I sat looking at the grim bulk of Masherbrum, I could hear Mal coughing in one tent, the goat grazing, and Shokat's blasted radio.

I was too keyed up to sleep. I crawled into my bag and, with the help of Sandy's diary and the evening's conversation, reconstructed the lads' activities since they first arrived at Base Camp eleven days earlier.

The first day after their arrival, as Kath and I were approaching the Askole rope bridge and Tony was sitting his last exam in Wales, Jon and Sandy went to reconnoitre the lower end of the Chagaran glacier. What they found was a shock – a truly horrible icefall riddled with crevasses, cornices, boulders, ice towers. When the sun hit it, it fell apart. 'Not too safe a way,' Sandy noted laconically. Meaning it was desperate. They felt the glacier must have deteriorated considerably in the twenty-eight years since Brown and company had come this way, for they'd made no mention of major problems and had even taken porters up it. No porter in his right mind would go near this, and even a mountaineer with only two brain cells left to rub together would hesitate.

They worked their way, roped together, up the left side of it, not at all happy. But after half a mile or so they came to a point where a natural ledge seemed to run down from the cliff on their left. 'Let's check it out.'

And so they found the Ibex Trail, so called because of the ibex droppings that littered it. It ran on an irregular natural ledge right round the cliff back down to Base Camp. 'A fine, picturesque and very safe route,' Sandy noted, 'lined with wild flowers, a small spring and a nice scramble.'

What it did was circumvent the entire lower Icefall. Without it we would probably have been unable to carry loads onto the Tower proper. 'Put this down in your book, Andy,' Mal said. 'The Ibex Trail is a piece of mountaineering genius.'

Next day they went up the Ibex Trail with Mohammed and Alex (Adrian suffering from boom-boom altitude headaches). The latter pair left a stash at a quartz block at the end of the trail, while Jon and Sandy struck on up the glacier – and in thirty minutes ran into the second icefall.

'It was quite difficult,' Sandy conceded. Meaning it was desperately desperate.

Moving together, they threaded a way up through it and plugged on, suffering, across a stretch riddled with visible and concealed crevasses. Some four and a half kilometres from Base Camp, they established Camp 1, put up a two-man tent on a small moraine bank at something like 16,500 feet, and thankfully turned for home.

'We tried to come down the left-hand side of the Icefall; this proved a very desperate and unsafe way.' Meaning it was totally fucking desperately desperate.

On the third day they rested. They needed to acclimatize, and no point in burning themselves out at this stage. Adrian, Alex and Mohammed carried gear up to the Quartz Block.

On the fourth day Alex, Adrian and Mohammed set out to stock Camp 1. They got seriously lost in the worst part of the Icefall and with some difficulty beat a retreat. Thus Adrian's intense dislike of that part of the glacier. It also pointed up the gap between Jon and Sandy and the others and how the Icefall was going to make support load-carrying much harder than anticipated. Burt would have a fit if he even saw this place, Alex thought to himself. He was fascinated by its unearthly, chaotic beauty, and decided to camp up on the glacier in the near future and let it get to him.

The fifth day:

The spirit of Light Dry Snow took the Spirit of Granular Snow as his mate and after a time she gave birth to a Mountain of Ice far to the North. The Sun Spirit hated the glittering child spreading across the land, keeping away his warmth so no grass could grow. The Sun decided to destroy Ice Mountain but Storm Cloud Spirit, the sibling of Granular Snow, found out the Sun wanted to kill the child. So in the summer, when the sun is most powerful, Storm Cloud Spirit fights with him to save Ice Mountain's life . . .

Is this our happy Highlander, smiling Sandy Allan? I wondered, and read on late into the night.

Jon, Mohammed, Alex and I walked up the Ibex Trail carrying loads, heading towards Camp 1. I was last in departing Base Camp, not because I was slow, but just making sure that I had all my correct and only necessary personal gear and expedition equipment. Jon shouted down from high on the Ibex path for me to bring some things that he had forgotten. This disappointed me more than it should have, and I must try not to get angry at these tiny little details. Aido not too well really, so needed a day off . . .

The glacier did not prove too much of a problem except for one steep serac part where we had to traverse on some knife edge seracs, down between them, then up some semi-steep black ice. The rest was quite good.

At Camp 1 they put up the four-man tent, brewed up after

Sandy had found running water by falling with one leg into a small crevasse full of it. Alex and Mohammed returned safely if somewhat apprehensively to Base. Jon hung his tiny external speakers from the roof of the tent and wired in the Walkman; while he gazed at the ceiling, listening to récherché reggae dubs and thinking of London, Sandy absorbed himself in *The Clan of the Cave Bear* and an existence even more primitive than his own. The day ended with the usual sequence: food, radio call, brew, alpenglow, sleeping tablet, sleep.

Day six. While half of our Expedition was stealing away from Askole in the race for Jolla Bridge, Sandy was brewing up and trying to rouse Jon at Camp 1. Neither of them was feeling too well – their first night sleeping at this level – but they forced themselves up and out into the wilderness. They could see their objective, the foot of the south face of the Tower, about one and a half miles away across the glacier, with a height gain of some 1500 feet. Jon remembered Patey had laconically noted that this section was heavily crevassed. It was.

We went up the left side of the glacier and then traversed to the centre, up through some seracs and crevasses, up a small valley between lots of seracs, waiting to fall in some holes but did not. Then round some small glacier green water beautiful pools, stuck in some wands as markers. I led up a steep slope, quite hard work, and we decided to take a steep line to avoid some seracs but once at the high point of that discovered we were in the middle of really bad and dangerous seracs and crevasses. We had to traverse left, but sank very deep in soft snow. We were both really exhausted and our heads boomed with altitude. We tried to joke but could not.

Eventually we placed two snow stakes and tied the tent and other loads to them and marked the site with a ski pole and one of the UK flags Jon had lifted from a service station in London.

We started back to Camp 1, both very tired and sinking deep into soft snow. Fell into several crevasses, tried to find an alternative route back but the one we took was really bad. We jumped some huge holes and had a bad time. At last we staggered to Camp 1, both of us tripping over our crampons, having problems. Sacks off, we sprawled out on the moraine, exhausted, lost. Half an hour elapsed before we could begin to get our acts together. Crampons off, start a brew, crawled into our pits and just lay there . . .

Lights out 6.00 p.m., alarm set for 4.30 next morning to go back up and pitch Camp 2 properly.

Enthralled, impressed and distinctly apprehensive for my own chances on the hill, I turned the next page of Sandy's diary. Shokat had finally turned off his caterwauling radio. Kath lay quietly snoring, her face blank and puffy with water retention. Tomorrow was a rest day for me. I'd check out the Ibex Trail. I read on.

My alarm gave a single buzz, my head throbbed twice to say good morning and remind me where I was. I pushed my hands against the tent and heard snow slide off the fly. I looked out – snow around, mist all over, a wind. Not so good.

'Okay, youth, want a brew?' Jon took it, swearing at his really sore head, trying to hold the pain in his forehead in one of his climbing-scarred hands. His eyes looked at me, they tried to be friendly but I could see he was suffering and had not really recovered from the exertion and altitude of the previous day. I liked this youth, I hoped he'd be okay. I knew he'd push it and say he'd be well enough.

He's a strong little bastard, I thought. I admired his determination as he tried to drink his tea. I radioed Base Camp. The lads there said that unless there was a vast improvement in the weather they would not be bringing loads up to Camp 1. I was disappointed . . .

Another brew. Jon came round though his head was still slow. We geared up and left round 6.30. I led, sinking into fresh snow, feeling like a blind man as I stabbed in front of myself with a ski pole. Often the pole would slip easily through into the emptiness of a crevasse, my feet sometimes left holes looking down into a black void. So we ambled on. Watching Jon I realized he was just coming along with me to be on the other end of the rope so that we'd be able to push up a new camp – for the good of the expedition. That was good.

Hourly radio calls, half-hourly stops for water. Several close calls as we slid down to our waists in slots. Energy wasted as we extracted ourselves. Up the steep col – hard this, my head exploded, pulsating pain as the blood pumped around. Jon must have been feeling like this at Camp 1, I thought. Push push on until up to my knees, each step a real effort.

We came to the cache of the tent etc – only the ski pole and flag visible. We picked up the gear and went on. We expected another half hour, but it was more like 1½ hours. Jon wanted to pitch the tent at one spot, but there was avalanche debris all around so I said No. Jon said he just wanted peace and quiet. My pounding brain picked this up to mean he wanted me to shut up. We argued and I burst on ahead because I knew and felt deeply we shouldn't site Camp 2 in that spot.

We were both exhausted at this point. Jon came after me and took the lead. After twenty steps he turned and said he was very sorry. Great and thanks, I said. I led another fifty steps in the deep snow, then Jon took over and we came to a safeish spot and sat down knackered. We could not tell if we were on flat ground or not because of snow and throbbing head illusions and fresh snow blowing onto our glacier goggles. Jon said we'll go on a few more steps and we did and finally came to a safe, flat place, no avalanche debris or hanging seracs.

We dug a tent platform. I said I was sorry that we'd argued and apologized for him having to apologize. Then we laughed a bit and worked well together putting up the tent.

. . . I pushed the pace back to Camp 1. A brew and a retort, then set off for Base. We got lost in one part of the Icefall and this resulted in some desperate glacier and serac climbing and dodging. We came through a happy team, joking over our argument. We both noticed how different we were. I take words at their literal meaning, Jon uses words very casually. We both agreed we'd have to learn to be tolerant, a big lot!

Base Camp was rainswept and coldish but felt like paradise to Jon and I.

On the eighth day Adrian, Alex and Mohammed set off to carry gear to Camp 1 while Jon and Sandy recovered. They got to the end of the Ibex Trail, but despondently turned back due to bad weather. In the evening the wind got up and nearly blew away the Mess Tent. They lashed it down some more and huddled round the stove chatting, singing, banging out rhythms on empty jerry cans and trying not to feel cold. For the first time snow fell at Base, but did not last long.

Their storm was a higher-altitude version of our downpour at Paiju. As they were struggling to hold on to the Mess Tent, Kath and I must have been baling out ours. Realizing this made me wonder what various friends in Scotland were doing at this precise moment, and I felt briefly homesick. Just altitude blues, I was learning to recognize them.

Next morning Adrian, Mohammed and Alex set off yet again for Camp 1, the latter two looking not at all keen but going anyway. Alex finally had to turn back, but Adrian and Mohammed struggled on, dumped their loads and returned. That night Sandy noted that all three looked worn out, sick and wasted. He wished he and Jon could have had the better load-carrying support, yet was very aware that the lads were doing their utmost. Some of the essential groundwork had been done, but not as much as he'd wanted. Do I hope for too much? he wondered. If I hoped for less from myself and other people, I wouldn't be disappointed so often. But would we achieve much then?

On the last day before our arrival, Sandy and Jon got up early yet again, packed their sacks with food and gas, snow stakes and deadmen and stoves, and set off up the Ibex Trail one more time. The aim was to spend the night at Camp 1 and push on to 2 to stock it up next day.

The acclimatization gained by having slept at Camp 1 and been up to 2 was making a considerable difference. The Icefall would never be a stroll, would always be potentially dangerous, particularly when descending in the heat of the day, but it took a lot less out of them than on the first couple of occasions. They arrived early, got the brews going, and lay out on Karrimats to pass the rest of the day reading, chatting and listening to music. Sandy's taste was largely what Jon scornfully called hippy music, and for the most part their partnership was soundtracked by Jon's tapes with Sandy once in a while vetoing some particularly depressing nihilist post-futurist experimental squeaks-and-pops band. ('If that's a band, youth, it's time they snapped.')

In the afternoon radio call Adrian announced that Mohammed had found Mal, Tony, Andrew, Kathleen and Shokat at Urdukas. Jon asked if they had the bleeding money, and Sandy asked what had happened to Burt and Donna. Though they were both keen to get back down to meet the others, catch up on news and get their mail, Camp 2 had to be stocked, so they stayed up that night.

Crossing the glacier and climbing up to Camp 2 came much more easily next day. Their blood was thick with red corpuscles that caught and carried what oxygen was available. The weather was fine and cold, and they confidently crossed snow bridges that in a few hours would become potential trap doors, depositing the unsuspecting climber into the depths of a crevasse.

They arrived at Camp 2 to find avalanche debris within 100 feet of the tent. They felt pleased that they'd made the effort to shift it to where it now was, and with their judgement of position. Of course, there was no knowing if it really was out of the line of fire, but it looked that way.

So they lit the stove, massaged their feet to get some feeling back in them and, after much discussion, decided to come all the way back down to base. There was little point in staying at Camp 1, for there was no fixed rope there to haul up to 2. Besides, Adrian had affirmed that there was mail waiting . . .

They hurried down. Letters for all, devoured in one feverish gallop full of chuckles, groans and exclamations, then reread more slowly, then finally read right through again alone in one's tent, savouring each word, the handwriting, the very feel of a letter from home. Letters are a reassurance that that half-remembered world still exists. Their importance is not in what they say, but that they've arrived at all.

I dropped Sandy's diary and lay back looking at the ceiling of the tent in the flickering candlelight. I was impressed by the amount of persistence and effort the lads had put in prior to our arrival. Reading between the lines, it had clearly been hard and at times painful and risky. And now Mal and Tony would be woken in a few hours' time to go straight on to the hill. They just don't let up.

I felt a certain resolution and confidence in me, a pale reflection of theirs, like the sun lighting up the moon that hung above the Lobsang Spire as I glanced out before finally going to sleep. The still night, glimmer of Masherbrum across the valley, the goat wandering on its tether, the dark wedges of tents . . . Base Camp Mustagh Tower. It is real. We've arrived. Now see where we go from here.

8

Move It On Over

*In which we learn to step high
with Alex*

12–15 July 1984

I woke next morning with rapid, shallow breathing and a racing
pulse. As I lay concentrating on slowing my breath, I could hear
voices drifting over from the Mess Tent. I sloughed off my
sleeping bag like a snake shuffling out of an old skin, and
stumbled over there. Tony, Mal, Mohammed, Jon, Sandy,
Adrian were sitting around in boots and gaiters and salopettes,
putting back the brews and porridge preparatory to another day's
Himalayan thuggery.

'Split the tent load, Tony?' 'How much gas for Camp 2?' 'See us
over another brew, youth.' 'Take a line up the ramp to the left of
the bungalow-sized boulder.' No rambling conversation this
morning, instead terse, practical details. We're on the job now.

Adrian is serious, methodical and preoccupied. He's very
aware he's going up for his last session on the hill, that tomorrow's Friday 13th, that the next day is his twenty-ninth birthday.
Though much more of a climber than I, we share a similar
attitude; the main thing is to get off with it. He's got other things
in his life, such as his marriage and his profession.

Sandy is dishevelled, amiable and strong. He greets me, as he
always does everyone, with a cheerful Good morning! Jon
sprawls back on the Gasherbrum 2 boxes, his eyes distant,
abruptly cackling at a remark. They both look worn but durable,
like their gear. Tony as ever vibrates with enthusiasm; Mal is
more controlled but clearly straining on the leash. They both
drain their mugs, say cheerio and leave. Some five minutes later,
the others follow them. 'Give us a radio call at two and six.' 'See
you.' Jon fools around briefly with Jhaved, a wave, then he and
Sandy set off. The partings are always casual, yet they always

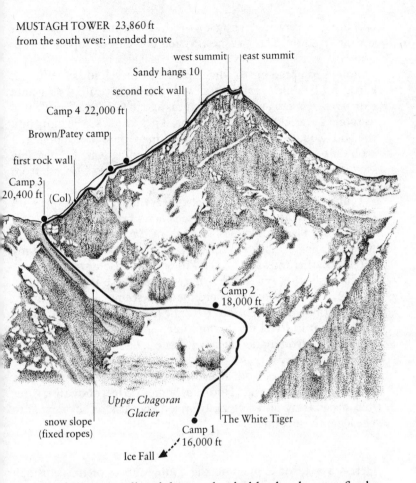

MUSTAGH TOWER 23,860 ft
from the south west: intended route

west summit | east summit

Sandy hangs 10

second rock wall

Camp 4 22,000 ft

Brown/Patey camp

first rock wall

Camp 3
20,400 ft (Col)

Camp 2
18,000 ft

Upper Chagoran
Glacier

snow slope
(fixed ropes)

Camp 1
16,000 ft

The White Tiger

Ice Fall

matter. If all goes well and the weather holds, they hope to fix the ropes up the Col and get the first look at the condition of the summit ridge. Then we'll know what our chances are.

I don't like this.

Ibex Trails are strictly for ibex. And for climbers who leave their brains in their rucksacks and their imagination at home. I don't like edging along this sloping ledge of grit and loose stone with the cliff on my left forcing me to the edge of the 500 foot drop on my right. The pulse in my ears beats its drum, my breathing is erratic. I cling to the rock on my left, take each section in short, sharp rushes, feeling the surface slip under my boots.

What prompted me to come up here by myself today? Why on earth did I think I could cope with climbing at all? I still hate exposure as much as I did six months ago in Glencoe. This fear is as total as seasickness and, like seasickness, attacks the mind and the body equally. It's not fear of anything – though if I slip here I wouldn't survive – it's just plain, unreasoning fear. In the same way some people violently dislike eating tripe, I recoil from heights. Shit, shit, shit!

I curse myself, Malcolm, all ibex everywhere, as I edge on. With every step upward, my unease intensifies. I really don't enjoy this at all. Only a form of amnesia makes me forget it. I know, though it doesn't help, that I will forget how unpleasant this is, and my total lack of enthusiasm, when I'm back at Base Camp.

The trail goes on and on. Every step I take is one more to retrace. I get to a point where the path seems to skirt round a boulder that sticks right out over the face. I cautiously sit down and look at it. I feel my commitment draining away, like water running out from under a glacier. I know I'm not going to go on. Not today at any rate. Angry and disgusted, I set off back down.

A rattle of stones from above. I duck in close to the cliff. They clatter past 20 feet away. I look up. Some 300 feet above me, three ibex are peering down at me from a higher trail. They appear to be elegantly sneering.

Here's a way of explaining the configuration of the Mustagh Tower, the approach glaciers and our camps.

Say the Tower is a detached mansion in an estate of enormous stately homes, and you are going to pay it a visit. Then the Baltoro glacier is the main approach road. The Mustagh glacier is a side street leading past the Tower. Base Camp sits on the kerb opposite the entrance. The Ibex Trail gets you onto the garden path of the Chagaran glacier. There's a lot of crazy paving here, mined with booby traps and trap doors. The Icefall is a cross between a maze and a dozen sets of iron gates. Clearly Mustagh Mansion aims to discourage casual visitors.

Camp 2 is the porch. You're standing on the doorstep, right

under the sheer walls. Will someone dump an avalanche on you from an upper-storey window? Fixing rope up to the Col opens the 2000-foot-high creaking door. In front of you now stretches the stairway of the northwest ridge, a two-day epic to the summit. At the end of that you will join a most exclusive party . . .

(Of course, you could try to sneak in by the easier northeast ridge, the one the French climbed and Covington's American expedition failed on, but really that's just the tradesmen's entrance.)

Friday 13th was a quiet day at Base Camp. The morning was sunny, blue and cold. Kath and I wandered up to the stream behind Base, which turned out to involve a fair uphill trudge across a couple of boulder fields. We passed the ruins of old rock houses that Mohammed said were left from the time the Mustagh Valley had been an ancient trading route into China, a couple of days' trek away. Peace and clarity came, as they so often did on the Expedition, from sitting quietly by the stream, waiting for socks to dry.

It is a world of absolute sensory deprivation where little moves, with vast canvases of blue and white and black. In this desolation, the tiny purple and yellow flowers astonish the eye. In the silence one's ears attune to the brushing of wind over stone, the distant clatter of rockfall, the croak of a chough drifting over the ruins. It is the same with one's palate. A finger of shortbread brought from home lingers the whole day.

Mal and Tony were back down for lunch, after dumping their loads at Camp 1. Mal told us he had been building cairns on a 'safe' area when, *crack*, a crevasse opened up between his feet and two seconds later he found himself 20 feet up an ice serac with no clear idea how he'd got there, and shaking with adrenalin. Neither of them liked the Icefall one bit, particularly when descending. Alex, who took an almost Scottish delight in death and destruction, shook his head gloomily. 'One day that whole baked-Alaska mother is just going to s-l-i-d-e away.' He cackled in the manner of the prophet Jeremiah pronouncing a particularly horrible doom in store. 'Of course, we mightn't be on her at the time,' he added, not very hopefully.

Wind me up, Scottie.

*

Adrian radioed to say he and Mohammed had made their first carry to Camp 2, but because Mohammed felt bad they might be coming down tomorrow instead of going back up again. Mal pulled a face, as I knew Sandy would when he heard. It was quite a serious setback. No one knew if Alex and I would be able to carry to Camp 2, and there was a limit to how much of their own support the lead climbers could do without diminishing the time and energy needed for a chance at the summit.

The gist of the message back to Adrian was typical of these situations: 'Do the best you can, but you decide.' There was no attempt to persuade or cajole or denigrate. By the sound of his voice – flat and dead with none of the 'old boy' humour – it had been an exhausting day. And as I read later, Sandy was lying in the tent at Camp 2 confessing to his diary how irritating and immature Jon had been all day. While Jon with his sore head was most likely thinking what a pain in the neck Sandy could be.

The lack of oxygen made cigarettes burn slowly, and the flies were sluggish. We spent the unpleasantly hot afternoons at Base swatting them, lying around trying to read, write or listen to music while Shokat's radio wailed, the three chickens squawked and the goat grazed half-heartedly. I began to realize that as in war, a lot of a Himalayan expedition is spent killing time. I was trying to enjoy the free time and the last few days of Kath's company, yet wanting the phoney war to end and to get into action.

A big meal of retorts, rice and dal in the Mess Tent. Jhaved lit the hurricane lamp, we pulled on our pile jackets and chatted on, enjoying the companionship and putting away one brew after another. About eight pints of liquid a day, Adrian had recommended back in 'Pindi. It had sounded a lot, but they went down easily.

Tony was enormously happy and didn't mind saying so. He was on holiday, surrounded by mountains, working on a severe mountain with the promise of real technical challenges. He seemed to love hills for their own sake more than any of the others. In his early teens, he told me, he'd done two newspaper rounds a day to be able to go to the Lakes every weekend and tramp 30 or 40 miles a day. Eventually he acquired an ice axe and learned how to use it, and gravitated inevitably towards technical climbing – particularly rock climbing, at which the others acknowledged he was easily the best in the party.

He trained as an engineering draughtsman, but kept on climbing. I gathered between the lines that he'd had a very rough time while training, on account of his being small and cherubic-looking. Maybe that had tempered his natural love of being in the hills into the hard, cutting blade of ambition. I wondered if the desire to prove himself as tough as anyone was what drove him. Jon, Sandy, Mal and Tony were all driven, for deep-seated reasons of their own. Initially I'd been curious to discover what those reasons were. Now I felt it didn't matter so much. I was becoming less and less able to stand outside them and analyse. Now I was beginning to accept that I was here and they were here, and that the doing mattered more than the why.

Finally Tony decided to go to Yosemite, to tackle some big wall climbing. He couldn't get time off work. He made the choice we'd all made, and left his job. For this absolutely pointless activity. To be able to sit in a tent in the middle of nowhere, with his fate out there on the dark Tower.

He was, of course, absolutely right.

The full moon hung impaled on the tip of Lobsang Spire, the wind was cold and clean. You could, with some difficulty, have read a book by the starlight. We said our goodnights and went to bed. 'I wouldn't have missed this for anything,' Kathleen murmured as we slid effortlessly down the slope into sleep.

Woke up at 5.00 a.m. full of nerves and purpose. A big day for the bumblies. Kath and I loaded our sacks with gas and hill food. We were only taking it to the cave at the end of the Ibex Trail, but it was a start and new territory for us. Tony was white and sick, so he and Mal took the day off and we set off on our own.

Climbing up the first section of the trail gave us a premonition of being ninety. We moved painfully slowly, gasping, unable to find the oxygen to move faster. Like the cigarettes, we combusted with difficulty. And 40 pounds on the back seemed to nail our boots to the ground. The trail itself made the heart beat faster, but I could view it more realistically now. Exposure apart, there were only a couple of genuinely delicate sections. Not speaking but glancing at each other now and again in silent empathy, we laboured on carefully.

After forty minutes I glanced back down; Base Camp was a little ring of tiny tents. The morning was so still we could hear the goat making goatish sounds and see the flash of water Jhaved poured from jerry can to basin.

We edged round the section I'd stopped at the day before – and the trail abruptly ran down onto a small boulder field above the glacier. On the left was an overhang with ski sticks, crampons, ropes and sacks clipped to an old piton. We unloaded our sacks and took some photos of ourselves trying to look indifferent yet heroic. The Tower looked much more fierce and abrupt from here, a monstrous pyramid slammed down across the head of the valley. I could see too what I took to be the Icefall, a jumbled, glittering slope half a mile or so up the glacier.

We lingered as the day grew warmer. More and more sounds from the glacier, slithers and rattles and crackings and hollow thuds. At her high point Kath was feeling slightly dizzy and light-headed; my chest seemed to be full of glue but I felt surprisingly strong – the benefit of having come up this way a couple of days before.

Kath took a last look. She wouldn't come this way again. We set off down; this time the trail was almost enjoyable. It felt good to walk back into Base Camp, back to the flies and flowers, to duck past 'Brew Me Crazy' and get a mug from Jhaved, having done one's bit for the day.

Before lunch we saw two tiny figures high up on the cliff. Half an hour later we ambled up from the camp to meet Adrian and Mohammed. Pat on the back, handshakes, the reassurance of physical contact, happy birthday to a beaming Aido. They were regretful not to be able to manage a second carry to Camp 2, but relieved and thankful to be safe and done with it.

They also reported that Jon and Sandy had fixed the first rope length up towards the Col. Mal whooped and punched his fist in the air. The door of the Tower was opening.

Mohammed pulled off his boots and crampons, handed them

and the helmet and axes to me with a tired smile, as if to say 'It's your turn now'. It was good to have my gear back. I remembered that what had really peeved Mal on arriving at Askole was not that the others had broken into his private stash of goodies but that they'd taken some of his climbing gear. Lay off my blue suede boots, matey.

I turned the fanged crampons over in my hand and wondered what kind of world they would take me to.

Meanwhile Jon and Sandy were suffering on the 1900-foot ice slope below the Col. They'd got away from Camp 2 early, tramped to the bergschrund and crossed it in that Rubicon moment that marks the beginning of the assault on the mountain proper. With 1200 feet of rope, snow stakes, ice screws, deadmen and pitons in their sacks, it was heavy going.

Neither of them had actually fixed ropes before. In Alpine-stylee climbing, it simply wasn't done. So they just used common sense. Jon led out the first 220-metre reel of bright blue polypropylene, securing it at intervals with ice screws and snow stakes. It was heavy work banging and screwing them in; beneath a thin surface of snow the ice was hard. Lots of little rocks frozen into the slope suggested a fusillade of stonefall in the heat of the day.

Sandy led out the second reel. Suddenly it was hot, with the sun reflecting back up from the snow they felt caught in the focus of a giant magnifying glass. The heat, the altitude and the heavy sacks drained away their resources at a frightening rate. They monitored their bodies and decided enough was enough; much more of this and they'd seriously deplete the reserves of energy mentally set aside for completing the mountain. That ability to assess realistically just how much go one has, and to know when to push on through suffering and when to call a halt, struck me as one of the most intriguing and essential Himalayan qualities. And like many Himalayan qualities, it transcends the physical.

So they secured the remaining rope and climbing gear to three snow stakes and rappelled down from their high point, and an hour or so later they plodded exhausted back to the tent. The heat was intense all afternoon, and due to it and the altitude of Camp 2 around 18,000 feet – they felt they were resting but not recovering. It was their fifth day of continual climbing and load-carrying. A certain degree of embuggerage was setting in.

And besides, they were beginning to smell.

We had a special meal – double retorts, rice and dal, and pink custard – for Aido's birthday. I gave him a can of peaches from my rapidly dwindling stash, and the advice to open it in the solitude of his tent – which, being at heart a canny Scot, he did. He was happy and relaxed now his time on the hill was over. It was hard for him to leave not knowing if we were going to make it or not, but his thoughts were turning now to getting back to Sue and starting his job. As always, those who were staying on part envied and part pitied him. He conscientiously went through our medicine chest with me. It contained an extraordinary variety of drugs and salves and potions, everything from pile cream to morphine and some wicked-looking tubes for carrying out a tracheotomy. We decided to pass on open-heart surgery.

As I'd got to know him more, I realized that for all his doctor's seriousness, he too found normal life lacking. He didn't like risk, yet he went parachuting, climbing and drove a Porsche very fast. He was an ideal climbing doc. We were all going to miss him.

With the possible exception of Jhaved. When Aido saw Tony's condition, still very pale and sick, and the state of Mess Tent hygiene, he expressed his opinion focibly. To mollify him, Jhaved made us pancakes. They tasted strongly of paraffin. 'This simply won't do, old boy.' They went to our goat.

While Jhaved sulked, Alex cleaned out the pan, rinsed it, and made a fresh pancake mix and presented them to the gourmets. We tasted them critically. Paraffin flavoured pancakes again. Adrian stormed, Alex was defensive, the goat got fat. When the same routine happened the next night, Jon occupied himself with a felt-tip pen and the lid of a cardboard box and twenty minutes later produced a memorable addition to our Mess Tent graffiti (I should add Alex's middle name was Brittingehame, and the paraffin miraculously speeded up bowel movements):

BRITTINGEHAME ALPINE SERVICES
The 5 Star Caterers
PUT A TIGER IN YOUR BELLY
STEP HIGH WITH ALEX!!

I did a lot of moonlighting that night. The paraffin runs. Squatting half-asleep looking over at the moon above Masherbrum, the sky holding light as if it was particles in suspension. It was peaceful and beautiful, but I would have preferred a good night's sleep.

I woke late to hear Tony and Mal saying their goodbyes to Mohammed, Adrian and Kath. As always, there was no knowing if or when they'd meet again, and as always it was very casual. 'Mind how you go, youth.' 'See you in Scottie.'

I finally got up, tired and weak. That day seemed full of goodbyes. Adrian and Kathleen packed up their gear and took their last walkabouts. I began sorting out my sack for tomorrow's glacier introduction with Alex. Jon radioed to say he and Sandy were coming down for a couple of days recuperation at Base. They passed Mal and Tony below Camp 1, compared news, then romped happily down the Ibex Trail into the green world of our Base Camp.

I want to quote Sandy's diary at some length because it gives some insight into his world, and also, I think, into how one is opened up inside after returning from five hard days on a Himalayan peak.

When I chatted with Andrew I wondered why he was surprised when I said I always keep a diary. Does he think because I don't talk too much that I'm as thick as two short planks? Like, I cannot spell, I speak porter-talk, but who in the world does not when one has spent two years with a no English speaking Yugoslav crew on an oil rig, and living with a French girl? Well, how can the man comprehend – he probably does. And such irrelevant but important thoughts pass through my head as I speak to him and Jon. One look into Jhaved's eyes and he knows what I want. One straight hit with my axe and I find a good ice placement. *C'est la vie*, Dominique would say. Don't worry, Sandy, she'd say. They'll never know you or what you've done.

. . . I fade away to wash by the stream. It's good to wash the sweat of the hill away, and I watch the dirty soapy water. What right have I to pollute the water here? But it soon turns clear. What right have we to hold opinions? Every right, I say to myself, and then I say if we have the right to opinions do we have a right to put them to other people to try and change their views? Do we have a right to build a small dam in the stream to make a convenient washing place, it's OK for us but by what RIGHT?

And Jon says, every right. He's an opinion holder, tells everybody his and puts them down boldly as he talks. I always think why does he, why should we? I wonder if he ever thinks this way.

Kath worries Andrew will not be OK on the glacier. I reassure her he'll be OK. We'll all be OK. I hope she finds that OK and reasonable . . .

. . . So, candle flutters in my tent. Slight wind tonight, nice alpenglow on Masherbrum. That's another point: why do we all compare things? Why are we all so narrow?

I thought like this a long time now, why does it start to fill my head and the pages of this book? And climbing is not so important to me, it's more the way I feel, the way I react, the language I speak and the words I scribe, the mess that I leave behind, the way that I eat my food . . . These suit my feelings.

Sign off now. Letters to write. Folks go tomorrow, the end of the Expedition for them. The climbing has just begun on the Col.

For Kath and me it was our last night together. We lay in our separate sleeping bags holding hands. There was little left to say. My head was full of tomorrow on the glacier, and her heart was full of leaving.

9

A Walk on the Wild Side

In which the author romps on the sleazy end
of the glacier, the Four Aces push open the door,
and we play high-altitude cricket

16–22 July 1984

Adrian, Mohammed and Kathleen left in the morning – along
with Shokat, who was going back to Urdukas for some kind of
LOs' convention. He'd seemed rather miserable, restless and
homesick the previous days. Here he had no duties, nothing to do,
no servants to wait on him, no army buddies to talk to. How
unselfsufficient army life makes people! You needed inner
resources to live here, and he didn't have them.

It was an intense parting for Kath and me, at once too drawn
out and too quick. We were all standing about in front of the
Mess Tent at 6.00 in the morning, our sacks packed for the hill,
theirs for the walk-out. My arm round her waist imprinted itself
with the memory of her delicacy and her strength. 'Look after
yourself,' she said. Her eyes held the sudden intensity of naked
feeling, as if a blue lid had lifted revealing a deeper, bluer eye
within. I nodded, wanting the moment to last for ever, wanting to
be away.

A brief farewell hug, for we were diffident about making a fuss
in front of the others. Adrian: 'Would you two like ten minutes
alone in my tent?' Laughter, handshakes with the others, the
usual promises and assurances – see you in Anstruther, meet you
on the Baltoro, when you get home I'll cook you steak and onions
and we'll drink red wine and then . . . It all seemed very iffy, but
we have to say these things.

They turned and walked away. At the crest of the slope down
to the glacier Kath paused and looked back at the camp, at the
mountain, at us. Unusual for her. ('Well, I didn't know if I'd ever
see you again.') Then she disappeared down the hill. Her slight
figure carried much of myself away with her.

*

I put Kath out of my mind. Big day today, onto the mountain at last. I checked my gear: harness, helmet, axes, down jacket, rope for prussik loops, a jumar clamp, gloves, camera, sun stick, goggles. Then a load of hill-food bags and gas cylinders to carry to the Brew Tent. How the weight adds up! Okay, youth, let's have a look at this glacier . . .

A clear, needle-bright morning as Alex and I pick our way slowly, gasping already, up the Ibex Trail. It feels like early days in Glencoe – keyed up, concentrating hard on detail, everything vivid and dreamlike, adrenalin buzzing. Pink flowers nestling under a ledge, caw of a raven, ski pole scraping on rock, watch this loose gravel, Base Camp tiny already, can see Sandy airing his sleeping bag, wish I was down there, no I don't . . .

We rope up at the Cave, tying our fates together for the day. A gesture of trust and solidarity, marriage by a 40-foot length of polypropylene. Mustagh is gleaming and severe and magnificently indifferent to our pranks. A little further and we sit down to strap on crampons and helmet, then gingerly climb up onto the glacier at last.

No gleaming blue and white here. 'The sleazy end of the glacier,' Alex drawls. It's all dark corners, rubble, disintegrating alleys, broken walls. My first sizable crevasse, a dark slot that goes down further than I care to look. Alex instructs on jumping technique: pick your stance on the lip, spot your landing place on the other side, picture the jump, then do it. Make sure you keep going forward.

I check it out, jump, clumsy with nerves and the weight of my sack and the unfamiliar crampons. Stumble on the far side, regain my balance. Alex relaxes and moves on. I feel like Lucky in *Waiting for Godot*, stumbling after an elongated Pozzo at the end of his rope. Moving together like this is new to me, all my Scottish routes had been done on belay. Rope's a bloody nuisance, always threatening to entangle with my front points, catch round a rock, or pull tight. There are dozens of crevasses up here. Most of them we step over, a few we jump. It's all happening too fast, too much to attend to. We come to a wide crevasse with a snow ledge in the middle. This one needs a combination jump – land on the ledge with one foot, tense and continue the jump to land on the other.

Picture it. Feel it inside yourself. It's not a heave, more like an ice dance, Alex says.

He goes ahead, making it look easy, positively graceful. He digs in his cramps and waits, takes in the rope till it's taut to me. Go for it . . .

Scarcely balletic, but I got across. Another stumble on the far side, still tending to catch on these crampons. 'Don't land on the front of your feet – you'll just trip over your points. Land on the heel, let your momentum carry you forward.' I try it over the next few jumps, feels a lot better. Then a double jump, to one leaf of ice, to another, then across to the far side. Not so bad this, could get quite into it. Sure makes the heart beat faster . . .

After twenty minutes of this, I begin to have time to look up from my feet. What we're in now is a fantasy wonderland. We move past great boulders perched like glowering skulls on slender snow pedestals. Around us are leaning towers of ice, slabs of snow some 40 feet high that must carry a hundred tons, wild gulches, broken pinnacles, white canyons curved like throats, caves like open jaws. All threatening, all inhuman, dead and wildly beautiful.

As the sun gets higher, the snow and ice surface is cut and scored by dozens of rivulets and streams. It's like walking over the hide of an immense white animal. Every so often we feel a shudder, hear the slither or thud as the animal stirs and another overhang collapses, or boulder finally falls off its perch. Alex grins maniacally, leans over a crevasse and bellows down, 'Wake up, Bertha!' Then we come on the first of the glacier pools, a strange blue-green, still as a watchful eye. It's a reverse of the natural order, seeing water on top of ice instead of the other way round. This whole place is a reversal, a negative of reality.

It's unreal, the product of a deranged imagination. It's the set of a low-budget sci-fi movie, *They Came from the Baltoro*. It's a blow-up of a world seen through a microscope – only there have I seen such chaos, breathtaking anarchy, a world in dissolution. It is so stunningly novel and bizarre and beautiful that I nearly walk straight into a crevasse for looking about me.

Alex's eyes are shining. This is his world up here. To the others it's an unpleasant necessity they'd rather do without, to him it's wondrous and inspiring. 'Right, time to go to school,' he says, and proceeds to give a crash course in glacier techniques.

He explains the procedure if one of us falls in a crevasse: the other kicks in with crampons and axe and tries to hold him. If he succeeds, he quickly makes a secure belay – a sling round a spike, or put in an ice screw. Then, if necessary, he can get out of the rope system and help his partner. Who, if not injured and still conscious, should either climb out with axes or tie prussik knots to the rope he's hanging from, clip them to his harness, and climb up the rope with their aid.

So I tried putting in ice screws, then prussiking up a 30-foot ice wall. It took ages, was very cumbersome. The knots work like jumars – push one up, step on the attached sling, push up the waist one, then sit back on it and push up the other. The kind of thing that's straightforward enough in rehearsals, but could be tougher on the night. I hoped that night wouldn't come.

Then we set off on a follow-my-leader through the lower parts of the Icefall, to become accustomed to hurrying down 45-degree ice slopes, traversing, contouring, jumping, chimneying. It's hard work with the pack on. It's very like learning to drive a car – an impossible number of details to coordinate and dangers to watch out for, demanding a great deal of nervous energy. Got to watch my feet all the time, keep the rope between us neither too slack nor too tight, keep it from snagging, and always the head turning, turning, checking out the possible dangers above – a tottering overhang, a boulder on a pedestal that could give, rocks frozen into the slope above that could start to roll any minute . . . Yes, exhausting but exhilarating as we hurry between leaning white walls, past glacier pools, through tunnels of green and white, across dark crevasses, stickleback ridges, following clear trickling streams. All is bright and glittering, it is wonderful to be alive and moving and solving problems with the sun on your back and the air so thin and clear.

Alex sets me at a couple of perhaps 80-degree walls of ice. I take the small axe out from the harness loop and, with the larger 'walking' axe in my other hand, front-point up them. Alex looks rather surprised. I explain that ice climbing is the one thing I've been trained to do and that in comparison with Scotland this ice is perfect, no problem at all. It's great to be doing something familiar, to feel with surprise and pleasure, 'Yes, I can do this.'

And from that high point we cut down to the Brew Tent. It looks unlikely and desolate, a blotch of blue slumped in a small flat area below the Icefall. Off with the sacks. Alex puts up the single pole, then starts raking out squares of cardboard, stove, billy, packets of cocoa, coffee, a couple of Granola bars . . .

Five minutes later, sitting on cardboard, propped up on our packs, stripped down to our thermal underwear, we're lounging in the sun with all the ease kings are supposed to have but seldom do. The brew is just coming to the boil, we take our rest and look around our kingdom. There's nothing to compare with the peace that follows endeavour – except perhaps the relaxation after making love, but without the occasional sadness we have at perfection not quite attained, or perfection gained and now slipping away.

No, this is peace, perfect peace. Even Alex is content to let silence have its way. A faint whisper of wind, a near or distant slither, the rattle of stonefall, a Whumph! as some boulder drops and sends vibrations through the ice and up our backs. The Mustagh behind us, shattered granite cliffs on either side, looking down the glacier to the soaring Up Yours of the Lobsang Spire . . . Ourselves lying back here on this little island of safety . . . The senses ripple out, then echo back. Inside and out, everything is clear and uncluttered.

I make our customary cocoa-and-coffee brew, pass one over. Alex digs out a packet of K2, passes one over. Reclining in this white world, I have a brief vision of the two of us as unlikely sages taking our ease on the cloud banks of heaven in our thermal underwear and glacier goggles. Our laughter rings in the silence.

We talk idly as the day heats up. Alex talks about his strange upbringing in the Caribbean, the marvels of Yosemite, guiding and load-carrying in the Cascades. We swap stories, talk of books, places, our plans and ambitions. His bizarre humour and constant clowning have perversely made him difficult to know; for the first time we start to become intimate. We talk of Mal the eternal romantic optimist, of Sandy the taciturn Scot with 90 per cent of himself kept below the surface, like a mellow iceberg. Of Burt whom he describes as a showroom jock – 'He wants to squeeze the mountains and put them on a wall. I like to let the mountains squeeze me.'

Eventually it gets too hot to be comfortable. The light is so powerful up here. It comes leaping off the ice, frying the skin and hurting the eyes even through goggles. So we pick up rope and axes and go for another jaunt, into rather wilder country this time. Alex keeps exclaiming over the changes in the week since he was last up here – a new crevasse here, a boulder disappeared there, the whole entrance to the Icefall changed utterly. We jump over the ruins of yesterday's bridges, tread gingerly on today's. Up here, the normal pace of creation and destruction is speeded up a hundred times.

One of my crampons comes off halfway up a 30-foot leaf of ice. I scramble up with difficulty, very annoyed at myself. Alex points out with heavy irony that this isn't too good a thing to happen in the middle of the Icefall. This training, as everyone emphasizes, is to enable me to move through the dangerous sections as fast as anyone else. It's as safe a place to hang around as the wrong end of a shooting range.

I refrain from pointing out that I was aware of this and I don't go about shedding crampons for the fun of it. I strap on the offending article so tight that I sprain my wrist and have to go easy on it the rest of the day. And still that crampon came loose again. Well, that's one thing I'll have to sort out.

After another hour's downright hard work, we return to the Brew Tent. I make another brew, feel good but tired. The day up here is good acclimatization as well as practice; another thousand feet up, next time we can sleep up here. 'Slowly, slowly,' as Alex always says. It seems to work.

Mid-afternoon, we rather reluctantly collapse the Brew Tent and set off back down. The crevasse jumps come more easily now, cooler and more controlled. It's the sort of thing that sounds worse than it is. I begin to see what Alex means about these jumps: don't try to heave yourself over, it's more letting your centre of gravity flow across the gap. A transfer rather than a leap. When I hit one of the combination jumps right, it feels oddly graceful and pleasing inside, as near to dancing as one can get, wearing crampons and a rucksack.

But our exit from the glacier to the rubble above the Ibex Trail is the most unpleasant move of the day. It has fallen apart entirely since the morning. We are faced with a semicontrolled slide down mud over black ice, hoping to brake on a couple of loose rocks, then without pausing jump right across a gulf between ice and rock. We have, rather foolishly, left our crampons back at the collapsing Rock House. So no grip. Again foolishly, Alex goes first, very tentative, then, slipping down the slope, just catches the rocks, twists sideways and is standing on solid ground, looking very relieved.

I look down at it. With Alex below me, there can be no belay. Only 30 feet down. But if I slip up here, it will put me out of the game. And the nearest hospital? This is stupid.

Slowly slowly edge onto the mud, crouched, keeping my centre of gravity down, not committing myself till the last minute, down we go . . . oh shit – jump!

Fine thing, terra firma.

'This Bertha bitch gets worse every day,' Alex mutters. 'One of these days she's gonna swallow somebody right up.' I smile, not particularly amused. I know the danger's there, I'd just rather not talk about it. But it's wonderful to sit again at the Cave, pull off the Koflachs, untie rope, unbuckle harness, swap ice axe for ski pole. Quiet relief, contentment, done for the day.

Arrive in Base Camp to be greeted by Jon, Sandy and Jhaved. They've been good to me, not patronizing, seeming to appreciate this is a big deal for me. Sandy's shaved off his beard – does this signify we're about to get serious?

Sitting in the Mess Tent tonight, I realize we're down to the hard core now. The Four Aces, a Poet and a Jester. Together we're going to crack this mountain.

You've got to believe it.

Mal radios at 6.00 to announce their safe arrival at Camp 2 with coils of rope for fixing the ice slope up to the Col. They've filled in the rest of the day playing chess – Tony is still winning – and listening to music. Thompson Twins: 'You Take Me Up'.

We sit up till 8.00, unusually late for here. The hurricane lamp lights on cheekbones, throws shadows round eyes. Hairy, dark-eyed Jhaved squats by the stove, Jon is sprawled back on massacred boxes, Alex spinning the preposterous yarn of Burt, Sybil and the possum, while Sandy grins and nods, hunched over his sewing, myself sitting on the bag of flour taking it all in. With the wind outside, the lamplight and the fluttering tent, it feels as if we're at sea, on some voyage of adventure through the dark.

This is what I've always wanted. It comes to me with sudden conviction as I look round my companions. There was a special warmth and closeness in our conversation this evening, a reaffirmation of our comradeship and common endeavour. The others noted it in their diaries too.

'Good value, eh?' says Sandy about something, as he says about almost anything, and laughs. He and Jon are clearly enjoying normality after six days on the hill, their faces look less swollen now. They want rest, lots of food, privacy and new company – the good things of life, to be stored away for the drawn-out famine of living at altitude.

I'm writing this by candlelight, my first night in Adrian's tent. Clothes, gear, tapes, letters all strewn where I bundled them in this morning when Kath and I packed up our old tent. She should be in Lilligo tonight, lying under the stars I shouldn't wonder, loving it. There's a curious, resonant hollowness inside, loving someone at a distance. 'But that's all right,' I hear Sandy say inside my head, 'it's all good jest, eh?'

I smile, write this down, blow out the light.

The next day was one of comparative inactivity. Mal and Tony radioed to say they were pretty shagged out, the weather looked dubious and the pressure was dropping, so they were coming back to Base. That was fine with us. They'd carried the fixed ropes to Camp 2; now it would be Jon and Sandy's turn to push on ahead with the arduous task of fixing them.

So we watched their tiny figures come round the corner of the Ibex Trail. As usual, everyone drifted out to meet the returning labourers. Funny how we always need to touch them – a pat on the back, a handshake – as if to assure ourselves of their reality. They do look a bit distant and strange at first, just as Sandy and Jon did. Their faces are swollen with water retention, their eyes slightly glazed with fatigue and distance, as if part of them were still up there in the white world.

'Here you are, youth,' Mal says, and tosses over his diary. They drop their packs and slump down in the warm sunlight to talk and drink their way back to normality.

A dull headache for me today, probably a reaction to yesterday's altitude gain. I sit on a rock above Base Camp, watching the summit of Masherbrum pluck white scarves of spindrift out of blue sky. Clouds come and go all day as the hours drift by.

Porters turn up with food loads from Askole – sugar, salt, rice, flour. They also bring news that the helicopter had come for Burt and Donna, who are presumably in Skardu by now.

'A nonchalant day,' Sandy recorded. 'Jon and I feel as though we've recouped our tranquillity. Reinstated our fundamental desire to assault this unremitting mountain again. Yearning now to scale to the Col, to see the remainder of the summit ridge. Will it shrug us or accept us?'

It's a rare night that finds us all together – possibly the last one till we're done here one way or another. Expeditions are a constant coming and going, and the different teams inside them tend to meet only briefly on the hill. So while this was just another casual evening in the Mess Tent of reminiscence and climbing talk as the reggae crackled and the brews kept coming, it was made precious by its transience.

We're all so typical of ourselves. Jon sprawled, Sandy smiling and planning, Mal hunched forward, smoking, Tony being earnest and enthusiastic. And me . . . Oddly enough, I think little of how I appear to them. Waste of energy, really. But I was forced to think about it after Jon brought me his notebook today and murmured, 'It's quite nice, really, like having a confessor.' I was pleased that much of his initial reserve about having A Writer along seems to have left him.

I opened it at random and read '. . . Candlelight has only two associations – expeditions and romance. Andrew and Kath a lovely couple though maybe they wouldn't like to be thought of like that! Kath bouncier and happier than I'd expected. Andrew receptive, professional, shy and modest.' Who, me? Really? Aw, go on . . . 'Some of the initial panic has left them as they relax into an environment they feel increasingly at home in . . .'

I lay back in my tent and considered this. Yes, when we set out I was probably trying too hard both to 'fit in' and to be seen doing my job. And only made myself obtrusive as a result. Now I'm simply here, caught up in it, getting on with it, feeling confident enough to be myself. How odd it is to read about yourself, to see your own name in print. I must remember this when writing about the others, how it must feel for them too. Must make it clear that whatever I write is not gospel, not judgement, just the mood of the moment. I'm not here any more to judge or analyse these people. Perhaps I was at the beginning. Now they're my friends and companions; I don't observe, I *react*.

Reading through Mal and Jon's diaries, I'm fascinated, and touched by their trust. Jon's is elliptical, shot through with curious insights and brief bursts of emotion. Mal's is detailed and solid, tender about Liz, straightforward.

Sandy that night was writing in his tent:

. . . An interesting realization which has only now penetrated the side-roads of my inadequate head. Andrew asked for access to our diaries. This I like but ask myself now Hey, youth! Are you writing as you normally choose? Am I recording my real feelings, or only ones that I think that other people think I should have? Good value, that, I enjoy when my head asks my head such questions. Another boulder to look under. Should I be clear-headed, or inebriated? Is this expedition permanent or transitory? Never been in this position before, find the idea entertaining . . . But I am as I am, as I have been educated and reared to be, slightly off-track but who the hell ain't? Anyhow, if I live long enough, perhaps I'll look back through these scribbles and shall be able to decipher my rudimentary simplicity. That's okay. Yes, I think so. Reality – fictitious word, that. What's it mean? I wonder what Alex's Zen dictionary says for it.

But sleep now. 'Me, Myself, I' on the headphones – why did Andrew give me that cassette? I wonder what he intended. Remember to ask the youth that . . . The more I know him the more I like him – or am I just writing false face words again . . . Don't know, I've only been here for twenty-eight years!

But sleep now, drift to a better place, an equally pretty paradise, hello, Dominique . . .

Four diaries, four inner worlds drifting in the mountains, touching like soap bubbles and bouncing away again. It's obvious that all the people we meet, even the most apparently straightforward, have their complex, fervent inner life. Yet we keep forgetting it. The diaries are a salutary reminder that we're each a unique world in ourselves, and that there are as many expeditions as there are members of that expedition. This book is even more subjective than I'd originally conceded.

Jon and Sandy set off this morning, 18 July, to fix rope up to the Col. One day to Camp 1, another to Camp 2, then probably two days fixing the ropes, and another day to come back. It seems so drawn out and laborious. This is the brutal, unspectacular stage of the climb, the time of sheer slog with little apparent gain, the real testing time. When it's hard to motivate yourself, when you can no longer remember a good reason for all this pain and repetition.

But get up they do, and as we watch them trudge up the Ibex Trail for what must be the tenth time, I think of Jon's summary of the three essential abilities of a Himalayan climber:

1. To get up in the morning
2. To keep putting one foot in front of the other
3. Tolerance.

All of which Sandy has in abundance. Massive competence and backbone, without the obvious brilliance of others I've climbed with. Very reassuring to sometimes sense his doubts, though! *Inshallah* we will emerge from this trip firm friends – we already behave a bit like a long-married couple, thinking similarly, tolerating each other's fetishes, arguments over in seconds.

– The sheer mundaneness of Himalayan climbing! Why should one have to physically suffer so much to appreciate this scenery? Is this why museums are always freezing?

Mal and Tony luxuriate in getting up late, eating and drinking as often and as much as they want. Tony, by far the cleanest and tidiest of us, sets off for a wash in the stream twenty minutes away. Today they're resting, tomorrow they'll be restless. I'm amazed and moved at these lads' stamina and persistence, epitomized for me in Mal's dogged, head-down trudging walk. It seems to say, 'This may not be fun or fast, and I'm not feeling very well today, and I've forgotten why I'm doing this – but I'm damned if I'll stop.'

Restless myself, on impulse I packed a light sack and set off up the Mustagh glacier towards 'China Mountain'. Good going at first, feeling strong and exhilarated as so often in the mornings here. Good to be alone, good to be moving and making my own decisions. Then the glacier became scored by fissures, which deepened into crevasses; I jumped them with increasing difficulty till I came on a fifteen-foot wide one with overhanging walls. No crampons, rope or ice axe. So I follow it along, cross lower down, come on another one, thread round it . . . In twenty minutes I was way off my course and could not really remember by what tortuous route I'd arrived there. Get out of this one, Greig.

There seemed to be an exit right that might take me off the glacier onto the rubble and grass beyond our washing stream. I do it, as fast as possible, over rubble-strewn ice, across a couple of narrow bands of ice like slices of a 500-foot-deep loaf of bread, a precarious slide and jump down a mud slope, quickly under an overhanging section, then clawing up the mud and boulder pinnacle on the far side.

I regained the grass, heaving, nearly sick with the sudden exertion. I'd been out of my depth, got into a bad situation, got out of it. All good training.

I carried on parallel to the Mustagh glacier, on the boulder fields and scrubby pasture below the cliffs on my right. A couple of hours later, I came to a sudden plateau. It was roughly the size and shape of a football field that had been crumpled slightly by a giant hand. The polo field.

Mohammed had talked about it. 'Up there,' he'd said, waving to the west, 'Afghan and Balti play polo with horses. Long time ago, big field.' And here it was. I wandered about its undulations, trying to picture the crowd that once jostled here, the fierce, boney faces, vivid scarves, the reek of horse sweat, the shouting and jeers . . . They still play Balti polo in Chitral and Gilgit, in a roughhouse stylee, and claim the game originated among the mountain people here. Lost in a dream, I passed ruins of rock houses, a rickle of stones that must once have been summer shielings or staging posts on the long trek between China and India. I'd seen those deserted, haunting mounds of stone before, in the ruined crofts dotted over the Highlands.

I sat back against an old hearth and dreamed in the sunlight while the wind crept over stone and grass. Up here in the mountains, human life and human time are so evidently of little account. We're a passing flicker across the land. This feels just right. I'm glad we don't stain it with our desires, our fear, greed, delusions of importance, money, arrogance, cruelty, hopes . . . All this must surely have passed through here for hundreds of years, and now there's only an unlikely polo field and some heaps of stone. So be it. That's what's so uplifting about these mountains – they're one of the very few parts of the world we haven't affected or fucked up. They're too big for us. And the few who come here come not to master but to be mastered, not to squeeze but to be squeezed . . .

It feels as if I've finally dumped a rucksack I've been carrying round for years. I feel light, innocent, uplifted. I've dropped the burden of my wasted, suffering, self-important race with its tragedies, hypocrisies and its near-mad leaders who will in all likelihood destroy much of this planet in the next thirty years. I've dropped the burden of myself.

For really we don't matter much, and this is a relief. My life is not important, my worries, hopes, losses, triumphs, are of little account. In the eternal, ever-shifting mountains, under the sky and wind, we flicker by like shadows.

For me now, there is the cool wind, the sun on my face, the warm rock at my back. I am alone on 'the roof of the world'. My happiness has a quality I can never describe.

We woke on the 19th to rain drumming on our tents and heavy cloud steaming up the Baltoro. Mustagh was completely blanked out. Jon radioed to say they were staying put at Camp 1.

So today was a festerday. We sat festering in the Mess Tent, talking fitfully. There comes a time when there seems little left to say. If this was the beginning of the monsoon bad weather we had been expecting, we could be here for a long time. Time hung heavy for all of us, but Tony seemed the most restless. He hated sitting about and fretted for activity. The rest of us were capable of retreating into books and solitude, but he always had to be doing.

Eventually we decided to make something, anything. At random I suggested a game of darts. An hour's ingenuity produced a missile constructed from an umbrella spoke, bolts, tent repair kit, candle wax and flights made from a John Players packet. On the lid of a cardboard box we drew in Mustagh, and situated little triangular tents at the appropriate places up it. You had to spear one tent before you could proceed up to the next one.

We were enjoying ourselves, like children on a rainy day, and competed seriously. After a couple of hours Tony and I had reached Camp 3, while Mal was still stranded at Base. Meanwhile Alex had given up in disgust and gone off to get stoned in his tent.

It didn't look likely that we'd ever make the tiny Camp 4 bivvy. We sat around after lunch while Tony made a ball. He knotted climbing rope, melted the ends in, then wound yards of tape over the whole. He threw it over to me; I caught it. It was very hard and heavy, not enough bounce for football. 'Right,' I said, 'anyone for cricket?'

Two porter staves bound together made a bat, an empty jerry can was the wicket, cardboard boxes were strategically placed fielders. It had stopped raining now, and Alex lay propped against a boulder, stoned and speechless, as we proceeded to play cricket for over two hours at 14,500 feet.

It was desperate and very serious and very funny. We believe it is a record for high altitude cricket, and can recommend it to any expedition as an ideal form of acclimatization training. With one batsman, one bowler and a wicketkeeper, there was no rest at all. We were all gasping for air, doubled up with laughter and exertion. I was heavily bruised by Duff's bodyline bowling, he put his knee out, and Tony pulled his forearm muscle. Eventually we hadn't the strength to bowl or hit another ball, and limped into the Mess Tent for a brew.

'English very strange,' Jhaved said, shaking his head.

'Too right, youth – but the Scots are worse.'

We were shattered, but we'd needed it. Now the clouds and barometer were rising, and Jon and Sandy radioed to say they'd be moving up to Camp 2 tomorrow. Over our evening dal and retorts we discussed the best game plan for Alex and me. Mal and Tony in particular disliked the Icefall. It was a concentration of what they called objective danger, that is, risk they could do little about. Stonefall, collapsing snow bridges, towers that suddenly crumble. There was an area near the top of it they described as walking over the dome of St Paul's, where they could actually feel the ringing hollowness beneath their feet. There was no way round it. It would have to fall in some time.

Listening to their stories, I agreed I should go there as little as possible, but the distinction between objective danger and normal being-in-control climbing didn't really exist for me. All my danger felt subjective, and I didn't expect to feel in control when climbing. What I'd seen of the Icefall so far was wild enough, quite disturbing; I could see it was dangerous but I didn't *feel* it. I'd been more gripped safely clipped to an exposed belay in Glencoe, which felt dangerous though it wasn't.

The upshot of our discussion was this: Alex and I should go only once through the Icefall. Once we'd gone through to Camp 1, instead of coming back to Base, we'd head on up to 2 the next day. Which of course could well create acclimatization problems: we'd be sleeping at Camp 1 without having previously been up there, then going further up to 2 and possibly trying to do the same there. That was a bit of a risk, but on the whole we preferred it to going up and down through the Icefall several times.

It was our sideshow. Obviously the lads, shorn of support climbers, had no time or energy to assist us. We must carry our own tentage, gas and food and bags. As long as we didn't impinge on the summit attempt, we could do what we wanted. At the same time, we wouldn't be able to help much in that attempt.

It was a delicate situation, and I was relieved to have our plan and position clearly stated and accepted. As usual, I was apprehensive and excited. The Col was my summit, trained and planned for and contemplated ever since Mal first walked into my kitchen in what now seemed another world, a world before climbing ... We'd go for it when the weather coincided with a natural break in the other lads' activities.

I fitted heel bars to my crampons so they wouldn't come adrift again, looked through all my gear and packed everything I'd need in my sack. Now we'd just wait for that opening, and go for it.

This is what I came for.

I stood outside my tent that night, looking at the moon shadow of Lobsang cast across the glacier like a stupendous spike on a sundial. I waited in the cool wind till excitement subsided and peace came. But my last sensation as I crawled into my bag was that of the sharp pang earlier in the day when I'd found Kath-

leen's nail clippers in the flattened grass where our tent had been.
I'd put her out of my mind for the last few days.

It's the little things that get under your guard.

Jon and Sandy woke at 3.30 to the whisper of snow on their tent.
They looked outside. Maybe one-and-a-half inches of fresh snow.
Which could create avalanche conditions further up the mountain, particularly on the White Tiger slope below Camp 2. At
6.00 they decided to set off in any case and see how it looked.

Sandy plodded ahead, remembering how when the weather
was bad in Chamonix he could nip down to the Bar National for a
beer, or drive through the tunnel and head for the Dolomites or
the windsurfing and sun-soaked beaches of the Calanques, with
Dominique, or shoot the breeze with the goatherds and wine,
pumpkin and apple growers in the Loire valley . . . He thought of
his brother fishing for marlin off Bermuda, must be good jest,
that . . .

Jon trudged behind, keeping an eye on the weather and the
build-up of snow. It was their third time up to Camp 2, so they
were reasonably acclimatized and moving well. Just the same, he
did rather resent the weight of his pack, stuffed with food, gear
and gas cylinders. If only Adrian and Mohammed had made one
more carry to 2 . . . But they hadn't and that was that. It's hard
work doing all your own support, too hard maybe. Who's going
to burn out first – Mal and Tony, or us two?

Tony was revving in frustration at Base Camp. Another day's
rain, probably snow further up, little chance of progress. Over
breakfast he confessed he'd been awake half the night thinking
about the summit ridge, envisaging all the possibilities and
problems. Not through fear, but pure mouthwatering anticipation and desire. The Tower was a beautiful mountain, daunting,
pure somehow, a worthy challenge. He was restless, distracted,
his imagination working overtime, his eyes distant.

The youth had summit fever.

'When I first got here, I was happy just to do some climbing.

But now it's definitely on, I want more than that. I don't care if I'm first or fourth on the summit, but I definitely want it.' He looked up from his brew, flushed at the thought. Typical of Tony, I thought as I smiled at his enthusiasm, always more ingenuous than the others. They're always very dismissive about their summit ambitions. 'I just like climbing' is the standard line – true, but a load of baloney as well.

Summit: at last the word had been said. From now on it hovered, unspoken, at the back of every conversation. They all seemed to have suddenly realized that if Jon and Sandy fixed up to the Col, the way would be open to the top. So whoever arrived at Camp 3 at the right time . . . Hmm . . .

I could sense their minds turning over the permutations, and hear it in Jon's voice over the radio. If he and Sandy had to come down after fixing the Col, then Mal and Tony would take a tent up and establish Camp 3. And then . . . Would they go on, could they continue with two weeks less acclimatization than Sandy and Jon? And would that be fair, after the extra work the others had put in? Did it matter?

Competition and cooperation. It was interesting to see these two highly developed impulses struggling inside each of them. We'd got to the stage now when carrying a load for someone else – food and gas, for instance – diminished one's chances of first crack at the summit. And with this deteriorating weather, there might well only be one shot at the top . . .

Mal hunches over his cocoa, distant and uncommunicative as Tony babbles on. He lights another cigarette. His eyes are directed at the dirt floor, but his thoughts are clearly not. He frowns, seems about to speak, doesn't.

I think this was the background to the tensions created by the midday radio call from the lads. They'd made Camp 2, where it was now snowing steadily. They were faced with the prospect of having to sit it out for a few days. They were getting very tired of trying to eat freeze-dried food and would like more and better munchies.

That is, will someone bring some up?

A notable lack of enthusiasm at our end as everyone calculates. Mal and Tony are already nursing summit hopes for the next time they go up; taking food for the others plus their tent for Camp 3 would probably rule that out. It would mean coming back down to 1, perhaps even Base Camp, before setting off again. Not a very exciting prospect. Alex is suffering from his recurrent bug and doesn't feel like going anywhere. I realize that if he and I go, to have any chance at the Col, we'd have to return to Base Camp for more provisions for ourselves, which would mean repeating the Icefall.

'Let them eat freeze-dried,' someone mutters. 'If they wanted more retorts and munchies, they should have carried them up themselves.'

That's how it looked from Base Camp. Mal and Tony had done all their own support, plus carried up more rope. They still had to take their own climbing gear up, and food for their summit bid, and the Camp 3 tent. So why should Sandy and Jon have any more support?

From Camp 2, it looked quite different. They'd been here two weeks longer, had put in more hard work, trailblazing and load-carrying. They were still the cutting edge of the Expedition. They should be able to call on support to maximize their chances. Sandy noted in his diary: 'I sincerely hope that the lads at Base Camp have not decided to forget about teamwork and just to get their own deal out of this Mustagh trip. It would be disenchanting if this were the case . . .'

Such conflicting viewpoints are inevitable on a trip like this. Each is quite reasonable and legitimate to whoever holds it. The quality of an expedition turns on how such situations are handled.

In this case, the situation is handled by not forcing it to a conclusion. 'We'll think about it,' we say. 'Please do,' they say, and sign off.

More rain. It's enforced idleness and boredom that lead to this endless speculation and these tensions. I feel suddenly fed up with the limitations and privations of life up here. I miss people to talk with about something other than climbing. I miss Kathleen and our easy intimacy. I miss writer friends, I miss wine and meals served on tables. Life here is so narrow and confined it's like living in the most severe of monasteries. One experiences very intensely, but in a very narrow range. Everything is black and white and blue – I feel acutely the lack of the warm colours, the subtle colours, the sights and conversations and affections that round out our lives.

Lying in this sleeping bag is a metaphor for life here: it's narrow and confined and I long for the double bed and the woman I share it with.

I spent the afternoon putting my tent in order. The Walkman, tapes, books and jotters laid out within reach of my sleeping bag. Candles, spare munchies, head torch, aspirin and sleeping pills all in their little pockets. Our tents are our kingdom, our refuge and our prison. They're the only solitary place on an expedition, the privacy we respect and guard, escape from, return to at night. Their contents shore up our identity; our letters from home, our books and tapes, the personal talisman we each have (in my case, a smooth stone picked at random from a Canadian beach), remind us who we are. Which at times, at certain times on days and nights like this, is something we feel slipping away like an avalanche slope.

Evening: Mozart on the headphones, rain on the tent. Together they empty the mind, displacing all else as I lie in the fading brown light. Till sleep comes I wander, an ironic, nostalgic ghost, through the streets and attics and bars and bedrooms, the fields and classrooms of my past.

Saturday
Sandy (21 July): 2.30 a.m., still snowing as I crawl in my sleeping bag to peer out the tent, also mist swirling and sneaking around. 'Today's off,' I thought, with probably four or five inches of new snow, powder lying up to the Col on the old hard snow. Classic avalanche conditions. I wondered what Mal and Tony were planning, they'd still be asleep right now. 3.30. Alarm went again, looked out, still snowing. Jon and I after quite profound consideration decided to go back to sleep . . .

That morning at Base Camp was all freshness after night rain. Wind, sunshine, blue sky and clouds – a world brand new and innocent. Jhaved and I sat looking across to Masherbrum while he talked about his village in the valley behind it, of clear streams, trees, apricots and girls. Like to go there sometime, it sounds like the Promised Land. Jhaved grins and nods. 'Mr Andy stay long time.' 'I'd like to.'

We sit in silence, full of a sense of spaciousness and ease. We've nothing to do and nowhere to go. Sitting with Haji Mahdi I always had the same feeling of peace, of the fullness of the moment.

12.00. Jon on the radio. He reported there's too much fresh snow up there to climb today, but they're hoping to fix rope to the Col tomorrow, weather permitting. The prospect of some progress raises our spirits – at times it seems as if we'll never move again. I remember the Spanish expedition we met on their way back from Gash 2 – out of twenty-five days there, they spent twenty confined to their tents. It could still happen to us. But this waiting too is part of Himalayan climbing.

Jon and Sandy still requesting more retorts and munchies. They must have a possible summit bid on their minds. We say nothing very definite, but indicate a certain lack of keenness. Alex is seriously sick today and can scarcely walk, so that rules him and me out. We'll see.

High point of our day was custard, solid pink kids' stuff. Biggest crisis: we're coming to the end of our tobacco. We hadn't expected to be smoking up here, so didn't bring enough. Never again! These enforced shortages don't break the habit, they merely confirm it. Yet I don't really miss alcohol. Our fantasies now are all about food. A pint of MacEwan's 80/- in the Athletic Arms, Edinburgh (the finest pint in Scotland and therefore in the world) seems as distant and unlikely as sex, which is another of life's goodies we scarcely miss up here.

Sandy: We read, listen to music, make brews. Jon breaks wind now and then, we chat occasionally. Then the sun shone through mist making a big yellow ring. Rock falling and powder snow avalanches. I pottered around awhile, inspecting some gear, checked out the bivvy tent, tried to get Jon to speak with a Black Isle accent. Spoke with the lads. Mal and Tony intend to come to Camp 1 tomorrow, but all plans tentative. When the mist cleared I could see traces of the rope we'd already fixed up towards the Col, and the red dot of lead rope at the end. Good to know it's still there. Tomorrow, *inshallah* . . .

Sandy woke at 2.00 a.m. on 22 July, by 2.30 his brain began to play the game. Lighting the Gaz stove, he knocked over the billy can of half-frozen water from last night, but was pleased to note he didn't curse or swear. His thoughts and emotions were in control. Good. That struggle for control in more and more extreme situations is the main reason for my being here, he thought, the reason for my breath turning to hoar frost in the head-torch light. We're moving on today. This is where it's at.

He and Jon set forth two hours later at first light. A fine, crisp morning. In their sacks was 220 metres of fixing rope apiece, pegs, krabs, snow stakes and deadmen. They jumared across the 'schrund and clipped into the bottom of the fixed rope.

Sandy: Being foolhardy, I was in front and had to excavate for the rope. Sometimes it was set very deep and I had to hack laboriously to see it, then pull and put my full weight on the jumar to free it. Twice I came to ice screws which were hanging loose, melted out by the sun on previous days. Replacing them, I moved on. Up with the jumar, hack at the ice – free the rope – up with the jumar – free the rope – move my feet, free the rope – up with the jumar, glancing back to check Jon's presence, checking the belays . . . And on it went till I came to the previous high point, about halfway up the slope. Felt some sense of achievement there, put in an ice screw and hung off. I felt very well then, very precise, very awake . . .

Mal: Definite lack of enthusiasm today, no drive, no strength, headache. Can hardly believe that it's altitude-induced because we've been up here two nights already with no problems. Most likely some kind of bug from Base. Could do without that for tackling the Icefall . . .

I sit perched on a rock above the Cave, looking up the Icefall towards the Tower. Alex was sick again this morning, so I decided to accompany the lads to the top of the Ibex Trail. It's hard to imagine that the trail was a big deal to me just a couple of weeks ago. Something's changing.

It's 7.00 a.m., the sun is moving down the glacier which is starting to wake up, groan and stretch. The whole mass of it falls apart on the Icefall slope as a loaf of sliced bread would if you took the wrapper off. I'm watching Mal and Tony pick their way over the crust towards the Icefall and Camp 1. It'll be my turn tomorrow, *inshallah*. Better try to memorize their route, though it might be quite different tomorrow.

Tony is in front, Mal clearly not feeling too well. In the back of
Tony's mind he's nursing summit possibilities that seem wildly
optimistic to Alex and me. They've only been once to Camp 2, for
God's sake, haven't even slept there. They can't have acclimatized
to a sufficient level. Tony's the one Adrian was most concerned
about – a total revver in the first flush of youth, a classic candidate
for altitude sickness.

A sudden, stomach-lurching crunch from the glacier,
somewhere up where they are now. I see their tiny figures pause,
then set off again. I've come to care about and respect these lads
so much. My friends in the distance and Sandy and Jon, who are
somewhere on the fixed ropes now, are neither gung-ho jocks nor
intellectual seekers of enlightenment. These are ordinary human
beings with an obsession. That obsession has brought out in them
qualities of persistence, patience, endurance, judgement and
courage. These largely physical qualities pushed far enough take
on a spiritual aspect and so become moving.

Enduring fear, danger, hardship and disaster has given them an
unusual degree of self-knowledge. They've lived over and over
the naked confrontation with the self. When life is hanging by a
thread on a mountain, there is no room any longer for evasion
and self-deception; for better or worse you know yourself as you
are. They have looked at death many times. They have known
absolute fear and the struggle to control it. They know how weak
and strong they are.

And yet in other areas they can be as immature, self-deceiving,
hesitant in dealing with life, as anyone else. Climbing a mountain
doesn't make it easier to speak in public or handle a dying
relationship. They're not heroes or sages. In their chosen field
they're aces; outside it they're bumblies, perfectly stumblingly
ordinary. If it wasn't for this I could only admire them, not feel
this affection. It's the coexistence in us of the exceptional and the
ordinary, the exalted and the petty – I look to my left and see the
Tower, its breathtaking purity of line, its inspiring upsurge, and
below it the shambolic mess one has to plough through to arrive
at it. As so often here, the place I'm in completes the thought for
me, embodying it.

Sandy: Aware only of the spindrift cascading, the occasional rock falling
from the South Face, the frequent cracks in the ice I was climbing, the
clouds and mist rolling in and out, snow flakes and Jon, the position of

the sun and how it shone, that was all that affected me, so it was nice but really exhausting. So I led up the first coil, and waited as Jon came up behind with the other coil of fixing rope. I took it as he looked wasted, and led out again . . .

The climbing was getting hard now. I'd come to the foot of the 100-foot chimney that Patey described as Grade 5. Joe Brown could not lead it at the first attempt and had to let the Scot [Patey] take over. That must have been good value without 12-point crampons and inclined picks!

I must admit I was not enthused at having to lead it. It was noon already, and it would be late by the time we got back to Camp 2. Also the snow was falling again, wind blowing, definitely unsavoury! But I decided to go on – I live in a fantasy world, you see . . .

Mal: Arrived Camp 1 round 11.20, very angry to find Jon and Sandy have taken the only spoon up to 2. As Tony said, it's hard to put up with selfishness when we've dragged more retorts up here for them, then find there must be twenty-five two-man packs of freeze-dried here anyway. Still, great news with Jon and Sandy fixing the rest of the rope. Waiting now for 1.00 call to see if they've made the Col . . .

To my right there's a ledge full of pink flowers like primroses. We always exclaim over them when we come up here, they fill our eyes like a silent explosion, a blooming colour in the iris. There's so little organic life up here that a flower or fly or ant seem miraculous. Astonishing how life grips to the smallest niche – a scraping of soil, some snow melt, and there's a scrappy, tenacious Eden: butterflies, bugs, flowers, grass, ibex, ravens, prowled by the invisible snow leopards.

Not only do we notice and delight in every scrap of life here, but our own sense of being is intensified too. At times I'm enormously aware of myself moving among this vast, elemental indifference, the only breathing thing for miles. We cannot but be aware of our weakness and insignificance in this desolation, yet it's oddly uplifting, like looking up at the stars in the blackest of nights.

We're so nearly nothing, but not quite. And that makes all the difference. The mountains teach us humility, but also how much we can achieve when we commit our all.

Sandy: I began to lead the pitch and found it worrying. Ice very hard below six inches of soft snow. Gradually I remembered how to do this, my arms reached and axes stabbed and investigated. Finding good placements, I moved up the main pitch of ice and came upon a length of old white fixed rope. It was frayed and worn by the weathering of twenty-eight years, for it could only have been the good Dr Patey's rope. Good value, eh?

Not much time to think about that, for a new squall hurried me on up. Coming onto the crest of the ridge I felt pleased and wasted. Ethereal. I took a few steps and saw into China. Hey, great, did not try to evaluate or label it, just felt really nice, my mouth probably wide open at the view of peaks shrouded in the mist, only the blue, grey, black and white streaks of the mountain flanks visible.

I took one more step onto the huge cornice – and fell down a hole that opened under my feet. Hell's Teeth, I thought, there can't be a hole here – even though I was in it! I pulled myself out. Looking down, I saw only darkness. My thoughts went to Herman Buhl on Chogolisa, to Pete and Joe on their last trip. I could not believe that I'd fallen into the cornice break. Desperate, yes, I was petrified.

I moved back the way I had come up; after three steps I fell in again, this time right to my shoulders.

Scared, the wind whipped me, although I had the fixed blue cord round my waist as a lead rope I felt LONELY. There was no logic behind these holes hidden below the smooth surface. I felt obtuse, deranged, I thought, Look, youth, you've spent ten years in the Alps, you were on Nuptse West Ridge – how in God's name can there be holes here?

These thoughts took two seconds, I pulled and levered myself out and moved back close to the rock, placed a deadman then a snow stake, tied myself on and took in the ropes . . .

When I returned to Base Camp, Alex looked thinner than ever and pale, but said he felt better. Tomorrow we'll go up to the Brew Tent, sleep there overnight to acclimatize, then go for Camp 1 the next day. Day after we'll go for 2, then return to 1. After that our plans are wide open. We've our own tent, and enough food for six days, so going up to the Col is still an option.

I'm excited and apprehensive as we discuss it. I've had enough inactivity, I want some action.

I also want to get it over with.

Shokat returned round lunchtime, much more buoyant than before.

1.00 p.m. Jon on the radio, the lazy, quasi-cockney accent drifting across the miles.

'. . . Well . . . At the moment we're lying flat on our backs on the ridge . . . We're pretty wasted.'

'So what's the Col like?'

'I wouldn't really call it a col, over.'

I play the straight man. 'What would you call it, then?'

'A tottering heap of shit.' Much laughter and head shaking over that one. Typical Jon, the only one who'll never admit to being moved by mountains. Like 'But have they got the money?', this became one of his classic remarks, applied from then on to everything from Jhaved's pancakes to the interior of Jon's tent.

'What about this tennis-court area that's supposed to be up there?'

'I think it might be in China at the moment . . . No sign of it here, anyway. We can see the ridge in all its awful glory . . . A piece of piss . . . It looks really hard, actually. It's great! And at the top there's loads of cornices, but we might be able to sneak underneath them . . .'

Sandy sat next to Jon, listening to the conversation. It depressed him. He had felt elated on arriving, then shocked to fall into two holes, then elated again. He thought it was wonderful up on the Col, the same Col Jon had just described as 'a tottering heap of shit'. How could this be? It was as if they had entirely different views. Must be the difference in upbringing, he mused, we're so different. I try not to be narrow, but sometimes it gets on my nerves. Then Jon said the summit ridge looked easy, while to me it looked desperate. I knew he was telling them a load of bull – he admitted as much – that I cannot understand. Why? Why must he take that 'I own the place' attitude? However, that's just me, don't worry about it, Sandy, Dominique would say . . .

They signed off, examined the ridge as it humped and soared towards the summit then set off down. Jon went on ahead, Sandy hung back, wanting to be alone. They'd done their bit; they'd fixed rope to the Col. The door was wide open.

It only needed someone to walk in.

So at last the critical phase is approaching; at last I've come to what I sought and feared. The test. Test of what? My skill? Luck? Nerve? I think it over as I wash clothes in the icy stream above Base Camp. Clear water, hot sun on my back, the wind, rattle of boulders over by Lobsang, these tiny flowers – as always, being up here clears my mind for reflection. Time to be honest.

Yes, I've probably come to test all these to some degree. But more than that. Simple curiosity. Not so much 'Because it's there' as *because I'm here*. I've come here not so much to prove something as to experience how I'll react in the face of genuine risk.

Then I catch myself and laugh. Isn't this all rather melodramatic? Well, if I get off with it, it will seem so. But I don't know yet if I will. That's the trouble with being a novice up here – I don't know what I'm up against. But the other lads concede there is real risk, particularly in the Icefall. 'There's maybe a 5 per cent chance of getting wiped out going through there,' Mal said a few days back. Then added casually, 'Probably higher than that for you.' Tony nodded.

That is enough to merit serious reflection. It would be foolish and narrow to suppress or deny the dangers and struggle up ahead. If I make a mistake, I'll be in serious trouble; if I get unlucky, I'll be dead. Acknowledging that and accepting it, as I feel myself doing now, is the most valuable experience that's happened to me on this trip.

Not to stare down into the crevasse till knees tremble and head spins. But to be aware of it, take in its breadth and depth – then jump.

10

The White Tiger

In which the author goes for his summit

23–27 July 1984

Sleepers, aspirin, Mogadon, Bradasol; camera, film; Walkman, notebook, pen; The Farewell Party; *sun screen, shades; Kendal Mint cake, toilet roll.*

Harness, jumar, krabs, slings; thermal underwear, salopettes, sweaters (2), socks (2); Thermafleece, windsuit, gloves, balaclava.

½ tent, 4 hill-food bags, gas, matches.

Lucky stone.

Right now Alex and I are being Glacier Slugs. Lying in our tent below the Icefall, listening to light snow needling against the fabric. Early afternoon in the yellow-brown light; Alex kneels in the vestibule contemplating the steam that signals our next brew. His bony face is calm but gaunt, he's still not too well and it was generous of him to come up today. I pass him a humbug which he accepts silently; I take one for myself – why do they always remind me of my granny? – and carry on writing.

A bit of a stagger up here this morning, with our packs weighing over 50 pounds. The weight and bulk tend to throw one off balance when jumping. As always when I'm keyed up, everything was superclear. Moving on the glacier seemed more natural, less impossibly demanding. The heel bars seem to have fixed my crampons. That's good.

Just one stumble, coming up to the widest crevasse. Wait, look at it, what if I slip, Christ, here goes, oh not so bad. And there's the Brew Tent already. Could really do with one . . .

So we stuck up the single pole of the Brew Tent by way of announcing our arrival, then hacked out a more or less level platform on the ice next to it and put up our tent. Good to unroll the Karrimat and sleeping bag, unpack the Walkman, pills, sweets and notebook, set up the stove . . . How little it takes to make a habitation in the wilderness! How little we need to make ourselves at home! Good feeling, propped up on one elbow here with the bare essentials of life around me. Warmth, the brew Alex just handed me, a cigarette – what more is needed?

Mal: Sandy and Jon just passed through, did the hospitality bit and borrowed the spoon back. They were obviously impressed by the summit ridge, although Sandy said it didn't look as hard as Nuptse – good news.

Very hot, stripped to Y-fronts, listening to Marley, Blondie and reading to pass the hours. Thoughts of home and Liz 5000 miles away. Sometimes this climbing lark seems so unreal, selfish and stupid.

Jon and Sandy came galumphing down through the Icefall mid-morning with the rapid, nonchalant mastery born of years of practice, on their way to Base Camp. 'Get a brew on!' floated across the ice. We had an affectionate reunion. They looked and sounded changed, after a week on the hill they had become true creatures from the Baltoro. Hoarse, glazed, faces burned and swollen, puffy round the eyes, their hair set stiff in the wildest of post-futurist styles, they looked *used*. They looked a fucking mess.

They were totally adapted to their environment.

We all sat on our squares of cardboard, drinking and talking and laughing for all the world as if we were in a pavement café and not amid the shifting wreckage of a glacier 15,500 feet up somewhere in Baltistan. A mood of gaiety and ease seemed to affect us all and our conversation was unusually lively as it ranged over poetry, our LO, the meaning of life and the marvellous futility of human endeavour, reggae dubs, the squalid nature of decaffeinated coffee . . . After a week's absence, we were taking pleasure in each other's company. I talked more than usual, more natural I suppose, not holding back so much for fear of boring them when they asked about my writing and this book. They seemed genuinely intrigued. 'Sounds good jest, youth,' Sandy said, 'do we get to your launching party?' It feels as if so many things have come clear the last few days – my own motivations, this book, Kathleen, what these friends of mine are about. And with that, an excited calm.

I feel balanced, committed and ready.

We went for another romp on the glacier this afternoon. Without packs it was a joy. We did a number of ice slopes in a Scottie stylee, then Alex showed me how effectively one can climb with just one Alpine-style longer axe. I liked that, it's more balletic, more about balance than hit-and-heave. More combination jumps, contouring across slopes, running down them, trying to make all the movements flow together. It's coming much more naturally now, easier to watch feet, rope, around and above as I followed Alex up, down, across, over, under, through the wild ice sculptures, caves, bridges, sweeping wings of ice.

It's as if we were thoughts dancing over the corrugations of a wintry brain.

Or as if a chef had gone overboard on free expression with 100,000 tons of meringue.

We've been chatting on the radio. Mal and Sandy wished us luck. The radio transmits a lot more than information; it gives us encouragement, laughter and support. It's good to hear the voices threading us all together: Mal and Tony taking a day's rest at Camp 1 while Mal gets over his bug, Jon and Sandy now happily piling in the calories at Base Camp.

Night comes suddenly, rising up from the valley below us. The stars are astonishingly bright, the Mustagh ridge glimmers by their light. It looks bigger than ever. It's wonderful to be here. I feel so tiny, yet full of strength.

Faint rustle of wind and water, the distant clatter of rockfall. Up here I always have a sense of stillness and silence, of the utmost gravity. And behind that these pale mountains offer and conceal a stillness and a silence yet more complete, the utter white and calm of death.

But we're alive. Bring us tomorrow! Take me to Camp 2!

Haven't I learned yet? Never assume.

Up at 4.30 in the half-light. Porridge, cocoa, munchies, lying in our bags. Cold up here, but wide awake. I packed carefully, a good way of calming nerves and establishing the kind of concentration needed all day. Gearing up is always quiet as we check and gather ourselves inside and out. Prussik loops, ice screw, spare gloves . . . Steady breathing, calm and steady . . . 'OK, let's go and mess with that mother.'

Our packs are huge, so high I can't tilt back my head to look up. A sharp pain in my lower back after 50 yards.

That was our first mistake of the day.

Then Alex's crampon came away. Something wrong with the straps. That was to recur at frequent intervals. As he bent over to fix it, I noticed how pale and sunken his face had become in the last week. He'd lost weight off his arms and legs too – in fact he looked like a human spider. I couldn't see muscle anywhere; he was running on willpower.

Still, we wound our way on up to the Icefall just as it started to wake up with the sun. 'The bitch is all scrambled since last week,' Alex muttered, and after a couple of false starts set off in a fresh direction. I followed on, as trusting as a conscripted peasant in a medieval army. 'Oh man . . .' Further muttering from up front. Alex backtracked and set off sharp right over a ridge of ice like a frozen wave about to break. All round us now the Tiger bared its gleaming teeth. A deep *whumph* round the corner up ahead.

Alex paused, hesitated, sniffed around like a giraffe suspecting the presence of lions. 'That big fucking boulder's moved fifty yards . . . Shit . . .'

I followed with rapidly diminishing confidence.

Twenty minutes later, after a series of moves that would be hard to reverse, we came to a complete standstill. We'd somehow got boxed into a narrow glacier ravine. In front was a 100-foot-long wall of ice, overhanging and peeling away from the main body of ice behind it. Behind us was a snow bank full of holes, topped with rocks from under which water was dripping on our heads. The left led deeper into country that made this seem tame, and the exit right, by which we'd come in, involved a front-pointing traverse for 30 yards around a wall studded with boulders that suddenly ended over a crevasse.

At this point Alex lost his presence of mind.

We spent forty minutes stuck in one of the most dangerous parts of the Icefall as he cast fitfully this way and that, changing his mind and changing it again. I resigned myself to luck. We were so completely hemmed in that if the overhang fell, or one of the rocks above our heads came out, there would be no way of avoiding it.

I tried to stand and say nothing like a good second. By now he'd thoroughly lost the place and was savagely cursing the weight on his back, the Icefall, the lads for sending him up here with a beginner, and, when I finally offered a suggestion, me. I was being led by someone who was not even pretending to be in control. It was scary as hell.

I saw leadership was not forthcoming and longed briefly for Malcolm's phlegmatic calm. Come back, Duff, all is forgiven! I felt at once resigned and anxious, had both resentment and sympathy for Alex who in turn was very worried, embarrassed and angry. Water was running down the slope hanging over us, a couple of rocks slithered and crunched into the ravine 30 feet away. The glacier was creaking and shifting all around us.

Finally Alex said, 'Well, you can see the options.' I could. I said, 'Let's get the hell out of here', John Wayne stylee. Alex looked relieved. With considerable difficulty we retraced our steps and made it back to the Brew Tent. Dropped the sodding packs. Sat down. There was an awkward silence, neither of us looked at the other.

Then he looked up and said, 'I'm really sorry. I fucked up.'

'No sweat, Alex.' He went and got a brew going, staring moodily into the billy.

That was big of him. I respected and appreciated his apology. But the truth was, yes he had fucked up. He'd got out of his depth and endangered both of us. My faith in him as a leader was shaken.

On the radio, we discussed our situation with Jon and Sandy. They suggested we come down to Base and go up to Camp 1 with them tomorrow. That sounded fine to me, but Alex opted to stay at the Brew Tent. He seemed depressed, angry at himself and withdrawn. So I said fine and set off down.

Wonderful to hit the Ibex Trail again, see the wind stir grass and flowers and smell warm earth. I romped down it in good spirits, looking forward to the usual chapati and mutton lunch. Base is wonderful; it's Shangri-La with flies. Here you can eat and drink and know the ground isn't going to open up beneath you.

Mal: Camp 2 is definite squalor after Camp 1. Ironic that just when you could do with maximum ease and comfort as you go higher, the reverse occurs. A four-man tent with loads of food, then a two-man tent with the unappetizing crumbs left by the scavengers, then a snow hole or bivvy tent with hardly anything. The average man's ambitions in reverse!

I'm neither put off nor desperately disappointed by today's abortive attempt. If that's the worst of the Icefall, I'm up to it mentally and technically. It doesn't freak me out and that's a good knowledge. I'm quite confident about going through it with Jon or Sandy. They've had a day of complete rest and are revved up to get back on the hill. This time they intend to stay up till they succeed or fail. The ropes are up, Mal and Tony should erect Camp 3. All they have to do is bring up more food, climbing gear and go for it.

Question is, will Mal and Tony stay up and try for the summit this time? That would inevitably put them ahead of the others. Does that matter? Is it fair?

And will the weather hold to give them all a chance at it?

Chatting with them tonight, I see the Expedition is accelerating. 'Summit' is a word we suddenly use. All the plans being formulated now are summit plans, after weeks of stocking and establishing this camp and that. This is where things get serious. They're now pushing altitude and pushing their luck.

Alex said it: 'It's like they've been playing checkers for a month, and suddenly today it's chess.' Chess in a hurry – against the weather, each other, dwindling food supplies, and the time they've set aside for Gasherbrum 2.

They're loving it.

So am I.

Sleep now prowling outside my tent. I'm tired, at peace, open to tomorrow. I blow out the candles and let it come in.

First things first – stuck my head out to check the weather. Cold and clear, high grey sky slowly turning blue as the light swells. We're on, then. The familiar pulse of adrenalin hits me as I push into the Mess Tent past 'Brew Me Crazy', and nod to Jhaved. I make myself a triple porridge which is like eating glue, wallpaper paste and a hint of sawdust, and think about the coming day.

Sandy (25 July): Entering the Mess Tent I expressed good morning to the lads with my normal good feeling. No real reply, Jon and Andrew sat there frowning over mugs of chai. Oh well. 'Hi, Jhaved, any chapatis?' 'Lunch only,' he said. I thought, that's no good. Jhaved handed me the chapati bag and I took one for breakfast. I felt that Jon was staring holes in me like the ones I fell down on the Col.

But still felt hungry, so asked Jhaved to make me an omelette. 'Omelette, no climb. Climb, no omelette.' But I took a firm line because I needed protein right then. Jon mentioned some immature thought about 'time'. I did my utmost to ignore this and asked in as open a way as possible if they would care for some also. After very little deliberation, they accepted . . .

It was a tiny incident, typical of a hundred others. The fact that we react to them and remember them may seem very petty but is indicative of the frame of mind one gets into up here: ultrasensitive to the slightest nuance of phrase or gesture, magnifying the smallest selfishness or generosity. So with Sandy's omelette, so with Mal's anger at the missing spoon at Camp 1.

That's why Jon listed tolerance as his third essential Himalayan quality. Without it, expeditions fall apart.

At the Cave we gear up in silence. The three of us tie on the same rope. I sit down to put on my crampons with great care. Don't want them falling off halfway and making a fool of myself. I tighten the straps to the last notch and stand up. Sandy looks at me.

'Ah, Andy, maybe you'd be better with the buckles on the outside.'

I feel a total pillock. I've put the crampons on the wrong feet. Today of all days, climbing with these Aces for the first time. What a bumblie.

So I sit down again and restrap them. Sandy very kindly tries to make me feel better by telling a story about how Mal climbed on Thamaserku for an entire day before discovering he'd had his boots on the wrong feet. I appreciated that – and was very aware of Jon's impatience beside me.

We set off and make the Brew Tent in good time. The crevasses have widened and some of the jumps are getting near our limit. The Rock House has collapsed completely. We found Alex packed and ready and in a slightly happier frame of mind. Still, I felt our relationship had been affected by yesterday's fiasco. He was reserved towards me, and certainly noticed my evident pleasure and relief when Sandy suggested I went through to Camp 1 with him, and Alex with Jon. And I found myself interrupting him a lot. I suppose I've ceased deferring to his experience, I no longer assume he's right and knows what he's doing.

I take on the extra food bags Alex has set aside to be carried up for the others, and find I can scarcely lift my pack. 'Let me feel that,' Sandy says. 'That's ridiculous, youth – you'll have to junk some of that. No wonder you had problems yesterday.'

So Alex and I junk some clothes and food. That feels better. Sandy looks at me, smiles. I nod. We set off.

It feels quite different being behind Sandy. He is so solid and confident, it scarcely occurs to me anything could go wrong in his company. But I work at it just the same as we wind our way up to the Icefall.

We enter the Icefall lower and to the right of yesterday's line. I need four pairs of eyes for this, to watch what Sandy's doing and the rope between us, concentrate on crampon and axe placements, look around and above for ice and Rocks Most Likely To. Into the danger area now. I'm gasping painfully, but there's no question of stopping here. Up, across, through, over another tottering heap of shit. We come to the bottom of a steep ice pitch, and arced across the top of it is a perfect tunnel of ice, blue sky showing under it, curved like the wing of an immense bird.

'Do you need to be belayed on this, Andy?'

'Don't . . . think so,' I gasp. He heads up, at once casual and careful, making it look easy and graceful. He crawls under the wing of snow and waits on the far side, grinning.

You know how to do this. Axe, bang in front points, next axe, step up, axe . . . Lovely ice this, slightly soft on top, firm underneath. I can do this, it's good . . . oops that placement isn't solid, slow down, look for it . . . Right . . .

I crawl under the wondrous wing and slump back. Can't get my breath at all. This really hurts. Sandy nods, a wide grin creases his face. 'OK, youth?' It's part question and part statement. It helps. I take a picture of Jon through the arc of snow which gives me an extra thirty seconds' breather, then we hurry on.

More front-pointing, a traverse that demands concentration – sudden flash of my first traverse with Mal in Glencoe, in the Lost

Valley – skirting past glowering boulders. I'm really starting to suffer now, simply can't keep up this pace. 'Not much further, Andy.' I grunt. I feel sick with exertion. I gulp air, but there's not enough there.

Finally Sandy comes to a halt, leans back on a rock. 'Hey, that's the worst of it done.' I've heard that before. I sling down my pack and lean over coughing and gasping like an athlete after the race. Jon and Alex come up. Jon looks at me and smiles warmly. 'You've cracked it.'

I shake my head, but feel better. Nice lad, Jon. I look around. Yes, we're at the top of the Icefall, just the long incline up to Camp 1 still to do. Top of the world, Ma!

We take a quick breather, drink some juice and munch a munchy. It's getting hot now, the reflected ultraviolet starts to grill us from all sides. Sandy and Jon take some six to eight pounds each from Alex and me. That feels good.

So it's off again. In two minutes I'm more shattered than before we stopped. Pain in the chest, sick in the stomach, legs leaden with lactic-acid build-up. It's crevasse after crevasse; many of them are too wide to jump so we must skirt round them or cross by snow bridges we can only guess are safe, uphill all the way. I'm definitely lagging behind. Only the hollow sound beneath my feet and Sandy's 'Don't hang around here, Andy' keep me hurrying on.

Sultans of pain, that's what these guys are, to keep doing it over and over and over. Because pain is what it is, nothing exciting about it at all. Just . . . pain. This is the persistence Jon wrote of, the ability to keep going when you simply cannot keep going.

Another break. My legs are starting to wobble and my whole body feels poisoned by the bitter taste of altitude. In two minutes I feel fine, then exhausted after the next twenty paces. I stumble on, following Sandy's bulk. The man's not human. Yes he is. He's just very strong and well acclimatized. This is new for me, it's bound to hurt. Fragments of songs and conversations drift through my mind like birds. To distract myself, I try to calculate dates, where Kath should be now, how long have we been at Base, when might we get home . . .

This is supposed to be my peak experience, and all I want is to be done with it.

After dozens more crevasses, we come to a melt stream beside a moraine bank. I'm forced to ask for a halt. 'Nearly there, two minutes, might as well keep going.' Heard that so often before – but this time it's true, there's a brown tent pitched among the rocks. We're here. Camp 1.

I dropped my pack and sat on the rocks. Sandy said something, I nodded dully. I sat and dumbly existed for a few minutes.

Then I slowly untied the rope. Bright red. Unbuckled my harness. Bright yellow. Bent forward wearily and started tugging at my crampon straps. Sandy dangled a blue bag in front of me. 'Like to fill this with water, youth?'

I got slowly to my feet. My legs had the weight and muscular elasticity of socks full of wet sand. I stumbled over the rocks and knelt beside the small, crystal-clear melt stream and stared into it with a mind as vacant as that water. But returning, I saw the tent and the lads sorting gear round it, the Icefall way below to the right, and straight ahead the great amphitheatre leading up to Camp 2, while above that the ridge and south face of the Mustagh Tower soared endlessly into the needle-bright morning, and a great satisfaction spread through me.

This is it. Into the mountain at last.

The first brew was almost orgasmic in the intensity of satisfaction it delivered. The second was nearly as good. I rolled two cigarettes, passed one to Sandy. We sprawled by the tent in the intense light, sun glinting off our shades, looking wild and dissipated on the outside and feeling relaxed and content within. It was 10.30 and we were done for the day.

The pleasures of mountaineering, I ventured idly, are similar to those of making love. The complete vivid absorption and adrenalin during, the wonderful sense of spaciousness and ease after, the body relaxed and the mind empty as a blown egg. You've been in contact with something though you couldn't now say what.

'You could be right,' said Jon, 'but that's too long ago for me to remember!' Our laughter rang out over the ice.

After a retort each, we felt much stronger. Alex and I pitched our tent on the glacier in a small area between two crevasses, one a couple of feet outside the front entrance, the other just behind the back. Not the kind of place you want to wander about at night. Again we unrolled our Karrimats and sleeping bags, laid out our personal gear and made our habitation in the wilderness. We were still somewhat awkward with each other. I wondered how we'd pair up for tomorrow's climb to Camp 2.

It was time for the noon radio call. Out of habit I began, 'Base Camp to Mal and Tony – ' then caught myself and laughed. 'Ah, Camp 1 to Mal and Tony, come in, please.' We waited, huddled round the radio. Then the familiar voice, 'Camp 3 here . . .'

Camp 3! It was the first time anyone had said it. It sounded foreign and novel to our ears, like a new country. We looked at each other and smiled. After ten days of seemingly getting nowhere, we had a new camp established. We were on our way.

Mal made his report. They'd had a hard slog up the fixed ropes, just as Jon and Sandy had the first time they went above Camp 2. At the top, they ran out the remaining 300 feet of rope in search of the tennis-court-sized platform the Brown-Patey expedition had used for Camp 3. No sign of it, and they could only assume it was somewhere under the corniced and fluted snow. They'd come across more mysterious holes of the sort Sandy had fallen down, and finally pitched the tent on a snow promontory. The site was not too good, and they'd secured the tent by tying the guys to boulders which they then lowered over opposing sides of the ridge – which gave me an idea of how sharp it must be at that point. Mal's assessment of the summit ridge was much as Sandy's – alarming at first sight, but on further study not as wild as Nuptse and it should go. With the extra 20 feet of snow on the ridge since 1956, the serac bands could be the major problem.

Still, the tent was now there, and whoever used it next would be on the way to the summit. At this point Jon made a new suggestion: what did they think of waiting a day or two at Camp 2, then all going together for the top? It was a good gesture, and should make the assault both safer and easier, with four to alternate breaking trail.

There was a pause, then Mal said carefully, 'That's an interesting idea, Jon. I'll talk it over with Tony and we'll let you know later what we think.' Jon tried to press him further, but Mal signed off quickly, pointing out they were very tired and wanted to get back to Camp 2 before the ice slope started releasing boulders down the lines.

It was an interesting suggestion. Before it, we'd all assumed the two pairs would go for it separately. We talked round it for a while. Certainly a good gesture of final solidarity; it made sense in a lot of ways. But if Mal and Tony were to stay up at 2 rather than return to 1, that meant a few changes. Alex and I would have to take a tent up to 2, so that both pairs could sleep there. And we'd need to take up food for them – and the only food we had was our own. Hm . . .

Alex and I went back to our tent and talked it over. In essence, if we did this, we'd be acting as support for the lads, rather than acting independently. Well, that felt OK. I wanted to contribute. But if we did that, we wouldn't have enough supplies for ourselves to go back to 2 a second time, sleep there and have a go at the fixed ropes to the Col – unless we went back to Base Camp. Which meant another trip through the Icefall, on our own this time. And we'd be tackling both the climb to 2 and the ascent to the Col on our own – terrain that neither of us had any experience on. And I'd lost faith in Alex's abilities.

But ever since Mal walked into the kitchen and announced, 'You can go to the Col, it's about 21,000 feet . . .', it had been my summit, my goal. Carrying this load for Mal and Tony would make it much more unlikely.

I looked at Alex. 'What d'you reckon?'

'I think we should carry for them and see how we feel.'

'OK. It's time I did something useful.'

So that was that. At 4.00 we all discussed the situation with Mal and Tony who were now back at Camp 2, thoroughly shattered. The game plan – an Alex phrase we'd all picked up – was for us four to go to 2 tomorrow, Alex and I carrying tentage and food for the lads. He and I would then return to Camp 1, because there wasn't enough tentage for six at Camp 2, and we'd scarcely acclimatized to Camp 1 level yet. The next day we'd go to Base and, if we felt like it and it fitted in with the lads' movements, we could come back up again. Meanwhile the Four Aces would go for the summit together.

Waiting for supper, we're all rather excited now – even Sandy and Jon, for the first time. The crunch – or at least the first bite – approaches. We can sit at our tent and look up to the summit, knowing that the fixed ropes, the tents and supplies are all there. We're coming together when it really matters.

Sandy is hunched over the stove, his ruddy face already

swollen, pushing his thin hair away from his eyes. Jon as ever is sprawled back with his hands behind his head, looking up at the roof where more esoteric reggae dubs crackle from his speakers. Alex is sitting cross-legged at the entrance trying not to be sick. And I'm tired and high, smoking a last cigarette – burns very reluctantly at this altitude – and thinking back on the Icefall today and forward to Camp 2 tomorrow. I'm right in it now and it feels fine.

We've passed the time with casual, rambling conversation. Much of it about food. 'Sardines on toast . . .' someone would say. A long pause while we consider this vision. 'Bacon . . .' We'd lie salivating at the thought of bacon we'd eaten and bacon we would eat again, crisp and lean, three rashers on a plate . . . 'With fried eggs and tomato,' another voice would add. 'Yes, but with croissants and pots of real coffee.' Coffee, elixir of life, taken in a Parisian café, all the quickening dream of life in its rising steam! 'And a pack of untipped Gauloises.'

How this deprivation sharpens the senses and the appetite! So many places to go, so many ordinary things suddenly so precious, haloed by memory.

When we can bear it no more, the subject reverts to climbing. Jon and Sandy eloquently persuade me I must go to Chamonix and do some Alpine routes. 'Good crack in the Bar National, youth!' And Jon adds, aware of my priorities, 'Cheap wine and fags – some nice easy routes too. You'd love it. You did all right today – if you were in Cham, we could already be getting into bacon and eggs in some café . . .'

It sounds tempting. I still intend to pack in climbing after this, but there are a few Scottish winter routes I want to knock off first. And maybe a fortnight in Chamonix, do a few of the easier classics . . .

I find myself talking about my dad and his death for the first time. Jon looked at me curiously. 'You really keep things to yourself, don't you?' Maybe I do. It had never occurred to me to tell them. I write instead.

We retired to our tent, took sleeping pills and read till sleep came to claim us. I lay awake listening to Alex's Cheyne-Stokes breathing getting slower and slower, then a pause that went on and on, and just when I'd be about to reach over and shake him, he'd take a deep shuddering breath and start up again. It was freezing outside and the stars were spattered brilliantly across the sky like an exploded diamond tiara. I was as happy and raised as a child on the first night of summer camp.

In the middle of the night, I woke to a sharp crack and a movement beneath me. 'Alex?' 'Yes?' 'Did you hear that?' 'Yup. Think it was some lil' Bertha opening up.'

I felt around the floor of the tent and came to a small decline where my fingers met no resistance. 'I think it's under the tent.' 'Can you be bothered getting up and moving?' I lay and thought about it. 'Not really.' 'Nor me.' So we didn't.

But we slept lightly after that.

When I looked out at 4.00 a.m. on Thursday 26 July it was very cold and snowing lightly. There was a fair amount of fresh snow on the tent and on the ground. I hoped it wouldn't cancel today, then put my head down, curling deep into the bag for warmth.

To be woken later by a call from Sandy. We lit the stove, got the water heating. Single porridge, two brews, a protein bar. Dressed, packed our sacks. At the last moment I stuck in an extra Kendal Mint bar. Could be a hard day. I took a last glance inside our tent – my Kundera book, Walkman, spare munchies, funny to think they'll be in exactly the same place when we come back here. Unless that narrow new crevasse opens up a lot.

At Sandy and Jon's tent we roped up for the day, Alex and I together. I'd have preferred it otherwise, but there it was. Sandy was in an unusually grumpy mood, positively sullen. Our cheerful good mornings had no effect on him. He wasn't happy about the time – round 6.30 by now – or the weight we were having to carry. (In his diary, he recorded that he had a sore head and we were all being particularly irritating, which just shows how desperately subjective all our assessments and reactions were.) We all took some of his load. It was the first time I've seen Sandy not 100 per cent and, as Jon said, it's something of a relief to see he's human. The snow had stopped and the sun made it a perfect spring morning as we plodded off.

Above the Icefall the glacier suddenly escapes the confines of the Ibex Trail cliff on the left and the spires on the right that run on to bisect the south face of Mustagh, some two to three miles further on. It widens out into a great amphitheatre, rising gently for half the distance between us and Camp 2, then curving up as on the rim of a bowl. A mile or so beyond the top of that rim, 100 yards out from the bottom of the southwest face, was our objective. I knew from listening that the two main danger zones were the threat of avalanche on the long slope out of the bowl, and that of collapsing seracs poised above the rim of it. It was this area of crouched menace that had been christened the White Tiger.

The first hour or two is exhilarating and relatively painless. We're moving past ridges and towers and still, ghostly glacier pools. Everything is on a bigger scale than the lower glacier, but less broken up. Most of the crevasses are too wide to jump, so we follow them along till we come to a snow bridge which we hurry over. I'm quite enjoying myself till Sandy points out that much of this area is riddled with smaller crevasses, only they're covered over so we can't see them. After that I'm very careful to walk exactly in his and Jon's footsteps.

Finally we come to the bottom of the White Tiger. We start zigzagging up it, glancing apprehensively at the seracs above us bunched like 100-foot-high paws. At once the incline starts hitting us, like a series of body blows. I gasp for air and energy, but there's none there. The gap between Alex and me and Jon and Sandy starts widening. We're down to a mile-an-hour plod now. What worries us is a massive build-up of snow running along the top of this slope. The sun is strong now and the snow is softening. There are several inches of soft snow on top of hard snow-ice; I don't know much about avalanches but I've a feeling this is a classic set-up for one. If the slope starts to go, we'll be lucky to get clear. Or if those massive white paws shift . . .

Worry wears away at our nervous energy. We try to move faster, but it's impossible. I keep looking up towards the crest of the ramp; it doesn't get any closer or look any safer. This is very unpleasant. But there's nothing I can do about it, so plug on and hope for the best . . .

It must be an hour or more later that we finally stumble over the crest and the incline slackens off. By now we're stopping every five minutes though it feels like an hour. We take another breather. The next section is one long heartbreaking gentle uphill, gradually traversing left. Somewhere under that towering south-west face is Camp 2. This is the section that the others always said seemed to go on for miles; the first part of it is strewn with hollow-sounding areas, and the second is exposed to the collapse of the massive seracs on the ridge that eventually bisects the south face. Again there's nothing we can do about that except be hopeful and fatalistic.

We look at each other. What we see looks dire. We set off again.

Now we seem to be wading through glue. The sun is needling down and smacking back up off the snow. Even through two pairs of shades, brilliant points of light are dancing across my retinas. The effect is one of disorientation, a timeless trance where everything hurts endlessly. When we stop every 200 yards or so, we begin to feel half-human. But as soon as we put one foot laboriously in front of the other, our legs ache with lactic-acid build-up. So much effort in just lifting boot and crampon out of a foot hole and moving it to the next.

How do these guys keep doing this? Whether they're crazy or brave or plain tough, what's remarkable is not the danger they accept, but the pain they embrace. I'd no idea it was like this. Jesus . . .

I'm sick in my stomach from gasping. Chest's pounding through to my backbone. Eyes smart and throat raw. I feel as if in the final throes of seasickness: all I want is for this to stop. We stop. We start again. It's worse than before. We're getting nowhere, better to keep going into this mindlessness. This is what all that running was for, pushing through the pain barrier along the Queensferry shore in fading light . . .

This is the real thing. The nightmare mountain, the endless snow slopes, the harsh grind of altitude. God it's horrible.

I can't go on.

I must go on.

I go on.

Pain isn't the right word but it will have to do. Does it hurt the others as much as this? How can we measure one person's pain against another's? Is Mal's 'wasted' equal to my 'shattered', equal to Sandy's 'pretty tired'? Are they braver than me, more determined or simply fitter? Let's think about this, anything to take my mind off what's happening now, this endless punishment, these white desperate hours beyond my limits.

Another stop. We lean, gasping, over our axes. I break into my Kendal Mint cake, hand some to Alex. He simply nods, too tired to speak. At least he looks as shattered as me. As long as he goes, I go. The sugar hits us. We straighten up like geriatrics in the last remnants of our pride and put our feet to the treadmill.

Somewhere along the line, when for the nth time I had gone on when I couldn't go on any longer, I decided I wouldn't come back up here. Forget about the Col. Okay, but let's get to Camp 2, you wimp, you bumblie, you staggering wazzock. You're not going to let a sick American outwalk you.

If only the light would stop needling my eyeballs. But no headache, that's good. You'll do it, looks like you're gaining on him . . .

The incline slackens off. Now we're in direct line of fire from the seracs. I'm much too tired to care. Bad sign, that. *Care, you fucker.* If we don't care, there's nothing left.

One thing the running taught me: there's always an end. Then I'll feel great.

Now this is odd: the footsteps in front of us suddenly diverge and move a rope's length apart. We look at it, mystified, then laugh out loud. Sandy's been in a bad mood all morning; we can picture the little irritations, the short, snappy argument, then the parting of the ways till the rope lets them part no further. In front of us in the snow is the very picture of a mountain tiff – and 200 yards on, the tracks converge again in conciliation.

Very touching.

Then round the corner comes a strange, wild-looking youth in shades. It's Jon. What's this he's saying? Just a short way now? Oh aye, Jon. But he's got an empty sack and insists on taking half a load from each of us. We're too tired to be proud. A good youth, capable of these sudden unexpected generosities just when you need them.

(Back at Camp 2, Sandy recorded, Mal had jokingly suggested that Jon just wanted a good mention in the book. Sandy shrugged at this. Big deal. Who gives a fuck? drifted in and out of his head. A good deed's a good deed.)

Suddenly there it is. A sagging brown tent in the wilderness below the south face, three ragged figures coming towards us, silhouetted against the sun. They look black and charred, ringed with fire. They're pointing cameras our way. I try to prepare a grin or a joke, but when we stumble up to them I can only look blankly through their cameras and nod as they warmly and generously congratulate and welcome us. 'Well done, youth.' 'Bleedin' good, mate! Seriously, I'm really impressed.' 'Not bad for an author.' Laughter.

I just manage a smile, sling my pack and camera into the snow anyhow. Jon, amused: 'You just don't care, do you?' I sense his affection and empathy. 'Nuh' is all I can say.

I sit oblivious to everything inside and out till slowly the greyness departs. I've pushed myself further than ever before, but I'm here. Wherever here is. Tony puts a lukewarm brew into my hand and smiles. This is it. My top. Like Kath arriving at Base Camp, I briefly feel tearful with relief and pleasure – then remember we've still got to turn round and go back.

Summits glow mostly in retrospect.

Camp 2 is a blur in my memory. I saw it for only half an hour, through a haze of fatigue. One tent, a second being put up, Mal standing with an absurd plastic shovel, a vague impression of the south face towering nearby and the more distant ice slope up to the Col – that's all I remember. Summits, wherever we find them, are absurd. Three months in Pakistan for this fragmentary half-hour. Of course making your summit matters. When they say it doesn't, what they mean is that getting there is half the fun. You can't extract the summit from an expedition any more than you can extract the smile from the Madonna: the meaning is in the whole. We need the summit to aim at, but the value of our journey is spread everywhere along the line. It's in the blank, painful miles and in the occasional milestones of outrageous happiness.

You may choose heads or tails, but in the end you pocket the whole coin.

I got to my feet and stood looking about for a last couple of minutes. The lads were busying about putting up the new tent and sorting gear. There seemed a new purpose and seriousness about them. This was where they get professional; this is where they stick their necks out. If you see a parrot in the jungle, its plumage suddenly makes sense. So it is with my friends the shuffling dossers. Their physical and mental qualities are adapted to these places. I'm glad I've been up here to see that.

Now let's just get out of here.

Alex and I shake hands with the Aces, all aware we won't meet again till they've succeeded or failed on the summit. They thank us again for our carry, we wish them luck. We pull on our packs – now wonderfully light – take a last look back at a place to which we'll never return, and set off down the hill, into the white.

The trip back to Camp 1 was another epic. After ten steps the soft snow had balled up under my crampons, giving them no more grip than dancing shoes. So I started knocking them with my axe, first one then the other, every second or third step, virtually all the way back. This was tedious and energy consuming but vital – particularly when we hit the ramp where a slip could well take us both away.

It was the heat that did for us. We were now walking through noon and the sun casseroled us from all sides. It softened the snow, weakened snow bridges, and our energy ran off us like our sweat. And we lost our way again.

It was a relief to finally get off the bottom of the zigzags down the ramp, to step clear of that poised avalanche threat. We were moving quite well at perhaps two miles an hour. It was very hot, and our arms and legs were weary from constantly banging soft snow off our boots, but our troubles should have been over.

They'd only begun. Alex's famed route-finding abilities took us off too far to the right. Because I'd lost faith, on the way up I'd tried to memorize our route and was sure it was more to the left. Alex pointed out he'd spent months in the Cascades doing this kind of thing. We held to his line and pretty soon lost contact with the prints from the morning.

There followed a frustrating and at times horrible couple of hours as we slipped and slithered along increasingly bizarre contours, followed bigger and bigger crevasses to more and more insecure snow bridges, tried to tiptoe over hollow-sounding slopes. Again and again we had to retrace our steps when a line was blocked. This sapped our energy and morale. I was frankly fed up with him. I was also anxious and very very tired.

Eventually we were lumbering along in something of a daze, Alex cursing outwardly and me cursing inwardly. All we wanted was to be back at Camp 1, and everything seemed to be conspiring to prevent us. I followed him across the umpteenth snow bridge, stepping carefully in his footprints – and it gave way.

It was all very clear. My right foot broke through, then my left. I started going down into this slot, as if being lowered vertically into my grave. I looked up and forward towards Alex. He'd stopped, half turned round, and with the swiftest and most graceful movement whipped our rope towards and round him. I was jerked out of the crevasse like a trout pulled out of water. One moment I was chest-deep, going down, the next I was kneeling on the far side, rubbing my knee where my axe had banged it.

I looked up at Alex standing 30 feet away. He'd been very quick. 'Thanks, Alex.'

'Aw, meester, it ees nothing,' in his Mexican whine. 'Eet is all right . . .'

The pain in my knee made me feel sick. I got cautiously to my feet. I could still walk. I looked back at the crevasse. It went down a couple of hundred feet, then it was too dark to see further. Well, that was lucky. Good value to fall in a crevasse and get out. Good for the book.

We set off again, slightly loopy with fatigue. I'd felt no fear, not even adrenalin. Too tired for that. Too much in the present to dwell on it, just one of those things . . .

Sometimes it gets so hard to care . . . Hard to care enough to keep banging that boot every second step instead of every fourth. Hard to care enough to follow this crevasse to a safer crossing. Hard to care enough to concentrate on feet, on rope, on the person ahead, on this tottering shit you're passing through. We've gone through all the Kendal Mint cake now; we've even stopped stopping. We stumble on in our own dazed worlds, a world of pinpricks, of light and voices in the head, curses and anxiety, memories. I feel full of holes like a Swiss cheese, riddled as the times. Long periods of blankness, on automatic, then suddenly returning to myself and wishing I hadn't.

We're wildly off course now, in an area where a gentle incline will suddenly end in an 80-foot overhung drop, where a contour leaves us standing on a leaf of ice in the middle of a huge slot. We're so far down into this wild patch that we can't see where Camp 1 is – or back to Camp 2. It's an ice maze that keeps shunting us further and further in the wrong direction, where every apparent shortcut is blocked, where all the time we're getting into more and more trouble and the sun gets higher and our energy gets lower.

'Look, Alex, this is fucking ridiculous!' I eventually explode.

'Any better suggestions?' he snaps back.

'Yes. We've got to get across to the left.'

He looks at me, then nods. We set off on my line which seems promising until we abruptly find ourselves on the peak of an ice tower that falls sheer on three sides. We retreat with difficulty and care. Alex pointedly says nothing.

We go back to his original line. It peters out in a torment of ravines, overhangs and ridges. It's like being a microbe walking over the face of W.H. Auden. We look at each other – and exchange sheepish grins.

No blame.

We backtrack and try again. I just want this to be done with. This is absurd – we're probably only half a mile from Camp 1, but we just can't close on it. Obstacle after obstacle seems thrown deliberately between us and it.

There's no option but to keep on trying. This day has gone on for years. And suddenly, quite clearly, Kathleen is speaking to me. I'd forgotten about her. 'Don't let go, Andy,' she says, 'I want to see you again!' 'Yes, Kathleen,' I mutter as she bullies, cajoles and nags me. 'Look, I'm concentrating. Look, I'm being careful.' 'Don't gibber,' she replies, *watch your feet.*

I can see her distinctly in the upper right corner of my mind. She is sitting looking out the window of a train. Rain streaks and wobbles across the glass. It is somewhere in England. She is wearing a blue hat and her French raincoat. She is thinking to me, telling me I must concentrate, I must care, that – she confesses with a wry smile – she wants to see me again.

'You will, you will,' I assure her. I make every step, every exhausted move for her, *to* her as in a dance one moves to one's partner.

The map of Auden's mug suddenly smooths out. We have come to a deep blue glacier pool, the colour of her eyes. All we have to do is a front-point traverse round the rim of it and the way ahead seems clear. Our Camp 1 tent is perched on the moraine a quarter of a mile on.

We sit down and drink the last of our Gatorade. We share our last Granola bar. We get up and carefully execute our last traverse. We arrive.

We're lying in our bags as the light fades and the last brew comes to the boil. We've eaten and drunk and largely recovered. We've spoken with the lads to confirm our safe arrival. Mal sounded almost envious when I told him about my slot-fall. 'Usually you've to climb for years to have one of them.' They're all set to move up to Camp 3 tomorrow for the final assault. We sign off with mutual good wishes for tomorrow.

I sit at the entrance of the tent, looking down the glacier towards Lobsang. I'm very tired, but somehow feel very steady. It wasn't that bad, was it? No altitude sickness, no headache. Right knee's painful and stiff, but I'll take painkillers if necessary tomorrow.

Tomorrow . . . Can't relax yet. Still the Icefall between us and Base. Let's hope we make a better job of it this time. Don't want to fall at the last hurdle.

'Hey, gringo! You wanta thees brew?'

I crawl in and take the mug. Alex's emaciated eagle face in the candlelight. It's hard not to appreciate someone who saves your skin, even if he then endangers it again. We gave it maximum pastry today, even if we got a bit flaky at times. Good value that.

'Goodnight.'

''Night.'

Asleep in seconds.

For the last time pull on the Koflach boots, zip up the Yeti gaiters. Harness, tie on. Prussik loops. Axe. As we prepare to set off, Alex tells me about his dream last night where he went up to the Col to fetch down Jon and Sandy's tent and when he got there they insisted he burn it. He did, and they stood back and watched it blaze, a beacon on the Chinese border . . .

We're at once flat and nervy, being so nearly finished but not quite. I mentally gather myself. 'Let's get it done with.'

A cold morning, the glacier dormant and no snow balling under our cramps. With light packs, we move fast, automatically, over crevasses and bridges, skirting pools and boulder pedestals. The ice is hard and the snow crisp; the most dodgy bridges hold as we hotfoot it over them. We come to the Bungalow Rock; it's still perched at the top of the chute, but only just. We face into the slope for two front-point descents. This is so much easier now. It's just climbing. Knee's painful from yesterday and have to go cautiously with it.

Brew Tent. We don't stop for one, just pick up a few things and set off again. We don't say anything, but we know we're home and dry. I almost feel regret as we make the awkward scramble off the glacier for the last time.

At the Cave in silence I slowly take off my helmet, crampons, harness, strap my axes to the sack. Slowly stripping away my climbing identity to emerge again as a regular citizen. Feel light, almost floating without it.

I walk down the Ibex Trail, savouring every step, noticing the flowers, the miracle of grass and dust and ibex droppings. I hear our goat baa, see the familiar circle of tents. Onto level ground. I wait for Alex and drink in the pure sweetness of being alive. Together we walk to the Mess Tent, drop our packs and walk in.

'Mr Andy! Alex!' A great beam from Jhaved, we hug each other, then shake hands with Shokat. I'm grinning like a simpleton. I feel very simple. Cleaned out. Released.

Jhaved hands us a brew each. 'Camp 1?' 'Camp 2.' 'Good climbers, very good!' He fumbles in his jacket, produces and lights his last K2 cigarette. He looks at me, his eyes dancing – then passes it over. I accept it reverently. These are as rare as snow leopards now, haven't seen one for a week.

So Alex and I slump across the tent from each other, wasted and joyful, grinning like imbeciles in the mountain villages as we answer Shokat's questions. I want this feeling to linger in me for ever. Jhaved hands us cheese omelettes. I unlace my boots and pull them off. I slowly take off my shades.

11

Summit Fever

In which we put it to the touch

26–29 July 1984

Mal watched Andrew and Alex set off down the hill away from Camp 2. He noted with approval how Andrew immediately began knocking off the soft snow balling under his crampons. He'd mentioned that to him once, when they sat halfway up Dinnertime Buttress in Glencoe . . . A brief memory flash of the Clachaig, of Liz frying sausages, of laughter and warmth . . . If Andy keeps thinking and concentrating like that, he'll be all right. Really, the youth did OK. And they brought up the loads that make our summit bid possible. And Adrian and Mohammed's work . . . Up to us to finish it off now. I think we can do it.

Mal, Tony, Sandy and Jon spent the afternoon of 26 July at Camp 2 establishing the second tent, sorting out gear, trying to calculate exactly how much food and clothing, rope and ironmongery they'd need. With every pound having the effect of ten at this altitude, it was important to get it just right. Carrying too much or too little would equally endanger the chances of success and of getting off the mountain safely. So how many pitons, how many friends? How much rope; stakes or deadmen? Pile jacket only or down jacket as well? Who carries the radio? Retorts?

They'd agreed the next day would be a rest day and they'd start the summit push together the day after. But somehow over brew and Jon's mum's precious fruitcake, they found themselves beginning to talk as if they were to go for it tomorrow. By the time they'd finished the cake, it was agreed. They were too revved up to wait any longer and, anyway, the weather must surely break soon. The new game plan was for a 2.00 a.m. start, to do the fixed ropes up to the Col while the ice-slope bowling alley was still asleep, then push up to Camp 3 before the heat of the day.

So they brewed and ate a retort each, and took a 6.00 p.m. call from Andrew and Alex who sounded tired but high to be back at Camp 1 after some adventures. Then they turned in, each to gather himself in his own world of calculation, ambition and apprehension.

Mal: Thought a great deal about home in that twilight zone between sleep and awareness. Semi-lucid plans for the future, all of course involving complicated ways of releasing Liz from work while allowing us both to earn a gainful income from some source or other. I need to see and be with her so badly sometimes. Each day on the hill I suppose is one day closer to getting home. Funny, this Himalayan stuff is so awful that the true wonder and fun and enjoyment only comes in retrospect. Trouble is, I suspect it's also a bit addictive . . .

Sandy woke up at 2.00 a.m., took his Bic lighter into his sleeping bag and gave it five minutes to heat up, then lit the stove. Jon woke up with his normal hill vocabulary. He said he hadn't slept much. Sandy poked his head out of the tent and grunted at the weather. Not too impressed. It was snowing some, light wind, very heavy clouds thickened the darkness over the Cathedral Spires.

Jon was still tired and showed no sign of stirring. Sandy talked with him and eventually they settled on staying put at Camp 2 that day. Jon put his head back down to sleep but Sandy suggested that as they were all a team it might be a good idea to communicate their decision to Mal and Tony.

'Hey, Mal, we're sleeping.'

'What d'you mean you're sleeping?'

Sandy told him they weren't going to go. He heard the zipper close on the other tent, and Mal and Tony conferring. Not long after, 'I think we'll go on up, and if the weather gets bad we can come down from Camp 3.'

Sandy asked Jon to communicate some, as really he'd played a major part in their not moving. Jon called out, 'I didn't sleep, so we're going to stay.'

'Yeah, no problem. We'll give it a go.'

A lot of subtle dynamics were going on at this point, only hinted at in their diaries. It meant that Mal and Tony, who had arrived at Base Camp two weeks after the others had done the groundwork, were going to get first crack at the summit. Well . . . okay.

Sandy bid them adieu, pulled off his Thinsulate clothes and went back to sleep, disappointed but philosophically accepting the situation. No point getting fussed about it.

So Mal and Tony set off into the dark on their summit push. Pools of light bobbing from their headtorches picked up swirling snowflakes. They felt isolated and lonely, dreamlike, their world shrunk to a few feet. They were each carrying some 40 pounds – five days' food, stove and gas, bivvy tent, shovel, rope. They crossed the bergshrund crevasse – that marked the beginning of the final struggle and plodded upwards to the fixed ropes on the ice slope. In the half-light they could see that the stakes and ice screws had melted out from the day before, then refrozen overnight, half out and at drunken angles. But they held and the stonefall was minimal at this hour, so they clipped in their jumars and doggedly plugged on up. Nothing challenging or interesting about this, just brutally hard work. Jug, step, jug, step, for three hours on the fixed line. An endless mindless plod. Then into the chimney at the top that Sandy had fixed. The line here had a nasty habit of dislodging loose blocks as one pulled or moved on it. Finally they were on the ridge, took a breather in the morning sunlight. The snow had stopped. If the weather held, their decision to set off alone would be justified. And even if they had to turn back, the trail they'd broken would give the second pair that much more of a chance.

And so it was all the way on Mustagh, the fruitful combination of competition and cooperation urging them on up the mountain.

Thus Mal and Tony plodded on to Camp 3. The tent looked awful, covered in blizzard snow, half collapsed and totally inhospitable. They dropped their packs and slowly set about putting it right, packing rocks and snow under the downhill side then stringing safety line round it, very aware of the surrounding cornices and those inexplicable holes in the snow.

That done, they melted water for a brew and chatted. Good to be done for the day. They studied the ridge above them. 'Hard,' Sandy had said, 'but nothing like as hard as Nuptse.' He and Mal had been rather over-ambitious on Nuptse West Ridge but the experience had been invaluable. It put the ridge above them into perspective and allowed them to look at it in an analytical, objective way.

Down below, Sandy pottered about to keep his red corpuscle-thick blood circulating, and read William Golding's *Free Fall*. 'This man knows what it's about,' he thought. Jon slept and kept the reggae dubs crackling out of the tiny speakers hanging from the ridge of the tent. Just dossing about, waiting, in an Alpine stylee . . .

Mal: 6.00 p.m. What Tony and I felt was a really emotional radio call to the others. Them wishing us all the best from Base Camp, including Jhaved and Shokat, almost brought tears to my eyes. Just hope we can make the push from here okay. If we grind to a halt, the second lot should have a reasonable chance. *Inshallah*. This one for Rocky, for Liz.

By 7.30 that night the lights were all out in Base Camp where Andrew lay smiling to himself in the dark at the sheer pleasure of being alive, at Camp 2 where Jon and Sandy were sleeping, and at Camp 3 where Tony revolved all the possibilities of tomorrow while Mal turned over, thinking of home as sleep drifted over him like the light snow on the outside of their tent.

Round 5.00 a.m., Tony and Mal were ready to leave Camp 3 for the final push upwards. In the half-light they could see the weather was not bad, though worse than for several days. Drifting cloud, light snow, ominous across the Baltoro. If it holds two more days . . .

The last brew, pack away stove, mugs, billycan, sleeping bag and Karrimat. Gear up, tie in on the rope that will link their fortunes all day. Both feeling tired but plenty left in reserve, no headaches or other altitude problems. Helmet, gloves, goggles, sling on the pack – about 35 pounds today. Ready. They looked at each other. 'Okay, youth?' 'Fine, Dad.' 'Let's go, then.'

It was good to be breaking new ground again. As he led the first few pitches, Mal's mood was one of suppressed excitement, total concentration and commitment. The ridge was initially steep but ill-defined and frequently obscured by cloud, so he found they tended to drift about on the southwest side in gullies and rock ribs. Don't want to take a false line this early in the game, must conserve energy.

He was aware of a slight apprehension as he kicked through surface snow into ice and began front-pointing up. Patey and Brown had taken three days to climb to their Camp 4, so it must be demanding. Probably not technically desperate – about Scottish Grade 2 or 3 at the moment – but this cruddy ice under cruddy snow made for slow, cautious going. The rock ribs were awkward and rotten, and protection was generally poor.

What this needs, he thought, is three days total concentration. Not one mistake, however minor. A slip or a small snow slide could take us over the south face with very little time to correct or brake. Looks like we're going to be mostly on the face or a few feet above it. Really relying on each other on this one . . .

Three weeks together on the hill had given Mal and Tony confidence in each other's abilities. Just as important, they'd quickly come to work together with the minimum of friction. Sandy and Jon's partnership was that of a long-married, constantly bickering couple; Mal and Tony's had taken the form of father and son, old head and youthful enthusiasm. It suited them to make a joke of it. Adopting and accepting these roles underlined their mutual reliance on each other; they were a pair, not two competing individuals who happened to be tethered to the same rope.

After five pitches Tony came up to Mal's stance, grinned through his sunburn. 'Great, isn't it?' Without any need for discussion, he led through onto the next pitch.

Meanwhile, back at Camp 2, Sandy and Jon had woken at 2.00 a.m., feeling as fine as one can at that time. To Sandy's grateful astonishment, Jon got the stove going and made the first brews, perhaps as a gesture of atonement for yesterday's nonevent.

They crossed the 'schrund and clipped into the fixed ropes.

They made rather good time up them, partly due to stonefall whizzing down the slope. The fixed rope limited room for evasion, and the effect was rather like being tethered at the wrong end of a bowling alley. 'Very scary,' Sandy recorded, 'but it gave us an incentive to move quite fast.' Fifteen hundred feet above him, he could see Mal and Tony moving on the ridge. They waved to each other. It felt good. Time to radio Andy . . .

I woke up, stuck my head outside the tent. A good enough morning – bright, fresh, a slight haze that would filter the sunshine further up. The weather's holding into the monsoon season, we've a real chance. The 'we' seems entirely natural. I began by observing this expedition from the outside, but now identify totally with it. A surge of optimism. We might just pull it off. Everything's come right at the right time since Mal and Tony arrived at Askole with the money. Even Burt and Donna's dropping out at Paiju helped Base Camp food logistics and made us more harmonious and coherent as a team. Then Mal and Tony's late arrival with fresh energy to build on what had already been accomplished. Time for the morning radio call . . .

'Base Camp here. We're now open to callers and improper suggestions.'

'____ ____'

'Sorry, youth, I've got piles and that would be difficult.'

Good to hear from Sandy. He sounds very well and elated in his casual Highland fashion. We exchange news and friendly abuse, wait for Mal and Tony to come in, but they don't. Probably too busy. But he can see them, and they seem to be going well. It's great having the radios, they allow us at Base Camp to be totally involved in what's happening up there. Over and out.

Sandy switched off and stuck the radio in his pack. Then it was head down, one step, push up the jumar, step, push, up into the dazzling morning sunlight.

As Mal and Tony worked their way up the ridge, alternating leads, to their astonishment pale lengths of old-fashioned hemp rope started appearing in the snow, in and out of lumps of ice. It must be the fixed rope of Patey and Brown, left there twenty-eight years ago. Some of it fell apart at the touch, but other sections seemed quite secure. Could use that at a push on the way down, Mal mused. There's going to be a lot of abseiling, and we

probably don't have enough gear. We always climb on the
achievements of the past anyway.

It was oddly moving and comforting to come on these signs of
the last living things to go that way. He came on an old Pierre
Allain karabiner. He reached down and tried the gate. It opened
and closed perfectly. He examined it more closely and saw
stamped on it: J. BROWN.

It was ten years ago that he'd read Patey's account of the first
ascent and begun to dream of repeating it. Now he was 21,500
feet up the west ridge, holding a piece of their gear in his mitt. It
seemed to say, 'Yes, it can come true. Yes, it can be done.' He
clipped the krab to his rack and slowly, painfully, climbed after
Tony.

At 10 p.m. Sandy radioed in from the top of the fixed ropes. He
could still just see Mal and Tony. 'Looks like they're on a difficult
pitch, so it's unlikely they'll radio in.'

'Yes we will!' Mal's amused voice sounded strong and
coherent, not too breathless. They had stopped for a brew, and
were now chatting and answering Jon's technical queries. How
many pitches, snow conditions, size of cornice, what technical
gear would they need?

'Immediately above us is the infamous 100-foot rock wall,
turned on the south side, by Patey's account. We're on the hardest
part of the climb . . . At least, I hope so! Sitting some three feet
from the edge of the south face, can see right down to Camp 2,
down the Icefall, Base Camp just around the corner. Better move
on now.'

'Good luck, youth.'

'Yeah, you too, Sandy. Over, out.'

The rock wall barred the ridge above them. On the right, a
several thousand foot drop down the south face. On the left,
seracs and the drop into China. Tony steadied himself and led off.

He levered himself cautiously up a couloir of avalanche-prone
snow that led to the foot of the rock wall. Then onto mixed
ground where his crampons screeched and scraped on bare, loose
rock, suddenly a liability. It was the first real technical climbing
he'd done at this altitude, and harder than he'd expected. On
shitty rock and insecure snow, with little protection, there was no

room for a slip or the smallest mistake. Not when you're on the tottering crest of the south face. Those old guys sure were good . . .

Tony: Finally got onto a notch about 18 inches wide and covered in scree. So I kicked it all off and stood on what was left. Then I ran out of rope, got a wire in a really good crack, and waited for Mal to come up.

Mal led a 50-foot level traverse out right, kicking out scree and tottering on top of the remains. Easy, but insecure feeling. Then a hard step down where he found an old peg. He clipped into it and studied the next move. He'd come out to a sweep of slabs straight onto the south face. Exposure no longer troubled him, but just the same the drop was impressive, and the slabs looked steeply angled and were probably rotten . . .

Mal: It was either the slabs which looked very hard with crampons, or there was a little rock groove above me, slightly overhung, that went up over the horizon. I said to Tony, 'It doesn't look right to me', but it seemed to be the only way. So I cleared away the loose stuff and pulled up into a shitty but easier angled corner. Loose holds all the way for 30 feet – typical Scottish buttress move, Grade 3 or 4 really, but quite hard at this altitude, in crampons.

He grovelled up this diagonal groove to an *à cheval* stance on a shattered ridge, directly above the traverse line and Tony. This left the rope behind him in a big Z. So he was ratty about the rope drag that kept pulling him back as he tried to move up, then Tony was ratty at him when *he* started climbing for not taking in the rope, and Mal was ratty at him as he couldn't pull up the rope because of the drag until Tony had made some progress . . .

Average mountain aggravation, brought on by nerves, fatigue and lack of oxygen. As Tony said later, if anything goes wrong, like the rope going tight behind you, at altitude you automatically assume it's your partner's fault. The lazy bastard! The incompetent wazzock! It never occurs to you it might be the mountain and the rope's just snagged. But irritation is a waste of nervous energy, so you try to put it out of your mind and concentrate on the next move, and the next . . .

Then one more pitch, heading diagonally upwards to get them off the south face and back onto the West Ridge. Scraping and levering up over very steep snow-covered scree, they found it rather gripping as the runners were more symbolic than functional, being placed in the larger lumps of loose rubble. It was with some relief that they finally regained the ridge.

'That was a bit hard, Dad.'

'You're not kidding.'

They pushed on another couple of pitches, and came to a spot where the old fixed rope ended in a tangle around a number of boulders, and a scree platform sloped out from the ridge. An old piece of polythene flapped in the breeze. It was the site of the Patey-Brown Camp 4. They dropped their packs and suddenly felt lighter and stronger. They'd made it this far. Time for a brew and the 2.00 p.m. radio call.

'How you doing down there, Andy?'

'Very comfortable, thanks. We've just finished stuffing ourselves on lamb and chapatis. Shokat's having a bit of a sulk . . . How are you, where are you?'

'We think we're at the site of the old Camp 4. We're a bit buggered, but no headaches or anything. We think we'll keep going a bit more and hope we find somewhere to doss higher up.' He looked at Tony, who nodded. They were both very aware that John Hartog had become badly frostbitten due to a night out on his summit push, so they felt they should gain an edge by doing several more pitches that afternoon. Four pitches today would mean eight less tomorrow and improve their chances of making the summit and back to the bivvy before dark.

Jon broke in to ask practical questions. What was the traverse on the rock wall like? Was it protected at all? How much abseiling on the way down?

'Getting down this is going to be the real problem. We'll have to abseil a lot of it. So it would help if you guys bring up some rope, ice screws, slings and general ab tat to 4.'

'Okay, Sandy and I will discuss that.' Pause. 'What does the rest of the ridge look like?'

'Well, the summit looks enticingly close.' For the first time, the suppressed excitement in Mal's voice broke through. He laughed. Even over the radio we could sense the hunger and anticipation. '. . . Though it probably isn't! We can see nearly all the route, and it looks easier than what we've done.'

'Really good news.' And a certain understandable envy and frustration seemed to surface in Jon's voice. He'd said he didn't care who got to the top first. That was as true as it can be among highly motivated, competitive people. But he was keyed up and very aware that the weather could break in the next couple of days and rob him and Sandy of the summit. 'OK, when do you want your next radio call?'

'Six will do us fine.'

'We'll keep in touch on the hour, just in case.'

There's always that 'just in case'. No one speaks about it directly. All the death jokes of the walk-in have dried up. It seems to be felt bad luck to talk about the things that could go wrong. So that 'just in case' is as near as we get to expressing our solidarity, our concern for each other. And for ourselves.

'Okay. Over, out.'

Late afternoon at Base Camp. Getting cool now, the flies wound down like tiny mechanical toys. I sit on the big rock above the camp, looking up the glacier to Mustagh in the last sunlight. Hard to imagine they're really up there on that ridge.

Mustagh is not a beautiful mountain. Not one of those graceful, soaring, ethereal peaks. It's big, hard-edged and unrelenting. I feel about this mountain as I felt about my father when I was ten. Respect, awe, tinged with fear. Well, I grew up, more or less, and the man mellowed. A heaviness in my chest as I realize yet again that I'll never be able to tell him about this adventure. He would have enjoyed it. He would have nodded and laughed and poured us both another dram . . .

Yet I find myself talking to him often, and he usually answers. Since he died he lives in me. I've internalized him. Part of me has his responses, his attitudes, his appetites. Like for whisky, for one thing . . . So I smile, nod at the mountain and light up a cigarette rolled with my mum's last letter to me. The radio crackles. It's Sandy, from Camp 3.

After the usual 'How are you?' exchange, he asks if we've heard from Mal and Tony, it's past 6.00. There's some concern in his voice as he agrees they could simply have lost track of the time. Or they could be asleep already. Or perhaps their radio's packed in. 'Yeah, I'm making up the same explanations.' Trouble is, none of them are very convincing. By now we're both definitely worried. Ten past six. They must have stopped climbing by now, they should be in their bivvy. So why don't they come in?

This must be how it happens. Friends simply fail to report in. A collapsing serac, a slip on a rock slab, a pin pulling . . . So easy. Sandy and I both have the same thing on our minds, but neither of us is prepared to say so. I ask if they're revved up for tomorrow.

'We're dead keen, yeah . . . It would have been nice to have heard from Mal, but . . .'

'Yes.'

Silence. Dead time on the radio. The sun has gone down, it is getting cold. I look up at Mustagh and shiver.

'Well, I'll say –'

Mal cuts in, 'We're somewhere just beneath the final tower now.'

Delight, relief in our voices as we take in his report. Such pleasure and affection in hearing the familiar voice. He sounds more tired and trudgy than I've ever heard him, but underneath that weariness is the lift of excitement.

They'd gone some five or six pitches past the old Camp 4 on knackering mixed ground. Floundering about in soft snow in the heat of the day, mostly moving together, sometimes belaying each other over difficult stretches.

They had exhausted themselves. Even the irrepressible Tony sounded weary and admitted he was 'quite tired'. But we all knew those extra pitches had put them in good striking distance of the summit. Tomorrow. If the weather holds. *Inshallah*.

They'd eventually found a possible bivvy site on a corniced ridge below what looked like the final steep section, and called a halt due to 'total embuggerage'. By this time they were at the staggering-about-and-useless stage of fatigue. So when they began shovelling out a platform for the tent they were short-tempered and ineffective. Tony seemed particularly feeble, to Mal's eyes at least, patting at the snow with the absurd red plastic shovel. 'If you don't dig, you can lie in the bloody snow,' he snapped. Tony bit back a reply and laboured on McKinley was easy compared to this.

Then, a foot down, they hit solid ice. A spasm of hatred at this bloody mountain, then they started prodding about elsewhere for another site.

Mal: We got another platform dug after maybe an hour. We were just about to put up the tent when I put my foot through the platform right into a crevasse. About a foot wide and right across this ledge we'd cut. So we thought 'Sod it' and just put up the bivvy anyway. Really we were too knackered to dig a third ledge. So we slept with heads on one side of the hole, feet on the other.

After the radio call we brewed and ate some. Big day tomorrow, but we've decided to treat it as just another mountaineering day.

At Base Camp, at Camp 3 and Camp 4, we set our alarms and turn in. A white moon rises over the Baltoro. The last light glows on the tip of Mustagh and the upper slopes of Masherbrum.

We lie waiting for dawn to rise on the final act.

First to stir is Sandy in Camp 3. It's 2.00 in the morning, Sunday 29 July, cold and dark. A dead world, and he himself half-dead it seems. He sits up in his sleeping bag. How often have I done this? Why do I bother? Why are we so narrow? Ah, but it's good jest! Better one still if the lads make the summit today. Our turn tomorrow . . .

He lights the stove and melts the ice-topped water from the night before. Jon slowly becomes more or less conscious, and as the first brew of the day goes down, they look at each other and inside themselves and decide they're feeling well. They melt snow for a second brew; just as the pan is nearly full of warm water Sandy adds a last spoon of snow and knocks the pot over.

'It's almost like a parable,' he remarks. 'Just that little bit of greed and you lose the lot.' Jon grunts, understandably not in the mood for this Highlander's philosophical musings.

They finally leave the tent round 4.00 in the first grey light, Jon leading. Following Mal and Tony's tracks from yesterday, they make steady progress up the gullies and rock ribs of the lower West Ridge.

It was 5.00 before Mal and Tony got going. This late start was to cause them problems all day. Their bivvy tent had proved a disaster, 'more like a casualty bag'. Hoarfrost had formed on the inside throughout the night and fell off in plates onto their sleeping bags and gear, then started to melt. Bivvies at 22,000 feet are never hospitable, and it was all rather cold and depressing as they began spooning snow into the billycan for the first brew.

Mal looked outside. Flurries of snow, and a deeper darkness massed over Lobsang and across the Baltoro. Not promising at all. He felt anger, real anger, realizing they could be robbed of the summit at this final stage. If the weather turns bad, we haven't enough food or fuel to sit it out, so it would be all the way back down to Base Camp. And even if we make it, will the weather hold for Jon and Sandy?

They were silent as they geared up, each summoning all their remaining will, concentration and experience. Harness, crampons, helmet, the rack of pegs and nuts and friends. The rope that will connect them all day as the partnership expands and contracts towards the summit. And all the time, suppressed excitement beating like a pulse beneath the skin.

Their sacks held the bare minimum. Shovel for emergency snow hole, stove, can, brew, some extra clothing. They sling them on, adjust to the familiar weight, then set off together on what they hoped was to be their last day heading up. The ridge here was fairly wide, gently undulating whalebacks, and the snow excellent as they trudged steadily up towards the first seracs.

In my dream Mal, Tony, Jon and Sandy are dancing round in a circle, holding hands. They are in full climbing gear, and laughing. They are chanting, 'Ring a ring of roses . . . Atishoo, atishoo! We all fall down!' and they fall flat on their backs in the snow, helpless with laughter. I stand outside their charmed circle, watching them. Then Tony shouts, 'Here, Andy – catch!' and twirling through the air towards me comes a purple karabiner. All I have to do is catch it to join their game. I very much want to. Here it comes, turning end over end in slow motion. If I concentrate, I think I can do it . . .

I blink awake. Yellow light in my familiar tent. Base Camp. Would I have caught that krab? I grovel for my watch. Ten to six. 'Ring a roses' – is it a bad omen? We get so superstitious up here.

'Morning, Jhaved.'

' 'Lo, Mr Andy. Summit today, yes?'

'*Inshallah.*'

Jhaved nods approvingly. I'm learning all things are in the

hands of Allah, all things are Maybe. 'Summit *inshallah* yes. I make prayer . . .'

'Aye, me too.'

We sit nodding at each other like pigeons, grinning, excited already, caught in the flush of summit fever. It's infectious across the miles. I switch on the radio and look out at the morning: nice enough down here, an odd haze over the sun, a lot of cloud across the glacier. Hmm . . . A light breeze ruffles the yellow flowers round the Mess Tent. The radio crackles . . .

'Morning, wankers!' Jon, of course, sounding very buoyant. And with good reason – he and Sandy are already at the rock wall that gave the others trouble yesterday midmorning.

'. . . We're tired, but no problem with the heads. So we're very pleased, we're going much faster than Mal and Tony did, I think.' A characteristic competitive note, though he immediately adds, 'Of course, we've had their steps to follow, which is an immense help. It's snowing slightly . . .' Pause. 'Actually, it's a great day!'

His exuberance sends smiles and optimism chasing round the circle of Jhaved, Alex, Shokat and myself as we crouch about the radio.

'It's going very well so far. The only problem is going to be coming down because we haven't got enough rope. So that could be very entertaining.'

Then the familiar Duff tones cut in. 'Good morning, we're on the West Ridge and we're on the final summital pyramid.' (This turned out to be an optimistic way of putting it.) More smiles all round. We may actually pull it off, after two years of planning, cock-ups and setbacks, and six weeks' hard labour. Glittering prizes . . .

Mal continues, his steady, emphatic Scottish voice just a little breathless. 'We've done the flat section above Camp 4, and we're now just passing the first serac barrier. We've probably got about a thousand vertical feet to go. We're not feeling too bad. Fucking cold, though.'

Jon: 'What are snow conditions like up there?'

'Bit heavy going, youth. We keep breaking through wind crust into deep powder snow, and there's more of those funny flounder holes. Not too bad, but then again, it's not perfect either.'

There's laughter at this typical Mal utterance. We're all feeling very good, very close to each other. With that we sign off, each to his own business.

Alex has packed his sack and announced he's going back up to the Brew Tent for a day's exploration and photography. I don't think it's because he's lost interest in the final push, but rather the reverse. He's been restless and distracted ever since we returned to Base Camp. He's got a touch of summit fever, and listening to the lads' progress inflames it. Well, we all have desires we'll never satisfy, though carrying them about is a waste of energy.

'Wish them luck from me,' he drawls, and the tall, emaciated figure plods off towards the Ibex Trail.

Meanwhile Sandy is tackling the rock wall between Camps 3 and 4. He'd climbed the first section much as Tony did till he came on an old Brown-Patey piton, tested it. Still solid after twenty-eight years. Thanks very much, he thought, clipped into it, then belayed Jon up. Now he edges with extreme attention along the crumbling traverse ledge and comes to the choice between the overhanging chimney above and the rock slabs on the south face that Mal had faced the day before. He opts for the slabs and with some trepidation scrapes his way across and up, trying not to be distracted by the 3000-foot drop below his boots. He remembers saying to Andrew a few days back, 'If climbing was dangerous, I wouldn't do it', and that youth's incredulous expression. He smiles to himself. This is not dangerous; a false move would kill me and Jon, so don't make one. Concentrate . . .

He runs into the same rope-drag problem as Mal and Tony had, and belays at about three quarters of the rope length. While Jon moves up towards him he looks up and spots Mal and Tony, tiny figures in red and blue, way up on the ridge. They look as if they're approaching the west summit of the Tower, but his Highland caution says, Don't bet on it . . .

'Hate this bloody snow,' Mal grumbles as yet again his boot breaks through the thin windslab crust and ends up knee-deep in powder snow. And again. It's like wading through mud or running a marathon under water, and at 23,000 feet the body is deteriorating all the time, white blood corpuscles and brain cells dying in their thousands every minute. One's physical and mental resources drain away like sand through an old-fashioned egg timer, measuring out the time one can still safely spend up here. That timer can only be reversed by returning to Base.

We've had 100 feet of névé and 1500 of powder snow. The whole route's changed beyond recognition since Brown and Patey. The Icefall for a start ... Twenty-five, twenty-six ... Twenty-seven ... Doesn't Tony ever tire? Twenty-eight ... Take a break at fifty ... Twenty-nine, I'm getting too old for this. No I'm not ... Thirty-one ... When I start counting steps it's getting serious ... Thirty-five ...'

By now they are on the couloir leading up to where rocks bar the ridge in front, and serac barriers are stacked up above and on the left. Neither of them like the look of those seracs. It's definitely a time for speedy movement, but the sun's softening the snow now and draining their energy down the plughole.

So round 8.00 Mal and Tony decide on a brew stop. They dig the space, get out the stove, fill the can – then look at each other.

'Got the matches, youth?'

'I thought you had them, dad.'

'If I do, I can't find them.'

In the depths of his fetid sack, Tony finally scrapes out five matches in a battered box. He tries them, one after another. The damp heads slide off the wooden stems. The ever optimistic, ever ingenious Duff tries to spark a light from the batteries of his head torch. No chance.

They look at each other, torn between accusation, apology and laughter.

'Ah well, all the less to carry,' Mal says finally. Tony shrugs, nothing to be done. So they leave the useless stove and pan, pick up their sacks, and head with some trepidation up towards those cresting seracs.

Sandy Allan is enjoying himself. Leading, he's come up against three tricky rock and ice pitches. He's feeling good and strong; the climbing isn't desperate, but hard enough to be interesting and exhilarating. Just the kind of stuff they came to the Tower for – the challenge of technical climbing at altitude. He makes the last few moves and comes to the end of his rope length. Finds a crack and bangs in a peg, clips in. Above him the ridge swoops on up towards the west summit, where he can still just see Mal and Tony. They appear to have stopped moving. Jon's coming up behind. He can see right over the Lobsang Spire, Mitre Peak, Cathedral, and across the Baltoro to countless ranges of unnamed, unclimbed peaks. A lifetime of climbing out there. This is good value. This beats working. This is possibly even better than Dominique. This is what it's about.

Kathleen . . . I've scarcely thought about her since she last spoke so clearly in my head as I stumbled down towards Camp 1. She should be back in Scotland now, doing whatever loved ones do when they are outside your ken. She should be here beside me on this boulder above Base Camp, looking straight up the glacier at Mustagh while the last act approaches its resolution. So should serious Adrian with his sudden humour, and Mohammed of the candid eyes and brilliant smile. And Rocky Moss . . . They're all part of what's happening up there. We're not really separate at all. The isolation of one person from another, so distressing at times, is only apparent. We're joined together by invisible, weightless ropes of affection, shared experience, cooperation, humour and love as we move together through the world.

The radio's on, but no one's come in. They must all be busy, concentrating, working it out. It's getting warm now, the first flies of the day. Jhaved is singing in the Mess Tent, praying perhaps, and Shokat's radio sails eternally from his tent. Do I wish I was up there too? No, not really. Making Camp 2 and back again was enough. Maybe if I'd had a chance at the Col . . . Forget it. My speeding pulse and summit fever are not personal now; it's for them.

Two enormous ravens circle low over our camp. Cawing derisively, they settle on rocks just beyond stone-throw. They are motionless, as if waiting. This has never happened before. What does it mean? Dead climbers return as these 'Himalayan budgies' . . . No one believes it, yet when we joke about it, it feels true.

A good or bad omen, their settling here today? Each of those black, yellow-rimmed eyes has an image of the mountain in it, the same mountain I'm looking at, the same mountain on which my friends are now struggling to get nearer their own obscure summits.

Tony is not a happy youth. He's cursing the mountain, this waist-deep powder snow, and Duff for sending him out on this crazy line. He is leading – more accurately, floundering – below the second rock wall. He is not enjoying himself.

Tony: Shortly after our non-brew brew stop, we came to another rock wall. It looked like it should be turned below some seracs on the left. Mal said, 'Just go up and wind your way up through the rocks.' I didn't like the line I thought he meant, but set off anyway. The first bit was névé, lovely stuff, then suddenly I was waist-deep in powder snow. I struggled around, then I was up to my neck in some sort of hole. I tried everything, swimming and rolling, but I just couldn't get to the rocks only 20 feet away where I could see a brilliant crack for a runner.

I exhausted myself there, and finally shouted down to Mal, 'Look, this is not on!' So he said, 'Just go across left below the seracs' and it was miles across this face, and I mean miles, like 100 metres or more, all avalanche prone and on belay and my thoughts going across there were, There's no way I'll do this again, ever. I was just gripped. I kept saying, 'Jesus, Mal, this is fucking ridiculous!' And it was. This was the slope that shuddered under Patey and Hartog, and it felt like it could go any second. And the seracs above us . . .

I reached some ice and put a sling over a spike, useless really. I set off right, back up across the rocks and that was horrendous because a slip there would have taken us both off. 'For fuck's sake, Mal, where are you sending me?' It felt like I was being sent. I was blaming him . . . Nerves really, I suppose. I finally found a good belay, and Mal led up through some ice and back onto the ridge. I was totally wasted, more tired than I'd ever been. I looked up at the west summit, it didn't look any closer than when we set out. If I'd have given up anywhere, it would have been there.

But they don't give up. They plug on as the day gets hotter and the hours slip away, pausing more and more often, to lean, gasping, over their axes.

10 a.m. Sandy radios in. He's in his 'Jolly good' mood. They've

cracked the first rock wall and are now getting close to the old Camp 4 site. He and Jon intend to go on past Mal and Tony's bivvy to give themselves less to do tomorrow. What's it like up there, Mr Porridge? 'Basically very nice.' Mal and Tony have just gone out of sight, and it's unlikely they'll see each other again until the Camp 4 bivvy when the lads come down from the summit this evening. That meeting seems a long way off. Over and out.

I sit cross-legged in front of my tent, radio at my right hand, recorder at my left. This is my vocation, and I enjoy it. I'm glad, overwhelmingly so, that Mal banged on my window and snatched me away from my settled life. This is good action.

Shokat, his hair oiled and brushed carefully into place, paces up and down. He stops every so often to stare at our goat. The goat stares back at him. It does not know it's scheduled to be the highlight of our celebratory meal when the lads return. Ignorance is a blessing of sorts. We who are not quite so ignorant can only plan and strive and worry. I am ignorant of what's happening up there, and wish I wasn't. Jhaved squats in front of the Mess Tent, scraping elaborate patterns on the ground with a kitchen knife. He knows it's all in the will of Allah.

We're all waiting, and there's nothing we can do but wait.

In the meantime there are sluggish flies to flick away, and this cigarette. I've smoked my way through my mum's airmail letter, and now start on a sheet from Dominique that Sandy left me.

It's the first time I've smoked a French letter.

Rough stuff.

12.0 Sandy on the radio. He and Jon are at Mal and Tony's bivvy. It looks slumped and desolate, so they're going on to a better site. Mal radios, but I can't make out anything for electrical interference. The weather is deteriorating again up there, and there's a thunderous feeling in the air. Bit worrying, that. Sandy relays that the lads think they're some 100 vertical metres below the west summit, are very tired but hacking on . . .

Mal: A small rock triangle started to figure in the game plan. The wading had become unacceptable. So Tony led off up a ledge system, our shattered bodies in tune with the nature of rock. I reviewed myself, control total thankfully, the urge to continue powerful, more powerful than worries about what would inevitably become an exciting evening descent. Already we should be turning back.

Up to join the lad, then diagonally up a groove – hardish rock climbing, and several very hard ice moves near the top. To me the most satisfying piece of climbing so far, a 70 degree corner, the left wall ice and the right wall rock. Bridged up, axes whacking away, the ice spray sparkling rainbows . . .

Back on the ridge again, the west summit proved not to be. Depression and determination vie against each other. We talk little but feel a lot, our lives inextricably linked now and for a lifetime. Companionship, irritation, worry, desire for the end of the uphill, a point where we could turn about. But not yet . . .

At Base Camp now we're raised, gripped by the nearness of success. It's remarkable how an expedition like this suddenly accelerates: two years' planning, the long walk-in, five weeks here slowly establishing and stocking camps – times when no progress seems to be being made at all, when morale slumps and no one feels like getting up in the morning – then it all comes down to three days feverish activity, succeed or fail.

The temporal shape of our adventure is mirrored by the physical shape of the Mustagh Tower. The huge, wide base, slowly rising, gradually narrowing and accelerating upward, then the final quick swoop up to the summit. It probably took the Egyptians years to lay the foundations of a pyramid, yet the last 100 feet would go up in a few days.

The breeze ruffles the yellow flowers dotted around Base Camp. I think of Kathleen, of Liz waiting and wondering back home, of the lads on the ridge, of my mother and father. They're all different distances away, yet whenever you think of someone they're as near as can be, beside or inside you. It's like our radios: however distant the point of broadcast, the voice is right beside you.

Mal: Overall impression of total tiredness, pure will, a bizarre desire to succeed no matter what, worryingly cold toes. A rapidly expanding vista to north, south and west, most of the peaks below us now. Slight weather eye on, yes, the weather. Hatred for crusty powder, counting steps, looking after the rope and the next place to stop (great – an old peg – good excuse to stop!). Gut fatigue and plugging plugging steps, will the rock handhold stay in place, oh well too tired to worry, use it anyway . . .

*

1.00 p.m. Mal on the radio. I snatch it up. He's loud and clear this time, but sounding breathless and flat with tiredness. We can hear the clinking of harness and rack in the background as Tony prepares to lead the next pitch. For a moment it's as though Jhaved, Shokat and I are standing right next to them, willing them on.

They've been ploughing up more knee-deep snow. The west summit seems to keep retreating before them like the end of a rainbow, but they're nearing some boulders that look as though they lead up to it.

'As long as these clouds don't wipe us out in the next hour or so, we'll be all right.' Pause. 'Tony's just started plodding off, so I'd better hold his rope. Over, out.'

Smiles all round. 'Summit near, Mr Andy?' 'Soon, *inshallah*.' We take a hurried lunch. Jhaved's made something special, but it's wasted on us. We talk as we eat, in quick bursts.

I think we're going to make Mr Covington eat his words. He was the American climber who supposedly said to Rocky, 'That Mickey Mouse expedition doesn't have a chance. They're not even serious.' Well, he'd tried the easier east ridge the year before and scarcely got off the glacier. We relished that remark. It gave us something to prove, and right now the lads are up there proving it. If we can get all four to the summit and back, a clean sweep . . .

Mal: A constant treadmill of false summits saps the will as efficiently as a bullet kills. 'What's it like?', my hopeful plea as Tony tops another crest. 'A long way,' he says emotionlessly, not even bothering to turn round or stop. A sinking, heavy, lifeless feeling as we go on for no logical reason I can remember, hope rising and falling with every step or setback. So tired, and all the time in my head a ticking clock, the sweeping second hand brushing away at our chances and perhaps our lives . . .

2.00 p.m. Sandy radios from their Camp 4 bivvy. They've arrived, shagged but safe, and are now brewing up and drying out gear. They can just see Mal and Tony. 'Yeah,' the casual, sleepy voice continues, 'they look about eighty feet below the west summit.'

My heart's banging away, we're all grinning and sweating in

the heat. Eighty feet! Surely they've cracked it. But no one dares say so, so instead I ask Sandy to describe his outlook up there.

'You mean the quality of life or how many glaciers we can see?' comes the reply.

He hands over to Jon, and we have a leisurely, pleasant chat. He's done for the day and is relaxed and enthusiastic.

'Actually it's been a really interesting day. Very similar climbing to one of the Italian ridges on Mont Blanc in that it's not easy and not hard. And as we've got higher the blocks, those tottering heaps of shit I told you about, have got bigger so you can pull up on them. On the China side there's this absolutely huge glacier just like a motorway with the streaks down the middle and everything, it's great. It's been very uncanny ... Everything's slightly pink and dingy and looks hand-tinted like one of those 1920s postcards. Yes, it's been a strange old day ...'

We chat on, enjoying the contact and hoping Mal will come in. He doesn't. I arrange to switch on every half hour from now on, then sign off.

> He either fears his fate too much
> or his deserts are small,
> that dares not put it to the touch
> to win or lose it all.

One of Mal's favourite quotations, from the Duke of Montrose. It expresses the attitude of those who are prepared to take a calculated gamble with their lives to achieve their goals. Then again, Montrose did in the end lose it all. When he was led down the High Street in Edinburgh to the place of execution, did he still think it had been worth it?

Very probably. It sounds as if he had a climber's mentality. That's why death isn't tragic for those who decide that, win or lose, life merits the gamble. It's excess of the life urge that brings us here, not a lack of it.

I watch the goat cropping the sparse grass at the end of its tether. The faintest breeze stirs the flowers nearest me. Something hovers on the brink of declaring itself.

2.30. Switch on. Wait. Flick away the flies. Suddenly Mal comes through and announces: 'We're on top of the west summit now and heading toward the main one.' Our exhilaration bubbles up in smiles all round, Jhaved bouncing up and down on his heels like a hairy leprechaun. The west summit! Surely they're going to make it now. Just a few hundred yards, a couple of rock steps, and a knife-edge finish. But Mal sounds quite wasted, and we can feel the effort he's making to breathe, speak and think coherently as he continues. 'Still a bit of a way to go and we're really tired and it's getting late . . . But I think we'll make it. We're leaving our rucksacks here in a small snow basin and going for it. We're just zooming off now.' He laughs. 'Zoom' is scarcely the word for it. They seem to have been moving in slow motion, like divers in lead boots about to tackle an octopus in an old B-movie. 'Get back to you soon.'

Radio silence, the distant swish of static.

We look at each other. Leaving their sacks is very committing. If for any reason they don't find them again – like if this threatened storm finally breaks – they've had it.

I get up and walk around camp to kick off adrenalin. All the empty tents waiting for their occupants' return. Scattered cassettes, letters from home, a book left open . . . I'm beginning to worry about their descent. They've been going over nine hours and have still to make the top, turn around and set off back to their bivvy on what sounds like a very accident-prone ridge, probably finishing in the dark.

Only Patey and Hartog made the east summit, after all. The other two had to turn back because it was too late in the day. Even at that, they were forced into emergency bivvies, and Hartog got frostbite. But there's no way these lads are going to turn back now. I hope they can still make the right mountaineering decisions while in the full grip of summit fever.

Down here we're fidgety and raised as expectant fathers, pacing up and down, totally involved and totally helpless to influence the outcome.

3.00 Jon. 'Well, the first brew's just coming to the boil . . .' He laughs, sounds very relaxed. But he too is concerned about the time, and can see Mal and Tony being forced to dig in overnight. And he's also worried that deteriorating weather might blow his and Sandy's chances for tomorrow. With the other lads' tracks to follow, there's little else could stop them other than avalanche or a collapsing serac.

'By way of further incentive, Jon, if you make it and get back to Scotland, you're promised from Kathleen as big a hug as is possible for a small girl to give. And as for Sandy, I'll buy him breakfast in the North British Hotel any time he wants!'

Laughter across the miles.

'Well, she's certainly one of my favourite ladies.' A big grin's just appeared all over Sandy's face . . . Ah, he says he wants Kath sent up here right away!'

We sign off after some more or less witty repartee. The radio is on all the time now, but no one comes in. Where's Mal got to? They've got to be near it now.

I pick a yellow flower and slowly shred it between my fingers. Waiting . . .

3.30 A burst of static on the radio. Then the familiar Duff tones, struggling for breath between words. 'Looks . . . about fifty feet from the top . . . Keep monitoring . . . Doesn't look far now – maybe fifteen to twenty minutes . . . Later . . .'

Christ, he sounds tired.

The LO keeps nervously smoothing back his hair with the palm of his hand. Jhaved squats, bobbing beside me, muttering under his breath. We feel we're pushing them every step.

I cut up the last of Dominique's letter. My hands are not entirely steady. Well, Mr Covington . . . What it must be like up there, all the slopes finally falling away . . .

4.00 'Just done a fairly stiff rock pitch . . . Wait till I untangle the rope . . . Okay . . . I think this is the summit ridge . . . I fucking well hope so.' Long pause, we bend our heads even closer to the radio. 'The west summit wasn't in actual fact . . . We've been over another one since then . . .' He's gasping for breath now, the voice hoarse. '. . . Very threatening clouds and an even more threatening time . . . Don't see us getting down tonight, bit of an epic, I imagine, later on . . . We brought up the stove and forgot to bring any matches or lighter – that's not brilliant, youth, now is it?'

I shake my head in silent laughter and affection. Pure Malcolm, that is. We'll remind him of that one for years.

'. . . Rope's just running out to Tony now, so I'll have to get moving . . .'

Surely they've cracked it. But like Scottish revellers waiting for New Year to strike, we daren't celebrate yet. I look around the camp. No wind, no sound; the two ravens are still perched on the boulder 30 yards away, heads cocked, expectant.

4.10 p.m. An explosion of static. My pulse leaps to 120. I pick up the radio. Malcolm comes through. He barely succeeds in sounding casual.

'At the moment we're sitting on the top of Mustagh.'

12

Thunder in the Mountains

In which Mal and Tony bale out and Sandy hangs ten

29 July–1 August 1984

Mal: Thank god we got here, I thought that ridge would never end. Pleasure; not intense, too much still to do to feel any bubbling joy. Just very happy at having reached our goal. Slumped astride the ridge, one leg in China, one in Pakistan – Tony a few feet away in his blue windsuit, K2 massive in the distance. A lot of peaks smaller than us. All around blue, grey-black thunder clouds twisting and churning. Shafts of light spilled through or under them, illuminating high hanging glaciers away out over China, mirror-silver bright. And odd twisting snow particles glinted in the air, caught like dust in sunlight . . .

At Base Camp, our wild and joyous cheer, the release of two days' tension and adrenalin, startled the goat from its grazing. It looked at us with puzzled, reproachful eyes as we babbled our congratulations. I sensed it was uncool, poor Himalayan stylee, to congratulate them at this point, but that was how we felt.

Jon cut into our euphoria to show how it was done:

'Hello, Mal. Jon here.'

'Hello, youth, how are you?'

'Oh, we're thriving. What we want to know at the moment is something rather practical . . .' And he went on with climbing business: what gear would they need, what was the route like, any problems? No congratulations, no well-wishing. Mal replied in the same vein, then Jon cut out of the conversation, leaving Jhaved and Shokat to express their happiness.

Mal: Radio a nice obligation, but as they dragged on, a rising sense of indignation – don't they realize that every second passing is critical to us? 'Okay Shokat, thanks, yes I'll tell Mr Tony as well, yes thanks okay, see you in a couple of days . . .' A raised eyebrow from the youth as he shuffles towards me, I move slightly to allow him to fix the rope for the first abseil, down a different face of the summit to a snow trough. Then I handed him the radio and took some photos . . .

So Tony came on the radio, his Lancashire accent bubbling from the crumbling knife-edge summit ridge of Mustagh to the parched green security of our camp. '. . . Extremely happy, Andy, extremely tired. It's an awful lot longer than I thought. The last 200 feet is *à cheval*, one leg over either side of the ridge. It's amazing! I can honestly say I'm well and truly knackered. I think we want to get down – there's not much daylight left, and an awful long way to go.'

Mal: Eventually Over, Out. A big grin from Tony as if to say great, well done, but the work starts now. Any fool can trog upwards but it takes craft and cunning to descend quickly and safely in these conditions. I view him critically – will he keep his concentration? I'm much more experienced at operating efficiently when fucked than he is – I'm fucked more often! So just a bit reserved. He knows my views on summit congratulations anyway, so we act as if we're only halfway on this mountain. Which we exactly are. I'm secretly glowing inside but suppress this to avoid alarming Tony. Urgency is the overriding theme, so we take a last look and turn our backs on this jewel . . .

They'd had some twenty minutes on the summit. Tony abseiled off a block, fixed the next placement. Mal whizzed down after him and pulled the abseil rope down as Tony fed the slack through the next abseil point. Everything on fast automatic now, precise, no need to speak. They soon regained their rucksacks and abseiled into the soft-snow gully which had nearly broken them on the way up. Two more pitches of swift downclimbing took them to the rock barrier. Suddenly thunder started to roll out over China, distant but not distant enough.

They faced a choice in the twilight – abseil down the rock, five pitches with the possibility of the rope jamming so they couldn't retrieve it, or follow the gully diagonally under the seracs on the avalanche-prone slope of the morning. To Mal, this was one of the most important mountaineering decisions of the trip. Down the rock led into unknown territory: a jammed rope or lack of belay placements could leave them desperately benighted. On the other hand, if it worked, they'd cut out an hour or more from the time it would take to traverse down under those menacing seracs. The pros and cons were perceived and weighed up wordlessly in the few seconds they stood still above the rock barrier while the thunder rumbled. 'Straight down, Dad?' 'Reckon so, son.'

They went for it, made it, and carried on down towards the haven of the Camp 4 bivvy in the gathering dark. Mal smiled, remembering the I Ching Kathleen had thrown before leaving South Queensferry: *Thunder in the mountains sounds much nearer.* Too right, youth . . .

I switched off the radio and recorder and was suddenly exhausted. Post-summital langour. Shokat tuned into the test match from England and Jhaved started making tea. We were the only people in the world who knew the Mustagh Tower had been climbed for the first time in twenty-eight years. It was already a fact, but no one else knew it yet. And it changed nothing at all, except us.

Elation glowed in me like whisky, but I was sobered by the knowledge that we couldn't relax and celebrate yet. I'd picked up enough between the lines to realize that Mal and Tony's descent would be the most hazardous phase of the climb. The majority of mountain accidents happen while descending. People are exhausted, their concentration slips, it's much harder to see what you're doing when downclimbing. Then Jon and Sandy still had to go for it tomorrow. A clean sweep . . . Only when all four had made the top and were finally reunited back down here could we finally call the Expedition a success.

Nothing I could do about it now. Might as well attend to these piles. I picked up water bottles and washing things and padded off towards the stream.

Alex was there when I returned. He seemed oddly tense and dissatisfied despite the lads' triumph and having had a good day communing with the glacier. He was still wondering if he could have gone higher on the Tower, and still unable to rid himself entirely of summit fantasies. He'd been sick on and off for two weeks now, and had become so beaky and scrawny he looked like an anorexic pterodactyl.

Jon radioed in at 6.00. No word from Mal and Tony. The air at Base was deathly still, the sky hazed and yellow, redolent with thunder. Jon asked us to start calculating how many porter loads we had for Gasherbrum 2, so we could send Jhaved off to Askole for porters in the next couple of days and minimize sitting-about time. Alex shook his head in mock astonishment and rolled his eyes. They haven't even got up this mountain, let alone down, and they're planning getting to the next one.

'Hey, *amigo*, these gringos they ees crazee.'

They intended to start shortly after midnight for the summit and follow Mal and Tony's tracks by head torch. Jon's cockney drawl was compressed with excitement; he knew that if the weather held, they had every chance of making it. It would take sleeping pills to let them rest tonight.

I lay in my tent. It was fully dark now. Ever optimistic, I'd drafted a telegram for Kath and Liz, and a press release. Now I was too restless to read, and too raised to sleep. All I could think of was Mal and Tony abseiling down through the dark. Had they taken head torches? Had they been forced into an emergency bivvy somewhere above Camp 4?

I grimaced, rolled a last foul French-letter cigarette and looked at the ceiling. I wanted my friends safely down. I wanted Kath and Adrian here to share in our success. I was singing inside, yet apprehensive. Three more days before we could truly relax and celebrate.

8.00 p.m. I speculatively switched on the radio, though I'd made no arrangement with either pair for a call. Dead time, it's called, when there's no transmission, only the endless swish of electro-magnetic surf.

'Camp 4 here, anyone out there?'

I fumbled, astonished, for the 'Send' switch. 'This is a pleasant surprise, Mal.'

'Yeah, well, it's remarkable how the prospect of being caught in an electrical storm on a Himalayan peak gets you moving. We got here five minutes ago. Tony's got the stove on and we'll have a brew if we can stay awake long enough.'

He sounded very relieved, and very tired. His voice dragged but was still ironic, still in control. We made arrangements for tomorrow's calls, and signed off. For tonight at least, they were safe. I could sleep now.

*

Mal switched off the radio, looked at Tony slumped over the stove. The last few hours had been a flickering movie on a tired old projector. He felt tired, more tired than ever before. Pleasure was there, somewhere in the background. A fifteen-year-old dream, two years' planning, all that slog and running around, the money . . .

It was certainly rather nice to get it done.

Jon had the stove humming as Sandy extracted his head from his sleeping bag. Five past midnight. The bivvy tent had proved desperate, hoarfrost everywhere that fell off the inside in plates causing damp patches and eventually total wetness. It was a bit depressing and miserable; the night outside was not much better, flurries of snow caught in his head-torch beam.

His mind was quite blank as they put down a couple of brews and dragged on their gear, nursing their fingers back to life. They geared up, selected a rack of pitons, nuts, friends, karabiners and slings, a figure-of-eight for abseiling, then roped together and set off into the dark.

Sandy: Jon led the first few pitches, my head nowhere special, a lot of concentration to crampon points and ice-axe placements and putting one foot in front of another. I followed the delicate beam of my faltering head torch, watched Jon and the complicated slopes he led upon.

He belayed so I climbed up to him, finding that initial part of the climb semi-hard in the early morning cold and darkness. He was tired, me too. We moved together most of the time as the light slowly crept in. We began sinking to our knees in soft powder snow, and Jon kept sitting down, quite exhausted. As is the mode of teamwork and friendship, I took up the lead . . .

I woke up late, round 6.30, went out to check the weather. Hazy, mixed cloud, very still. Our luck is holding, I thought. Just give us two more days.

At 7.00, Jon radioed in, sounding determined and businesslike. They were well up the mountain, not too far below the west summit by the look of things through drifting cloud and snow. 'A couple of hours, I should think.' And signed off.

Mal came on the air. They'd slept in after yesterday's efforts and were just having their first brew. He asked immediately after Jon and Sandy. 'That's fantastic.' Best wishes. Over, out.

When Tony and Mal finally got moving, their descent was a long history of dragging weariness and automatic action. They abseiled a lot, but downclimbed together at times for speed's sake. Finally Tony's concentration faltered; he slipped on snow-covered ice and only stopped himself from shooting over the southwest face by grabbing a rock on the way past. Mal was unamused; if Tony had gone over, so would he.

It happens again and again in climbing. It makes one at once trusting and extremely critical of the least error or piece of carelessness in one's partner. Climbing partnerships are often marriages of convenience, all too frequently followed by a quick divorce on return home, but at the time their intensity is total.

Well, we got off with it that time, Mal reflected, controlling his anger. Let's hope Tony learns from it. You must go on a mountain with an absolute determination not to make a single mistake.

Still, they moved quickly and well until, having abseiled down a 100-foot rock wall, the abseil rope jammed and they couldn't pull it back down. Mal borrowed Tony's knife, climbed back up as far as possible, asked Tony to pull on the rope to stretch it, then cut it through. They now had less than half of their original rope length. Their longest abseils could be only 35–40 feet. No need for words; they both knew this would add to the time, energy and the likelihood of accidents on the descent to Camp 3, and that there was nothing to be done about it.

They pushed on down, feeling the extra oxygen revive their minds and bodies. I hadn't realized till Mal pointed it out what a precise technical business descending is, especially when you're short on gear to abseil off. With each abseil, you're forced to leave something behind – a nut, a couple of pitons, a friend, at the very least a sling and a karabiner. Which leaves you all the less to choose from on the next abseil placement. And if you run out of gear too soon, you're in trouble.

Knowing this would happen, Mal had memorized all the likely abseil points on their way up the summit ridge, and was now ticking them off one by one. They'd need this big nut for the crack on the next ab, so use the small one here . . . Got to keep at least three pegs back . . . We could use that old peg of Patey's on the ab after that . . . Maybe even some of the old fixed line, it seemed strong enough in parts . . .

A very mental business, a kind of climber's Pelmanism or Kim's Game. A feat of applied memory. I found later that Mal could visualize exactly every abseil point of the descent – and indeed all the important ones on every route he'd ever climbed. It reminded me again there is a lot more to mountaineering than courage and strength. To be good one needs tolerance, self-control, route-finding ability, understanding of weather and snow conditions, memory, meticulous attention to detail, absolute commitment set against the capacity to judge when one is stepping over the knife-edge ridge into unacceptable risk.

On top of this, Himalayan climbing demands more sustained physical endurance than any other pursuit. Perhaps only single-handed long-distance sailing compares to it. A marathon runner gives it everything for a few hours. A pentathlon is held over a few days, but at the end of each day the athlete can bath, eat a normal meal, sleep normal hours and thus recharge. Above 20,000 feet one does not recharge, can eat little and usually sleep less, in conditions of great discomfort. And then the next day get up and do it all over again.

It is this combination of absolute mental and physical demands that makes mountaineering the total experience. That makes it so addictive. That makes my bin-men friends so moving and impressive to me.

Right now I just want to see them all back down here at Base, lounging among the flies and sunshine and green grass.

Sandy: After a brew I led on up a steep couloir, finding it quite hard, almost Grade 4 Scottish. It was more bold than difficult, snow on rock slabs, not really secure placements just gravitation on poor rock. But came to the top of it anyoldhow and once close to the West Summit, belayed Jon. I took out my sunglasses. Later I realized Jon had his on but I hadn't noticed at the time. He was there, sure, but just a person – I wished we could have communicated more . . .

We moved on. I let up the side of the ridge and came to the bump of the west summit. We climbed up mixed rock, belayed one pitch, then another. It was a delight, a steepish rock wall then into a gully. Then we moved on together, ever closer to the summit.

Mal: Camp 3 – a hovel transformed to a haven, even a heaven, in three days. Inside to brew, rest, even relax for half an hour. Then junk some spare food into a crevasse and then clip into the fixed line and set off down again.

The slope was horrific, all anchors needing replaced, the odd rock whizzing down with a manic whine. I saw a large boulder plunging down towards Tony below. He heard my yell and started scampering off sideways. But the line was fixed and was about to pull him back like a bowstring. The rock shot past him, then the rope whipped him back across the line it had taken a second before. It looked really funny from above, like something in a cartoon – but probably not so amusing to the little fella!

We continued on down as fast as possible, eyes and ears straining upwards all the time. Going-down syndrome, getting more edgy the nearer to home and safety.

Back at Base Camp, the same routine as yesterday. Smoking, walking around restlessly. Irritable with flies and piles, waiting.

Sandy: I led up taking my time and enjoying life in general. Once I thought I was on the last summit ridge I stopped and belayed to a block and took in the rope as Jon came up. I wanted to let him lead, just the one pitch to the top, but he was obviously not really in great form, he was happy but not enthusiastic. So he made a radio call to report our position. Andrew down there at Base Camp – with the flies, I thought, but also good food, omelettes and chapatis.

After the call Jon did not give any indication of wishing to lead, so I took the technical gear and led on up to the top – the summit. I placed my foot on a rock and on the snow and stood there on the summit of Mustagh, then sat down, legs on either side of the ridge, placed a friend in a crack and took in the rope. We felt good, well I felt great, not so much about the summit or even the place, just felt well. Looked out of my eyes and saw only clouds really, most of the mountains shrouded. Occasional windows gave us views of Base Camp, Gasherbrum etc., but no fantastical views. But they would have been materialistic views anyway. I am not here for that, for consumer durables. Be as well walking in the rain, I thought . . .

And so at 9.30 a.m. our radio sprayed saliva-static at Base Camp and we heard a very cheerful Jon:

'Well! We had a nice knife-edge finish to the route and are now sitting on the top. It's really wicked here, and we're really enjoying ourselves. To my left . . . (static) To my right . . .' (More static – we could hear about as much as they could see.)

A shower of congratulations across the airwaves. A clean sweep. All the lead climbers have made it. All they have to do now was get back down safely and we've a rare total success in the bag. Happy? We were radiant.

Sandy came on, the same greeting as always, whether in South Queensferry, the North Sea or the Himalayas: 'Hello there, youth, how's it going? Over.' He asks me how it's going? How's it going up there? 'Really good, actually. Yeah, it's really good. Quite happy . . .'

So they sat up there cracking jokes and watching the clouds part to let them see into China. Sandy had a sudden picture of himself as a tiny blot, a fly on the summit of the Tower, and his Highland nature waited for a huge hand to come out of the sky to swat him off, booming, 'Who the hell are you, Allan?'

As they prepared for the first abseil he thought of his family and wondered 'Is this what I get instead of a MA, BSc., B Com., Vet. surgeon MRCVS? Do I care? Yes I do – but differently!' He began the descent by slipping 20 feet when he thought Jon was holding him on the rope and it turned out he wasn't. 'Should I trust this youth from south of Hadrian's Wall?' he wondered, and began to concentrate again.

So while a deeply fatigued and relieved Mal and Tony stumbled towards Camp 2, and Alex and I started working out how many porters we'd need for Gasherbrum 2, Jon and Sandy abseiled and downclimbed through the clouds towards Camp 4. And on the way down, as Sandy reported laconically a couple of hours later, Jon saved his life. Both of their lives.

They'd come off one abseil and found a new peg banged into a crack. Obviously one of the first pair's, it would save using one of their own. After a moment's chat, Sandy abbed off:

. . . the peg pulled out, I got a shock as I fell very fast before I stopped with an effective and impressive view down the southwest face under my dangling feet.

'Hey Jon, do you have me or is it the peg?'

'The peg's come out – I've got you.'

'Oh thanks very much' as I reglued myself to the face and climbed back up. We replaced the offending peg and I thanked Jon for saving our lives. Teamwork at its best. Okay, in mountaineering one is always saving one's mate and hence oneself, but I was glad he was on the ball when it really mattered. I owe him a pint of beer.

In the early afternoon radio calls assured us both pairs were safely at the Camp 4 bivvy and Camp 2 respectively. Once again I found myself tired and restless, and it was with some pleasure and relief that I finally withdrew into the tent, into myself and music and my journals, at the end of the day.

Automatic now to check the weather first thing: still holding. Misty on the summit ridge, but no sign of heavy snow. There'd been some radio discussion the night before about how to clear our gear off the mountain; the nub of it was that if Alex and I didn't go up to Camp 2 to bring some tentage, food and gas down, some would have to be abandoned at 1 and 2. Neither of us were keen on sticking our necks out. In Mal's opinion the two summit pairs should take down what they could and leave it at that. People have been killed before now going back onto the hill to clear it; he saw no point in taking that chance for some £50 of gear.

He probably regretted that decision as he and Tony tied on bits of tent and gear to their already bulging sacks and stumbled towards the White Tiger. They were full of down-going nervous tension, just wanting it safely done with. Ten days now on the hill was long enough. They came alongside the White Tiger to find it had pounced and obliterated our trail. Just another of those lucky things. They picked their way down the slope and carried on across some very shaky snow bridges in the general direction of Camp 1.

Jon and Sandy passed by the old Patey–Brown Camp 4 site, wreathed in shifting mist, and left the mountain to a solitude interrupted only twice in eternity. Their passing was itself just a flicker, a puff of cloud.

But real and precious enough to them. They came to the abseil where Mal and Tony had lost half their rope, and picked it up on the way down. Which was just as well, because their rope in turn jammed and they lost more than half of it. So they tied the two bits together which allowed them to make restricted 40-foot abseils, just long enough to reach Mal and Tony's abseil points –

without which they didn't have enough gear to get down. Again, good luck and good practice.

All in all, their descent was, as Sandy described it, 'rather intense'. The margin for error was small, the weather miserable, the belays seldom secure. On the way up, this is more acceptable, but on the way down one's thinking is entirely defensive, there is nothing to hunger for but safety.

In time they came to Camp 3, had a brew and mentally prepared themselves for the fixed-rope descent – to Sandy's mind, considerably more dangerous than the Icefall.

Sandy: I stopped and took some final photos of that high place. I felt fine but sad, goodbyes always being difficult, as a chough circled above, the wind whipped me, and the tent fly bellowed.

I attached my descendeur to the fixed rope, very aware of all the safety steps to take and I took them all. The slope was desperate: the snow crystals were large and independent of each other like sugar; the ice screws fixing the rope had melted out and lay against the slope, useless to anybody. I had to replace them all, as boulders the size of washing machines tumbled by . . .

The last couple of abs were in and through a death zone, projectiles flew and the snow-ice was soft and desperate. I slid on my knees trying to spread my weight and fell through the bergschrund, looked up just waiting for something to hit me between the eyes. But it didn't, so I climbed out and thrashed down to the end of the rope, took a bum-slide, then walked on a little to be out of range – and then water touched the rim of my sunshades and I was aware that I was crying and I sat on a mound of ice and looked up at the Mustagh Tower, the boulders falling down the southwest face, Jon sliding down, Camp 2 in the distance, the thin line of the fixed rope. Relieved and so glad, smiling internally now. We'd cracked it.

Alex, sick and restless, packed a small sack and set off up the Mustagh glacier again towards 'China Mountain' for a couple of days. When Mal radioed at 9.00 to say they'd safely made Camp 1, I set off up the Ibex Trail with an empty pack to meet them.

How could this trail ever have bothered me? It seems months ago that I first groped my way up here. Now happiness, suspense and a certain sadness at our imminent departure shift around inside me as I sit waiting at the end of the trail in hot sunlight. The Tower looks as uncompromising as before; we climbed it but in no way conquered it. If we conquered anything it was ourselves, each in our own way.

I watch and listen as the glacier below me falls apart – boulders abruptly dropping out of sight, stones rattling, a wall of ice collapses. I begin to get nervous for the lads. They're late, this tale's still unfinished . . .

It's the clinking first, clear across half a mile, the unmistakable sound of axes on rock and jingling racks. Then I see them, two little blobs linked together coming slowly, very slowly towards me across the glacier. My heart leaps up like a lover's.

I watch them approach. After ten days on the hill, they are scarcely recognizable. Huge packs, lumbering and stumbling along, encased in windsuits, heads totally obscured by helmets, beard, glacier goggles, scarves. Could be anything or anyone under that.

I get slowly to my feet as they cover the last few yards. 'Welcome back.' 'Good to see you, Andy.' We only shake hands, but the air is resonant with emotion. Mal looks exhausted, and Tony's face is peeling, scarred and swollen with water retention and sunburn – but grinning as always. They sling down their packs and slump. I give them humbugs, pass Mal a hoarded K2. He smiles, again the emotion is tangible, pure affection and relief.

'Thanks, youth, haven't had a fag for five days.'

Then he digs into his sack. 'Here, I've got something for you.' He hands over a small chunk of summit rock. It's on my desk in front of me as I type this. It's just a rock, of course, but it took some getting.

We sat chatting at the Cave, leisurely now in the pure pleasure of being alive. Mal was still peeved at himself for tripping in the Icefall when a crampon hooked some gear hanging from his harness: an elementary error, the only false move he made on the mountain but still one too many. They exclaimed over the flowers and thin grass in the ledges behind us, and I briefly saw it through their eyes – liquid colour to parched senses, the glowing evidence of life.

I loaded my sack with their gear and we set off down. Tony was soon way ahead, and I realized Mal was moving desperately slowly, with the exaggerated care of a drunk trying to walk in a straight line. As if reading my thoughts, he quietly admitted to being shattered, not so much physically – he can recover from that in a few days – as mentally and emotionally burned out. He didn't think he'd go on to Gasherbrum 2, it was too serious a peak to start with anything less than total enthusiasm and commitment. He hadn't told any of the others yet, but was pretty sure in himself it was more than the last few days' exhaustion. All the rushing to and fro, having to go back to Britain and come out again, had taken its toll. He'd done the main thing he came for, any more would be out of a sense of duty rather than desire.

He was silent then as we plodded on. I could understand his feelings – the same inner knowledge had grown on me somewhere on that endless haul to Camp 2, a knowledge that this was enough, that one's appetite for achievement and pain was sated.

I suddenly realized I wanted to go home too. Up till now I'd assumed I'd go on to Gash 2 with the others and sit around Base Camp there while they went for it if weather permitted. But I wasn't really that keen. The mountain itself was out of my league to tackle Alpine style, it didn't sound spectacular, and Mustagh had always been the core of the trip for the book and myself. The only reason for going there would be to see K2, and Mustagh from its 'unclimbable' side.

My time here, I reflected, is physically and emotionally used up. I've had the experience I came for – any more would be because I feel I should rather than genuine desire. Yes, I'd like to see K2 and be around while the lads go for Gash 2, but there's things I'd like even more: to be with Kath again, friends, Scotland, to pick up my life again.

Imperceptibly, as we picked our way down towards the oasis of Base Camp, we found ourselves talking about Queensferry, about the Edinburgh Festival and Liz and Kath. That world which for a long time seemed faint and insignificant compared to the Tower became more real and present in our minds, a new gravitational pull that asserted itself even as we stepped down onto the grass of Base. As Jhaved emotionally hugged Mal and Shokat congratulated them, and Mal and Tony finally shook hands amid much emotion on the verge of tearful for us all – even at that sweetest moment I knew I was ready to leave.

Jon and Sandy radioed to say they were at Camp 2 and to discuss porter loads and extra provisions for Gasherbrum 2. When it was clear that no one down here was going back up to clear the mountain, Jon was peevish at the thought of the load he'd have to carry, while Sandy was upset at the thought of the mess we were leaving on the hill: each in character.

Jhaved set off mid-afternoon for Askole with a list of provisions and the number of porters required, letters, telegrams and a press release. The news of our success would spread down the valley and out to the 'First World'. Not that it was important, but it would bring relief and delight to people that mattered to us: Liz, Kath, Aido and Rocky.

It felt like the end of term at Base, our minds were full of departure. In the evening we found ourselves in the yellow pool of the paraffin lamp, talking about what we missed most. It was not, as before, things like food and beer. What we yearned for now was human values and human contact. Tony missed his family and friends, for Mal it was Liz and home. And I suddenly felt how intense and narrow life up here had been, as narrow and all-enveloping as the sleeping bag I slid into every night. So much missing – all the gentler emotions, all the warmer colours for the heart and the eye. Here it was only black and white and blue, and our lives had been monkish in their single-minded harsh simplicity. It had brought extraordinary elevation of thought and feeling, but at the cost of leaving behind the fertile valleys of the world, and all the life that flourishes there.

Time to go home, Andrew. Soon as the lads are off the hill.

I was with Mal in deepest South America, looking for a legendary sea monster in an inland sea. We were guided there by a crazed old man who looked like an ancient version of the film director Werner Herzog on a particularly manic day, a raving scarecrow who insisted over and over that the monster existed. There was an unearthly silence in the air, the lake lay deep and green and motionless. Then the surface began to wallow, great waves boiled up from beneath. It was clear the beast was about to appear and it was going to be gigantic. The ancient lunatic capered and gibbered on the shore. We were about to see something completely outside our comprehension, beyond the very bounds of possibility.

Then to the left of the disturbance, a tall figure arose directly out of the water to about waist height, something between a demon, a god and a man, with wild yellow hair streaming out from his head, and his eyes bored into mine in a crucial, demanding way. His power, and the power of the challenge he was offering me, hit me like a blow. If I could understand his message and generate in myself the right response, I would be able to face out the monster whose huge grey back was at that moment rising up into the sky. If not, I would die or go insane with terror. He was on my side, but his eyes were so demanding –

– I woke with a jolt as if I'd stuck my fingers into a power socket. What the hell was that about? And why now, rather than before the climb? What is the monster that really does exist, and who is its stern counterpart?

I tried to put it out of my mind and groped for the radio. Sandy came through to say they were setting off soon, and I arranged to meet them at the top of the Ibex Trail. In the Mess Tent Alex, who'd returned the night before, was struggling with the kerosene stove, in as much of a state as he'd been in the Icefall. Support climber, Base Camp manager, photographer, glacier lover, jester – he'd been trying to be too many things and was not doing too well at any of them. And his recurrent bug had struck again.

I finally got a hot brew and sat staring into the steam, wondering what was going on with my mind, what monsters wallowed under the untroubled surface and what challenge I had yet to face. Why do we know so little? God, I'm starting to think like Sandy Allan.

So I wandered up the Ibex Trail to meet Jon and Sandy. The purple flowers along the way were withering. Autumn and bad weather were just round the corner. Time for us to move on.

Once again I had a long, nerve-racking wait. And once again, the faintest clunk and ring of axes, then the tiny figures stumbling over the glacier's spine. My pulse hammered while I watched them carefully climb off the ice onto rock, good old solid, reliable rock. Actually it was completely rotten and broken up, but a great improvement on the glacier, which was at its sleaziest that morning.

Sandy's steady 'Hello, how's it going?' as we shake hands, a grin of pure delight from Jon. Nearly home. I take some of their gear and mention that they seem much less wasted physically and mentally than Mal and Tony. Sandy mutters something about it being easier to follow in someone else's footsteps, while Jon puts it down to their greater Alpine experience – 'A piece of piss, really' – and I realize it's competitive time again.

As he walked down the trail, eyes delighting in grass and flowers, Sandy wished Jon would leave him out of such conversations. Really, who gives a fuck, he thought. Mountaineering is personal, I don't wish to expand my ego by it. Sure it's nice to appeal to the world, for folks to read Andrew's book and think, Well, these guys are okay – but to compete, don't need that. Need my girlfriend, one or two good books and to remain friendly with Mal and Tony and Andrew and Jon, to be able to participate in other ploys and adventures with the lads. That to me is where life is at . . .

And so we walked back to camp. All the handshakes, the smiles, the sense of pleasure and achievement finally allowed expression. A clean sweep, I thought as we sprawled on our packs. All four up, all four down. The kind of success that seemed unlikely when we set off, and a complete fantasy at times like our Skardu crisis. We've knocked it off.

'Right,' Sandy announced as he took a brew from Alex, 'let the bullshit commence.'

13

Coming Down

*In which we go our ways, the author
discovers a new reticence, and Malcolm
makes an outrageous offer*

1–17 August 1984

The bullshit commenced. We had four perfect days with nowhere
to go and nothing to do but clean ourselves up, eat, sleep and
shoot the breeze. Long, leisurely conversations comparing
incidents of the climb, discussing the next climb, Scotland, Irish
politics, books, pubs, childhood, good times and bad times. The
first evening we were all together was largely spent debating
which mountain to go for next. Annapurna 3? Changabang?
Amadablam? Six months ago this would have been largely pie in
the sky for the lads; now with Mustagh under their belts it all
seemed possible.

That they should sit and talk like this demonstrated to me not
only their continued appetite for climbing, but that through all
the inevitable tensions they still valued and respected each other
as part of a team. It was simply assumed they'd all go on climbing
together. After three months in each other's company, this
seemed unusual and remarkable, a real success in itself. It was
probably that cohesion and cooperation in the midst of competition which had finally yielded the Mustagh Tower – and a sense
of achievement which was only now beginning to sink in and
glow, like the embrocation I rubbed on my knee every night in
preparation for the walk-out.

Only Tony fretted at our inactivity. 'I'll go mad if we spend
another day here without climbing anything.' His face was
burned out, but not his hunger. He lacked the others' talent for
happily lying in a sleeping bag for days. Jon and Sandy were
winding up for Gash 2, while Mal kept his thoughts to himself.
On the third evening he came to my tent, ostensibly to ask for a
roll-up but really to discuss arrangements for our walk-out. He

said he felt physically recovered but the motivation, that hidden and mysterious source of power, had burned itself out. That night he announced to the others he wasn't going on and explained why. They were taken aback and disappointed; for a while they tried to change his mind, then accepted it. 'I'm sorry you're not coming, youth,' Sandy said, 'but I understand why you're not.' 'Yes,' Jon cut in, 'he's a raving woofter!' but his laugh was more sympathetic than usual.

Tony congratulated himself on his powers of recovery, as the innocent lad was prone to do. 'I'm like a battery – small and rechargeable.' 'And ninety per cent lead,' Sandy added. Pause. 'That's not a pun', but it was a beauty and five minutes later we were still laughing and spluttering.

The days remained astonishingly blue and the nights a pale explosion of moon and stars. Now we'd soon be leaving I saw again how wildly beautiful the world was up here. I sat for hours gazing across the valley at Masherbrum, letting it imprint itself in me. I had no expectations of coming this way again.

We all had our plans and futures mapped out for when we went our separate ways. Myself back to writing this book, cleaning up a book-length narrative poem, doing writing workshops in schools. Mal had to find some casual work to start recovering the money gone on the trip, then the winter guiding season in Glencoe, then a guiding trip to Kenya. The LO dreamed of rejoining his unit, of clean linen and hot showers. Sandy would go back to the oil rigs, Tony would go rock climbing until his college term started. Jon would work in a climbing shop in London. Alex planned to stay on in Baltistan, working with Mohammed towards becoming an accredited guide.

We'd meet again, but probably not all together like this. Though my thoughts now were all of going home, I felt, as we all did, sad at the prospect of parting.

Sandy: . . . And from Base Camp to the stream there is a path now, worn by our expedition's feet, and the grass is yellow in the centre of the path. There are flowers, blues, greys and yellows ever changing, and big boulders with chips knocked out as they fell from the cliff that holds the Ibex Trail. I thought of the last few days, how good they were, then of the future and the jest on Gash 2. That ought to be good value, but who can tell as yet?

On the afternoon of the fifth day, Jon shouted, 'A sail! A sail!' and we saw a procession of porters straggling across the Baltoro in our direction. Jhaved had made good time. He'd brought our porters and, most important of all, he brought K2 cigarettes and mail. A note from Kath to say she was having a great time walking out with Aido and Mohammed and that she wasn't worrying because she for some reason felt certain we were going to make it. A letter of Anstruther minutiae from my mum, and a long funny letter from a friend in the insanity factory of New York City.

We were jerked out of clouds of smoke and letters to confront another last-minute crisis: we had four more loads than porters. Reluctantly we pulled together, went through all the Gash 2 loads and rationalized them, i.e. gave half of them to the porters, stashed one load of kerosene, and spread the remaining weight hoping the porters would accept it.

It was the goat's last night on this astonishing earth. We'd all become attached to it and none of us wanted it killed. But it was the LO's goat and he wanted a farewell feast, so Jhaved led it away and came back with a bloody knife. The Balti method of cooking goat is to fry it for some ten minutes, and because it's a lean mountain beast, it is quite inedible. It could be they cook it that way so we can't eat the little bit we're given, then they take the rest away and do it properly.

Our last supper. It was a little poignant – certainly for the goat – but our minds were dominated respectively by Gash 2 and going home. For me the great adventure was nearly over, but I had no real regrets. Leave when the party's at its best. We were happy, relaxed, completely successful; Gasherbrum 2 might well detract from that. I always felt they were unlikely to make it.

I took a last look at our camp by night. It was cold and clear; the moon had set behind the Lobsang Spire and threw great shadow-mountains across the face of real mountains, confusing the eye, surreally clear cut and dramatic. In the same way I was already struggling to distinguish what had actually happened from the creations of memory and the vivid projections of the imagination. All I really know is the heightened clarity of moments like this – the chill wind, the mile-long shadows, the stars frozen in silent detonation, myself hunched entranced in a pile jacket above the glacier, smoking a last K2.

4.15 in the morning, pitch dark. Jhaved has the stove going. Time to break camp and leave this place.

We burn all our rubbish in a kerosene pyre, a miniature Lobsang Spire, an upward-leaping twisting tongue of flame. We stand round and watch it burn, in a hurry to get away yet reluctant to leave. The fire marks the end of our time on Mustagh. Once it is reduced to ash, we set off down the hill to the glacier and come to the parting of the ways. We joke in the pale early sunlight, wish each other well, shake hands, take one last look back at the Tower, and walk away.

My walk-out with Mal was a vivid succession of blue, hot days, of leisurely conversations and hour-long silences as we turned over the events of the last three months and anticipated the future. Glare of the sun, ski pole rattling on rock, sweat tickling under the arms, wind in the ears: the trance of walking.

Once on the Baltoro we began meeting people again, were slowly welcomed into the wider world. This time we were the hard-bitten ones on the way down. 'Summit?' we were asked over and over. It felt good to be able to say yes.

Walking out is an extended decompression, an easing back into normal life. Part of the addiction of climbing is that it makes the ordinary world marvellous and desirable again. I associated everything I wanted now with items of furniture: bed, chair, table, settee. The casually intimate embrace of a familiar lover; the company of friends, shared food and drink, laughter and conversation, the cats sprawled out, books, the guitar . . . Back to the warm, human world – not for safety and shelter, not running away from something, but a return to the complex, human life that's there.

And yet part of me acknowledged that in another six months I'd probably be dissatisfied, wanting something more, something challenging. It's the absurd pendulum of the heart, always restlessly swinging from one desire to another. Always wanting something else. Sitting above Askole I'd felt the urge towards Buddhism, the desire to gradually prise oneself away from desire, to cease to be ruled by wanting, to stop the pendulum. Yet even then – and now, with Askole in sight and my steps gladly accelerating and leaving Mal behind – I knew I wasn't ready. I am still in love with desire and commitment. They yield us, if we're lucky and work at it, a relationship that endures, a mountain climbed, a book written. I hurry into Askole.

The trees are dense with ripe apricots. The fields are stacked with yellow wheat, erect as schoolmasters, rapping my knuckles as I wander through them towards the village square. 'Remember me, boy,' they seem to insist. I will, I will.

It's autumn in the mountain villages. The mills are working again. Hadji greets me with the quietest of smiles. We shake hands, he touches me lightly on the back, murmurs how happy he had been to hear of our success. Askole feels almost like home, I am full of joy to see houses, trees, livestock, the rhythm of a life that is not climbing. On the way up I had been entranced by the foreignness of the way of life there; now I loved it simply because it was life.

We bought six fresh eggs and ate a miraculous omelette. Then one of our porters invited us to his house for omelette and chapatis. When we saw Hadji in his cool, dim parlour and he offered us more eggs, we were struggling to fulfil the duties of a guest. Both stomach and mind need time to adjust to the sudden richness of life in the valley.

We continued on down, through the villages and air thick with oxygen. We found ourselves increasingly cautious the nearer to safety we became. The paths above the river and below the mud pinnacles were obstacles rather than challenges. With our porters lagging hours behind we frequently were unsure of the way, whether to take the ascending or descending path. There were sections we didn't recognize at all though we must have walked up through them, others that had become telescoped or enlarged by memory. The whole trip must be like that, a reflection not so much of what actually happened as how we happened to feel at the time.

We were cut off by a raging melt river an hour above Chaqpo. The hours passed, it grew dark and still our porters didn't show. We had no food, no water, no tent, no sleeping bags. We did have cigarettes. Luckily the night was mild so we just took a sleeping pill each and lay out on our Karrimats. It felt curiously exposed, lying in the middle of nowhere with no shelter or cocoon about one.

It didn't bother me that much, just another of those hitches. As

I lay waiting for sleep to hit me, I tried to remember what I was like before all this started. Do I feel different? Have I changed? There did seem a new inner confidence, or at least a resilience. I felt more self-possessed, more patient, less anxious, more fatalistic. I didn't know what was coming up next but I knew I'd deal with it because I had to. That was a difference.

I can't quell legendary monsters with a glare, but I don't panic either. That felt good to know, even as the rain started falling and we had to look around for a ledge to lie under. The morning would come, the porters would show up, we'd get home sooner or later.

'Sure climbing a mountain is a challenge,' Sandy had remarked, 'but the biggest challenge is leading a normal life, eh?' In a curious way the past nine months had been the most simple and unstressful of my life. All the problems were immediate and had immediate solutions. All you had to do was get up early in the morning and keep going safely till the end of the day. Everything else, the past and the future, was lost in amnesia.

And crouching under this ledge, shivering slightly and extremely thirsty, was a minor nuisance that would pass. Beside me Mal hunched and lit another cigarette; in the flare of the match I saw his face was stoic and untroubled as we waited for dawn.

It came. It always does. We crossed the river, found our porters and set off on the last leg, to Dassu.

Two miles short of Dassu, we were overtaken by one of the Norwegian team that we'd met at Jolla Bridge on their way to climb Trango Peak. He was limping with tendonitis and seemed agitated. We soon found out why.

They'd had a rough trip. One climber had to be helicoptered out with oedema, and the wife of one of the other climbers fell in the river and was injured while accompanying him to the chopper. They flew out together. The remaining four climbers got high on the peak, then ran low on supplies. Two of them abbed off to leave enough for the other two. The other two were finally spotted on the summit. At that point one of the first pair set off home with the good news while the other, Dag, who was now hurrying along with us, went off to film for a day. When he returned there was no sign of the summit pair. The descent route was visible, but there was no one on it.

He waited another day. When there was still no sign of them, Dag left their LO at Base Camp and set off for Skardu and an army helicopter.

There was nothing very adequate we could say. As we hurried on to Dassu I was reminded how fortunate we'd been. Sandy's escape when Jon held him over the southwest face, the rock thundering past Tony, my crevasse, a dozen other occasions when we'd got off without even noticing it . . . There had been three other deaths on the Baltoro range that we'd heard of already. I fervently hoped the lads were going to be all right on Gash 2.

Dag shared our jeep on the grinding, sliding, bone-shaking ride towards Skardu. We were quiet and thoughtful, Mal and I just beginning to relax in the knowledge it was all over, beginning to feel the fatigue and the pleasure of achievement. Only four out of forty-odd expeditions had been successful in the Karakoram this season, and we were one of them. We did all right. I did all right. Didn't make the Col, but I got far enough to make Adrian raise an eyebrow, and I had carried a crucial load. In my sack now were three volumes of journals plus three of the lads' diaries: the makings of Rocky's book.

It seemed a lifetime ago, that innocent, joyous, uplifted day of our jeep ride out from Skardu to Dassu, Mohammed's hat raised against the sky. Now we were weathered and worn, skinny but resilient, all our movements economic and controlled. We were tired but not weary, for who could feel weary with a Himalayan summit behind him? I felt older now, more centred and self-possessed, curiously at peace with myself and the world around me. It wouldn't necessarily last, but it felt good now, and that was enough.

So what's it all about? Why do climbers climb, why did I do it, what does it mean? Somehow I no longer want to talk or think about it. I'd begun climbing eager to analyse my companions, myself and climbing; now I'm reluctant to draw any conclusions at all. There is no clear answer to these questions, and even if there were it would not be very important. It is in the experience itself that the value lies. I can only really talk about it with other climbers, and with them there is no need to explain. So, standing up on the back of the jeep as we slither through the desert in the brown twilight, cool wind in our faces, I content myself with thinking that the meaning is in everything that happened, and it is the texture of these last months that I wish to convey in the book. There will be no message.

With self-possession there comes a certain reticence.

At dusk we came to the outskirts of Skardu. The first faltering electric lights, first shops, first telephone wires. Then scooters, vans and beat-up cars. On the way up, Skardu had seemed the end of the line, as basic as a dwelling place could be. Now it was a hustling metropolis that bewildered the senses. At the K2 Motel, the first shower for two months, the first table and chair, food served on a real plate. It was pleasant but rather baffling.

I lay sprawled in my first real bed, thinking about home, the Norwegians, my friends. Our connections are so fragile and tenuous. There is no security; climbing just dramatizes this, but it's as true at home. A peg pulls while we're abseiling, friends move away, a rope is cut by stonefall, our parents age and die, snow bridges collapse without warning, love drains like water through your fingers.

I tried to face the truth of the matter: our lives are erected over crevasses and we thread our way through visible and invisible icefalls. Our faith and our sanity hang belayed from a tottering heap of shit.

And yet we press on. Our protection may be illusory, but we use it. We go places, we achieve things in the face of our fear. With our friends and lovers we live our lives, and laugh and feel happiness more often than ought to be possible.

Creatures of hope, living on amnesia, riddled as the times.

Midafternoon on Friday 17 August Mal Duff and I were sitting on the veranda of Mrs Davies Hotel, Rawalpindi. It was the monsoon season and humidity dripped down our arms and tickled our backs. Flies crawled over peeled mangoes, ants zigzagged across the old black and white tiles, the fan whirred overhead. The old flat-footed wallah shuffled past. Peace. Stagnation. We had four days before the flight home; it was all over.

We'd had some body-swerves to negotiate in 'Pindi. Burt and Donna had left Flashman's after a week there without paying. They'd also failed to reinsure for helicopter rescue. Burt had in fact written the Pakistan Army a cheque that bounced, and the authorities were considerably less than amused. It took a lot of sweet pastry to placate them and reinstate helicopter cover for the lads on Gash 2. Even Mal, who is forgiving to the point of sainthood or idiocy, was upset about the mess we'd been left to sort out.

But now it was done. If we were thinking of anything that afternoon, it was of the cool air of home. If we were planning anything, it was making a phone call home. If we were waiting for anything, it was our next jug of coffee.

I should have known.

The fourth climber from the Norwegian Trango Peak team flopped down beside us. He'd been waiting for news of his friends. A helicopter had flown past the route and seen nothing. They were certainly dead, but none of us said so; that was in the silence after he gave us the news.

Voytek came over and joined us. I'd read about this near-legendary Polish mountaineer in the climbing magazines; meeting him I was struck by his youth, his absolute composure, and the startling direct intelligence of his eyes. As we chatted, the Norwegian told us they'd had plans for a north-south traverse of Everest next spring. They had the permits and the trip largely organized, but now two of Norway's leading climbers were, well, missing. It was doubtful if they could mount the whole expedition. Maybe they'd concentrate on securing a Norwegian First Ascent by going for the standard south side route, and let the China side go.

There followed some discussion of high-altitude traverses. Mal was lounging back in a cane chair, making an occasional contribution but looking vague and bored. I thought he had a headache or was thinking of Liz.

Eventually Voytek and the Norwegian drifted away. I went for more cigarettes. When I returned, Mal looked up with a mock-serious, half-challenging grin I'd seen somewhere before.

'Andy, how d'you fancy helping raise twenty grand and coming to Everest?'

I pretended to give his jest serious consideration. 'When?'

'Next spring.'

'Sounds all right. I didn't know you were interested in Everest.'

'I am interested in the Unclimbed Ridge with the Nord's permit.' Pause. 'Shall I count you in?' He poured out two coffees.

I sat down, lit a cigarette, felt the familiar rasp in my throat, considered this latest fantasy for a couple of seconds.

'Yes', I said.

'For fuck's sake, Mal', I said.

Postscript

Sandy, Jon, Tony, along with Shokat and Alex, set up a Base Camp for Gasherbrum 2. And not long thereafter they one by one got sick with dysentery. They made it up to a Camp 1 but were all still ill and wasted, so came back down again.

And that was that. They were disappointed but philosophical. At least they had the satisfaction of Mustagh. That would have to be enough for that season.

The next time we met at the Tinker house in London, it was not so much to reminisce about the trip as to discuss the northeast ridge of Everest.

Twice a day, every day, an old man hobbles with his bent legs and a stick down and up the cobbled lane outside my window. I take a break from my writing to watch him work his way back up, plastic carrier bag in one hand and stick in the other.

There is no need for him to shop twice a day. He does it to get out and about. He moves very slowly, with great concentration and care, at much the same speed as we did at altitude. His face is expressionless under his flat cap; his patience is absolute.

For some reason today my heart goes out to him in a wave of empathy. He pauses halfway up the lane and leans resting on his stick. His legs are very thin, the trousers flap loosely. I think painfully of my father and how he wasted away in the last months. The old man calls to someone passing at the top of the lane; they wave and walk on briskly.

He shifts his stick, looks up at the top of the lane and moves on, eyes fixed on his objective. As he tackles the last steep ramp his head goes down and he pauses, rocking, between each step. I'm sitting tense at my desk, willing him on. He makes the top, wobbles, then steps down off the pavement and he's made it. His shoulders sag, he looks around at the trees, the newly returned swallows carving up the air, the kids playing football and the mechanic bent over the car. A perfectly average precious morning.

Then he straightens up and hobbles on along the road to the right, inching out of my line of vision.

I am proud as hell of him. It is not sentimental to say that his daily walk exceeds in patience and stamina and stoical courage anything we did on the Mustagh Tower. This is the real thing, done daily, humbly, for no fame or applause, to no end but self-respect and the purchase of daily bread.

Acknowledgements

The author and publishers would like to thank Routledge &
Kegan Paul Limited and Princeton University Press for kind per-
mission to reproduce material from *The I Ching or Book of
Changes* translated by Richard Wilhelm and rendered into
English by Cary F. Baynes.

Index